THE WARREN HOUSE TALES

THE
WARREN HOUSE
TALES

A SOCIAL HISTORY SINCE 1865

V. K. L. GOOD

THIRD MILLENNIUM
PUBLISHING, LONDON

© 2014 Third Millennium Publishing Limited, Warren House
and V. K. L. Good

First published in 2014 by Third Millennium Publishing Limited,
a subsidiary of Third Millennium Information Limited

2–5 Benjamin Street
London
United Kingdom
EC1M 5QL
www.tmiltd.com

ISBN: 978 1 906507 82 4

British Library Cataloguing in Publication Data
A CIP catalogue record for this book is available from the British Library.

Managing Editor: Janet Sacks
Designer: Helen Swansbourne
Production: Bonnie Murray
Reprographics by Studio Fasoli, Italy
Printed and bound in China by 1010 Printing International Limited

PHOTOGRAPHIC CREDITS
The publishers would like to thank all the companies and individuals
who have provided images, and apologise in advance for any
unintentional omission.
akg-images 142; Alamy 6, 87T, 87R, 104, 191T; Bonhams 20T, 46;
Bridgeman Art Library 7, 8B, 9, 17, 21, 25, 52T, 56R, 65, 75L ,79, 83T,
99, 102, 105L, 108, 156B, 158R; The Trustees of the British Museum 86;
Churchill Archives Centre 100, 146B; Reproduced by permission of
English Heritage 71B, 72, 73TL, 72B, 82, 84, 132, 175, 176; Eric Lyons
Cunningham Partnership 193, 195, 197, 199B; Getty Images 15T, 67,
75R, 76, 80, 81, 89R, 109, 113B, 134, 136, 139, 141, 146T, 149, 158T,
160, 166, 168, 171L, 177, 190; Imperial War Museum 161, 164; Joshua
Tucker Photography 202C, 202BL, 202BR, 203T; Library and Archives
Canada / S.J. Thompson 89L; Library of Congress, Prints & Photographs
Division 165; Mary Evans Picture Library 8L, 18, 24, 26T, 36, 38, 49, 58,
62, 66, 103, 110T, 112, 115, 123, 143, 148L, 151, 170, 171R, 172; Media
Wisdom Photography 1, 2–3, 4, 6T, 10, 11, 27, 28B, 32, 33, 35B, 41, 42,
44, 45T, 54–55, 57, 69, 70, 71T, 73TR, 92, 94, 95, 97, 107R, 125, 128,
129, 130, 131, 133, 144, 154, 155, 184, 185, 194B, 196T, 199T, 200,
201, 202T, 204; National Museum Stockholm / Erik Cornelius 56L;
National Portrait Gallery, London 12L, 12R, 14, 23, 29B, 31, 37, 51, 83L,
101, 138, 156T; RIBA Library Drawings Collection 26B, 35T, 113T; RIBA
Books & Periodicals Collection 29T; Reproduced by kind permission of
The Royal Bank of Scotland Group (2013) 39; Royal Geographical
Society (with IBG) 80; Royal Horticultural Society 28L; Reproduced with
permission of the University of Sheffield 34; V. K. L. Good 203B;
Victoria and Albert Museum, London 114, 117

CONTENTS

INTRODUCTION

Hidden in the thickets of Coombe Wood, a gang of highwaymen rested while their horses drank from the nearby brook. Their leader, Jerry Abershaw, would rob and terrorise travellers along the Portsmouth Road that ran from Putney Bottom up Coombe Hill, towards Kingston, until he was hanged in 1795. From a nearby roadside tavern, The Bald Face Stag, he and his notorious gang of thieves planned their villainous acts; armed with pistols, they held up the post chaise and robbed the wealthy passengers travelling to and from London on this lonely stretch of road. They were not the first to prey on the wealthy inhabitants of the area: 50 years earlier, Dick Turpin and Thomas Rowden had attacked a coach party and stolen their guineas on nearby Kingston Hill.

Highwayman Jerry Abershaw robbed and terrorised travellers between Putney and Kingston

Red Rover Coaches carried passengers through Coombe on
their journey between London and Southampton

Since the 16th century, the London to Portsmouth
Road had been an important link between the
capital, the coast and the Royal Palace of Hampton
Court. Furthermore, Kingston Bridge was the only
crossing point over the Thames after London Bridge,
and Kingston grew into a thriving market town and a
centre for trade. The fertile arable farm lands and
natural springs of Coombe, set high on the hill above
the town, had long appealed to the nobility.
Elizabethan statesman William Cecil (Lord
Burghley), William Cokayne (once Lord Mayor of
London) and Jacobite MP Edward Harvey all owned

land at Coombe. They, their friends and their fellow
wealthy merchant travellers, making their way west
from Putney Heath, were prime targets for the
highwaymen.

In the early 19th century, newcomers to the area
cleared the ancient woods to create grazing lands,
enclosed by fences, hedges and ditches, and in so
doing, they cut off the once open landscape across
which the robbers had made their getaways. Toll-
house keepers living at the newly created turnpikes
improved security, and the highwaymen turned their
attention to other forms of criminal activity.

Left: Sir William Cecil, Baron Burghley, Chief Minister of the realm of Elizabeth I, owned land at Coombe

Left: Sir William Cecil, Baron Burghley, Chief Minister of the realm of Elizabeth I, owned land at Coombe

Below: Prime Minister Robert Banks Jenkinson, 2nd Earl of Liverpool, lived at Coombe House 1802–28

However, entertaining was a social necessity for the Prime Minister and, in 1812, Queen Charlotte and the Prince Regent, accompanied by various princesses, visited Coombe House. In the run-up to the Battle of Waterloo, the King of Prussia, General Gebhard von Blücher and the Russian General Platov had meetings with Liverpool at Coombe House. The same courtesy was extended to the Duke of Wellington on his way to Belgium in 1814 and after his victory against the French.

Sometime after the Earl of Liverpool's untimely death in 1828, Coombe House, together with neighbouring lands, including some owned by 2nd Earl Spencer, were bought by HRH Prince Adolphus, Duke of Cambridge, for his son Prince George. For the next hundred years most of the freehold titles on the estate at Coombe Warren remained in the ownership of HRH Prince George, Duke of Cambridge, and his sons. The Duke was a grandson of George III and a cousin of Queen Victoria. Like many of the royal family, he was a

By then some of the wealthiest men in the country owned land on Coombe Hill. These included the Whig politician George John Spencer, 2nd Earl Spencer. In 1822, Spencer gave one acre of his land on Coombe Warren to the Admiralty for the building of a semaphore station connecting the lines of communication from Whitehall to the naval dockyards at Portsmouth. Coombe was also favoured by Robert Banks Jenkinson, Baron Hawkesbury, 2nd Earl of Liverpool. He was a Tory politician and Prime Minister from 1812. Liverpool lived at Coombe House from 1802 until his death there in 1828. This extract from his diary explains its attraction: 'Yielding to a sudden impulse to get away from the noise of London, went off one evening in a chaise with cold meat for supper. Reached Coombe around 9, with a feeling of comfort not to be expressed, slept. Next morning had above an hour's walk and potter in the midst of workmen, pigs and turkeys, before returning to the parliamentary grind.' His ministry was long and eventful, and he did not particularly enjoy the company of house guests. Indeed Coombe House was described by a fellow politician Charles Williams-Wynn as 'unquestionably the dullest house in which I ever passed a day'.

Poster advertising
the Red Rover
Stagecoach

soldier by profession, and in 1853
he found himself waging a battle
of his own against the local
population over the right of way
of a turnpike which crossed the
Duke's Coombe Estate. Dubbed by
the press 'the Battle of Coombe
Warren', the whole affair became
the subject of a satirical comedy
entitled *All's Well that Ends Well;
or the disputed road on Coombe
Warren* (five acts in verse) by
Philip Horatio Inkpen
(pseudonym). Indicted in court for having illegally
stopped up a public road, the Duke defended his right
to protect his land. The verdict was a victory for both
sides. The local people were given the right to cross the
estate on foot, while the Duke maintained control
over the rights of access for vehicles.

> My loyal Kingston subjects give me cause,
> To feel assur'd they all respect the laws;
> And while defending rights which are their own,
> Do well maintain the honour of my throne.
> Behold those glades and that embower'ed walk:
> Where simple swains and maids hold am'rous talk,
> Where gallant knight's reign up their fiery steeds;
> And some old man, his lazy donkey leads.
> Where ladies and their lap dogs freely roam,
> And ploughmen plod their weary footsteps home.
> I will not shut that noble avenue,
> Or hide the landscape from my people's view;
> Nor stay the gambols of those boys I see,
> Who soon may be my dashing cavalry;
> For all the pomp when peers around me bow,
> Or gems that sparkle on my regal brow.
> Go make some reparation for your ways,
> And earn a monarch's love, a nation's praise.

All's Well that Ends Well, Act IV, Scene 1, the Queen to
the Duke of Cambridge

Some years later, a little
way up from the entrance to
Warren House, the Duke
erected toll-bar gates to
maintain the privacy of the
roads within the estate. They
were always closed during
the Epsom Derby race week
in order to discourage
travelling gypsy caravans and
other undesirable traffic
making their way towards
Epsom. The only people
permitted on to the estate were residents and their
visitors. Tradesmen paid an annual charge for the
right to use the roads. Red Rover Coaches, owned by
Watney's, were, however, allowed to travel through the
Warren, Coombe Hill, on their journey from London
to Brighton.

While the Duke maintained a residence at Coombe
House and was often to be found with his gamekeepers
and guests shooting on the covers within the Warren,
he also successfully leased various properties and the
rights to parcels of land on the estate. Although coach
companies and some landowners succeeded in
blocking the development of the railway to Kingston
until 1863, the Duke had little problem attracting
buyers. The notoriously steep gradient up the hill from
Kingston Vale was eased by the creation of a cutting
and London was thus brought within an hour's ride by
horse-drawn carriage. Coombe soon became popular
with fashionable London society – bankers, politicians
and aristocrats – who built a number of large houses
alongside the existing Regency properties such as
Kenry House (belonging to Lord Dunraven) and
Coombe Hurst (the home of Samuel Smith, Florence
Nightingale's uncle). These included Coombe Croft,
Coombe Leigh, Coombe Warren, Coombe Court and,
of course, Warren House itself.

1

1865-84

THE TALE OF THE ARMY AGENT AND THE DUKE

HUGH HAMMERSLEY (1819-84) AND PRINCE GEORGE, 2ND DUKE OF CAMBRIDGE (1819-1904)

'A man of very cultivated mind and refined tastes and by his gentle and affectionate nature greatly endeared himself to all who came into contact with him.'

Graham Milne, from his Hammersley family notes

HUGH HAMMERSLEY was pleased with his new country house on the Coombe Estate. It befitted a man of his years with a growing family. Hammersley had been fortunate, thanks to the influence of his great-uncle; he had made the right connections and the Duke had been most obliging. In the words of Prime Minister Disraeli, 'One secret of success is for a man to be ready for his opportunity when it comes.'

Opposite: One of the waterfalls in the Japanese water garden, established in the 1860s/70s

Above: The Hammersley-Eden Crest at Warren House

Warren House at Coombe was the Hammersley family's country retreat, just 12 miles from their London home in Kensington and the offices of Cox & Co., agents and bankers to the British Army, where Hugh was a partner. Even though Kensington was relatively rural in 1865, Coombe was an idyllic spot, where he and his family could escape the noise and activity of Albertopolis. Hugh Hammersley was in good company: most of the land around Coombe was owned by rich arable farmers like Mr Francis Garner, who owned 750 acres of Coombe Farm and employed 20 men as agricultural labourers, dairymen and shepherds. In the 1840s and 1850s a growing number of large houses were occupied by wealthy professionals, such as John Sim on the Coombe Estate, a timber merchant and Justice of the Peace, living with his son, a solicitor; Robin Hood Farm was occupied by Colonel and Lady Wemple, and Coombe Hurst by Samuel and Mary Smith, who were the uncle and aunt of Florence Nightingale. These large houses were also home to the

Thomas Hammersley (1747–1812), Hugh Hammersley's grandfather, from a painting by Hugh Douglas Hamilton, Dublin, 1812

Charles Greenwood (1748–1832), Hugh's great uncle, by Thomas Lawrence, 1828

domestic staff who served in them: butlers, lady's maids, cooks, grooms and coachmen. The Duke of Cambridge, who owned all the land on the Coombe Estate, employed gardeners and gamekeepers to look after his estate. Many people had been drawn to the area, as road improvements eased the gradient of Kingston Hill, with a cutting near the summit and an embankment below, thus bringing the City of London within an hour's ride by horse-drawn carriage. By 1861 various civil servants, the banker Bertram W. Currie, and another army agent, Edward Septimus Codd, lived among the large farms and the dairymen, carters, gamekeepers, foresters, gardeners, butlers and lady's maids that made up the local population.

THE HAMMERSLEYS

Like the rest of middle-class Victorian England, the Hammersleys had prospered since the early days of the Industrial Revolution. The family wealth had come from banking, though not all of his ancestors were as

lucky or successful as Hugh. His paternal grandfather Thomas Hammersley (1747–1812) and maternal great-uncle Charles Greenwood (1748–1832) were among the pioneers of private banking in the 18th and 19th centuries. While some bankers facilitated the investments of wealthy merchant-capitalists, Thomas Hammersley and his partners, Ransome and Moreland, lent money to the wealthy aristocracy, including the Prince of Wales, the future George IV. Charles Greenwood was already an established figure in the world of banking as a controlling partner at the army agents and bankers Cox, Cox and Greenwood since 1783. Both Greenwood and Hammersley were wealthy men in their own right by the time they established a new banking partnership, with Messrs Montolieu, Brooksbank and Drewe in 1796. However, Thomas Hammersley became too accommodating in attempts to attract customers amid tough competition, and overstretched himself financially. Sadly, even his pleas for patronage to his customer the Prince of Wales fell on deaf ears. He died in 1812 leaving the bank and its debts in the hands of his partners and eldest son

Hugh Hammersley (1819–84)

Charles Hammersley, Hugh's father, from a painting by John Prescott Knight

25 Park Crescent was home to Hugh Hammersley and his family in the 1840s

Hugh (1774–1840) and third son George (1785–1835). By 1823, the bank was known as Hammersley, Greenwood and Brooksbank. Hugh Hammersley spent the rest of his life trying to liquidate the charges on property held by the bank. He was let down by his partners after Greenwood's death in 1832, and after his own death in 1840 the assets of 'Hammersley's Bank' were acquired by Coutts & Co.

Fortunately, as it transpired, the second son, Charles Hammersley (1782–1835), had chosen not to join his father and brothers' banking business, preferring instead to join Charles Greenwood at his other venture, the army agents Cox & Co., where Hammersley became a co-partner in 1814. Greenwood was also related to the Cox family through a great-aunt. It was the wealth, connections and good business sense of Charles Greenwood that propelled Charles Hammersley and his son towards great wealth and status of their own,

and ultimately the timely alliance with Prince George, Duke of Cambridge, which brought Hugh to the Coombe Estate.

Hugh Hammersley was born in 1819 in Dulwich, the seventh child and second eldest son of Charles Hammersley and Emily Poulett-Thomson. Hugh's mother, Emily, came from a well-established middle-class family whose rise in wealth and social standing was characteristic of the age. She was the daughter of John Buncombe Poulett-Thomson, a senior partner in an important and successful London trading firm, J. Thomson, T. Bonar & Co., which together with Baring's merchant bank had obtained a highly lucrative monopoly of Russian Government copper out of St Petersburg. Her brother Charles was the first Governor of the United Province of Canada, while her brother Andrew became a director of the Bank of England. Her sister Frances also fared well, marrying

Hammersley and Co. Bank cheque, dated 1831

first William Baring, fourth son of Sir Francis Baring of Baring's Brothers Bank, and then four years after his death in 1820, marrying Arthur Eden, deputy Comptroller of the Exchequer and ancestor of a future British Prime Minister.

Charles and Emily Hammersley had a large family of 11 children. By 1841, when Hugh was 22, their wealth had enabled them to purchase a home at 25 Park Crescent, London, an elegant Regency semicircular terrace, designed by George IV's associate John Nash, on the southern edge of Regent's Park. They employed at least ten staff from butlers to housekeepers, lady's maids to footmen, and cooks to kitchen maids. A family note says of Charles Hammersley: 'The prosperity which attended him throughout his career as an army agent was mainly due to his personal intelligence and energy, to his unbroken devotion to his work and to the confidence universally inspired by a character in which a rigid sense of honour and justice was ever tempered by the impulses of a benevolent and generous nature.'

BANKERS TO THE ARMY

Army agents made their money by charging a commission based on the amount of money that was passed from the Exchequer through their bank to the soldiers and regiments on their books. As their role developed, agents also became the intermediaries for the buying and selling of officer commissions, under the 'purchase of commission system'. This system existed within the Cavalry, where two-thirds of commissions were made through purchase, and in the Infantry, where around half of the officers had paid for their rank, and it was universal in the Household Cavalry and the Foot Guards, socially prestigious regiments with higher pay. Within the purchase system, the officer class had to fund them-

selves, rather than the state paying them a proper salary – an obvious advantage to the Treasury. Officers also had to pay for their own uniforms, kit and civilian clothes and those in the Cavalry had to provide two riding horses as well. For non-commissioned officers, warrant officers and troopers, however, horses, uniforms and equipment were paid for by the Army. The Duke of Wellington said, 'It is the purchase of commissions which brings into the service men who have some connection with the interests and fortunes of the country.' His implication was that only the aristocracy with their connection to the land would serve as dedicated officers.

The regular army expanded from 40,000 personnel in 1793 to over 250,000 at the peak of the Napoleonic Wars in 1813. At the outbreak of war with France in 1793, Cox's was the largest army agent, employing 35 clerks serving 14 cavalry regiments, 64 infantry regiments and 17 militia. It was an enormous logistical challenge for the leaders and army commanders to mobilise troops, let alone maintain rations, bedding, clothing, weaponry and ammunition during a military campaign, but it was met well by the trusted Cox's. In 1801 a warrant was issued for Cox & Co. to receive monies from the East India Company for soldiers transferred from regiments to the company's service.

For 30 years the army agents' business flourished under the management of Richard Henry Cox, Charles Hammersley and Greenwood. They were not only bankers to the higher echelons of the Army but also to the aristocracy of the nation. As early as 1768 William, Duke of Gloucester, brother of George III and a military commander of the Foot Guards, opened an account with Cox's, and persuaded other members of the royal family to do the same. They included the Duke of Cumberland, a military field marshal; the Duke of Cambridge, also a field marshal and a member of the Privy Council; Prince Edward, the Duke of Kent, father to Queen Victoria, a soldier and

Prince Fredrick Augustus,
Duke of York and Albany,
held an account with
Cox's

in 1791 Commander-in-Chief of the Army in Canada; and the third son of George III, William Henry, Duke of Clarence, who was the future William IV and by 1790 a retired naval admiral.

It was Charles Greenwood who held the greatest influence with customers, and in particular with the Duke of York, who had heavy financial obligations to Cox's. When Greenwood had entered Cox's as a clerk in 1771, he had brought with him the account of his friend Frederick Augustus Hanover, the Duke of York, subject of the nursery rhyme and favourite son of George III. Apparently when the Duke introduced Greenwood to the King as 'the gentleman who keeps my money', Greenwood drily corrected: 'I think it is rather his royal highness who keeps mine…'

By 1795 the Duke of York had been appointed Commander-in-Chief of the British Army and over the following 20 years was to be responsible for many of the changes to the way the Army was run. He established the military college at Sandhurst and insisted on improvements in rations, medical care and accommodation, as well as a new approach to discipline and penal codes. However, when a scandal broke in 1808 relating to the Duke of York's involve-ment in his mistress Mary Anne Clarke's scheme to sell army commissions, his future involvement in the Army was threatened.

As early as 1803 Commissioners, appointed by the Government, had been examining so-called abuses of public money in the Army, Barracks and Ordnance departments, abuses which had been aided and abetted, it was said, by the Duke of York and army agents such as Greenwood, Hammersley and others. Thomas Creevey MP, diarist and later Treasurer of the Ordnance, said of Greenwood, '[his] tricks with money in these departments would whitewash those of Trotter by comparison' (Trotter had been accused of fraud and financial abuses in the Royal Navy).

The system of purchasing commissions was complex. There was a price for every rank and for every promotion or transfer and, where possible, retiring officers sold their commissions in order to raise a pension. By law, the purchase of commissions was only to be handled by official army agents, appointed by the regimental colonels. However, some ex-officers who understood the system and had influential friends would identify possible openings within the officer ranks of certain regiments, obtain the necessary endorsements from senior officers for the candidates, then liaise between the official army agents, such as Cox's, and the would-be soldier purchasers, and charge a fixed fee on top for their services. This form of commission broking was illegal.

This widespread system of corruption in the Army blocked the promotion of competent men who did not have the right social connections or enough money to pay the artificially inflated prices. It was well known that army agents openly traded commissions through a string of intermediaries such as Mrs Clarke, and while there had been an attempt to ban this kind

THE SALE OF COMMISSIONS SCANDAL

Mary Anne Clarke

In 1804, Mary Anne Clarke, the mistress of Frederick, Duke of York, was also having an affair with a commission broker from whom she took bribes to gain promotion for officers within the Duke's regiments. On discovering that his mistress was prospering illegally, the Duke of York left her in 1806, and bought her silence with an annual pension. However, he could not keep up payments so Mrs Clarke let her activities be known and the scandal broke in 1809. There followed a House of Commons Inquiry into the activities of Mrs Clarke, who testified that the Duke was fully aware of all of her business regarding the sales of commissions. At the same Inquiry Charles Greenwood swore that he reluctantly acquiesced to the Duke's orders in such cases. The Duke, although acquitted of corrupt practices, was forced to resign as Commander-in-Chief of the Army, but was reinstated in 1811. Mrs Clarke tried to raise more money by writing a book that revealed the conspiracy against the Duke of York, which she claimed had been orchestrated by the Duke of Kent's private secretary. She was prosecuted in 1813 for libel and sentenced to nine months in prison, after which time she fled to Boulogne, France, where she spent the rest of her life.

of brokerage in 1806, without proper enforcement no one was ever prosecuted. The case of Mrs Clarke prompted the introduction of the 1809 Brokerage Act, which was more rigorously upheld.

The Duke of York recovered his reputation and went on to make the first reforms to the system of purchasing commissions by increasing the number of free commissions, thereby opening up the service to more than just the wealthy aristocracy and landed gentry, enabling the middle classes to join the Army as officers, and insisting on a minimum level of experience before promotion to higher rank. His relationship with Cox's put them in a highly advantageous position right at the forefront of army reforms, as well as the social and political elite.

By 1815 and the end of the Napoleonic Wars, Cox's had become bankers to the whole of the Household Brigade, nearly all the Cavalry and Infantry regiments,

the Royal Artillery and the Royal Wagon Train, which was later to become the Royal Army Service Corps. Their accounts were audited by clerks at the Ordnance to avoid further accusations of corruption.

GREENWOOD'S DEATH

Charles Greenwood died just before Hugh turned 13, in January 1832. He had been on a visit to the Royal Pavilion in Brighton when, while with the new King William IV, he was suddenly taken ill, and died within a few hours. The Earl of Munster, a Privy Counsellor and soldier, the eldest natural son of William IV with his long-term mistress Dorothy Jordan, wrote a fitting tribute to Greenwood in a letter to Charles Hammersley: 'I have double reason to regret my excellent, lamented kind friend, not only for his qualities as a man, but from the circumstance of his being in Brighton on my account, being engaged in a most delicate discussion with the King and myself, and God only knows where I shall (I am sure the King will feel the like difficulty) find another in whom we shall both place the like confidence.'

Charles Greenwood's death may have led to expectations of a large inheritance. However, most of his fortune had already been spent on penniless royals, lavish hospitality required of his status, and a 'generosity towards all who claimed his help'. The greatest amount of money had been spent trying to stop the collapse of Hammersley's bank in 1840. Instead of inheriting a fortune, his nephew Charles Hammersley lost £25,000 as sole Executor and residuary Legatee.

HUGH HAMMERSLEY

Like their father, Hugh and his eldest brother Charles were educated at Eton College, as were the sons of other banking families, including the Drummonds, Montolieus and Cox's. At the time it was probably the best boarding school education a gentleman could provide for his sons, the choice of generations of British aristocracy and royalty.

By his early twenties, Hugh had joined Cox's and was living with his parents in their large, elegant Regency house on Park Crescent, on the southern edge of Regent's Park. Here Hugh lived until he married in 1855. His bride was a first cousin, Dulcibella, daughter of Arthur Eden and his mother's sister, Frances Poulett-Thomson.

By then Cox's was responsible for the administration and accountability of the pay and personal incomes of around 5,000 officers stationed both at home and around the world – a very important role. The Hammersley family notes explain:

The boy gazette to his first commission, the field officer aspiring to the command of his regiment, the veteran contemplating retirement and the officer's widow claiming her poor pension, alike addressed themselves to Cox and Co certain to find sound counsel, effectual help and kindly sympathy. It need hardly be pointed out how much business experience and capacity, how complete a mastery of the regulations and practice governing the army, how strong a grasp of a vast variety of technical detail, and above all, how great a degree of unfailing tact in the intercourse with men of all ranks, classes and conditions, were indispensable for the efficient performance of such services.

The family notes also highlight the fact that these soldiers were not particularly well paid; indeed many relied on additional family wealth merely to maintain their place in the ranks.

Military officers, more especially in their earlier years, are not noted for the exercise of strict economy in their private expenditure, and with the imprudent or unwary subaltern who after an unsuccessful attempt to retrieve his position by a desperate resort to Epsom Downs or money lenders saw ruin staring him in the face, it was to Craig's Court [Cox & Co.'s address] that he instinctively bent his steps. There he was sure of an indulgent hearing, and of such material help as the case might admit of, and often when the strict exigencies of business compelled them to harden their hearts against the appeal, the generosity of an individual partner would come to the rescue, and by timely aid, accompanied perhaps by a paternal warning for the future, would thus save a young life from wreck.

The duties performed by Cox's kept them in continuous communication with the British Government and all military departments. This included both the Secretary of War and the Commander-in-Chief of the British Army, who in 1856 was none other than Prince George, Duke of Cambridge, owner of the Coombe Estate.

HISTORY OF COX & CO.

'Uncle' Richard Cox, founder of Cox & Co.,
by Sir William Beechy

'Uncle' Richard Cox, as he was known not only to Charles
Greenwood but also most of the British Army, had, from
humble beginnings, become a very successful and wealthy
man. In 1746 Cox was appointed private secretary to Jean
Louis (or John) Ligonier (1680–1770). Then, in 1757, the Right
Hon Sir John Ligonier, Field Marshal and Commander-in-
Chief of the British Army, was appointed to the richest and
most influential position in the country, Colonel of the First
Guards, and as such had the right to appoint his own agent.
Impressed by the way Richard Cox had corresponded on his
behalf with under-secretaries of government departments,
colonels of regiments, treasury officials and the like, Ligonier
awarded the rights of the agency to his faithful secretary.

From 1759, Ligonier also held the post of Master-General
of the Ordnance. It was an office of great dignity and
influence as the Board of Ordnance
was responsible for all British artillery,
engineers, fortifications, military
supplies, rations, bedding, clothing,
transport, field hospitals and medical
supplies. Richard Cox was also
appointed his Secretary at the Board
and given the agency of the Royal
Regiment, adding to his increasing
fees considerably. Cox also secured
the agency of the regiment of
Colonel Eyre Coote, protector of the
East India Company.

Initially Ligonier and Cox transacted their business in
Ligonier's house in North Audley Street. Later, as the agency
work increased, Richard Cox hired two clerks and working
from Cox's home in Albemarle Street, just off Piccadilly, they
began to keep the accounts of the regiments. They were also
responsible for logistics and the general welfare of the troops,
for example the provision of clothing and special requests
from the regimental adjutant, like the shipment of personal
effects or the requisitions of supplies or weaponry.

During this time, Cox also continued his role as private
secretary to Ligonier, who as Master-General of the Ordnance
was also a member of the inner war cabinet during the Seven
Years War, the first truly global conflict. Cox worked with
Ligonier to ensure that the deployment of British military
power was sufficient and correctly balanced, even when
resources were stretched.

Conditions for the troops abroad were dreadful – tropical
diseases killed more troops than died in action. The care of his
men was the basis of Ligonier's success, and much of the
medical assistance was paid for out of his own pocket, while
food supplies were improved. Advancements in ordnance
research, and development in artillery and weaponry were also
made possible under Ligonier. He improved the previously
hazardous system of military purchase, giving commanders
greater authority over buying and sourcing supplies.

In 1765 Henry Drummond joined Richard Cox, establishing
Cox and Drummond, and the offices were relocated to Craig's
Court, off Whitehall. They became agents for the Dragoons
and eight more infantry regiments, and by 1768 turnover was
£345,000 per annum. Business grew aided by the huge
increase in the number of regiments needed to police
America between 1774 and 1776. Henry Drummond had left
Cox's by 1772, so in need of
business partners to share the
risks, Cox was joined by Mr
Arthur Mair, and then his own
son Richard Bethel Cox. When
Mair died in 1783, Cox's cousin,
Charles Greenwood, became
a partner, at which time the
company was known as Cox,
Cox and Greenwood.

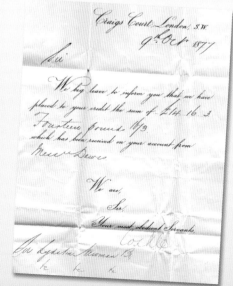

Letter from Cox & Co.,
Craig's Court, dated 1877

Having emerged victorious from the French and Napoleonic Wars, Britain and Europe remained at peace for 40 years. Cox's looked after an army which provided colonial defence in British North America, Canada, India, Mauritius, Ceylon, Cephalonia, South Africa, the Caribbean and New Zealand. The agency charged fees based on the amounts of money they were handling, either approved for Ordnance or as pay and allowances for soldiers. Cox's were also responsible for maintaining an army reserve fund, which until 1826 was partly made up from the sale of commissions, but by 1856 was much diminished. Between 1830 and 1841 sums amounting to over £40,000 from the purchase and sale of commissions in the Army were credited to the Paymaster-General in aid of army services.

Cox's thrived in spite of the onset of reform in the British Army and the abolition of buying and selling commissions. Even in 1892, when the government fee for disbursements was cancelled and agency profits had to be made entirely from banking services to officers, Cox's capital reserves were still £400,000 with deposits in excess of £2 million.

In the years 1905 to 1911, Cox & Co. expanded their business by setting up five branches in India, serving the British garrisons stationed there. The volume of work increased with the onset of the First World War and not surprisingly staff numbers increased from 180 in 1914 to 4,500 in 1918. In 1915, a separate company Cox & Co. (France) was incorporated, with London and South Western Bank (LSWB) subscribing to half the share capital. In January 1918, LSWB merged with London and Provincial Bank and subsequently with Barclays Bank (Overseas) in 1922. By then Cox & Co. (France) had branches in Paris, Boulogne, Le Havre, Rouen, Marseilles, Lyons and Amiens, while over the next two years branches opened in Cologne, Algiers, Nice, Menton, Cannes and Monte Carlo.

Although post-war branches opened in Alexandria, Egypt and Rangoon, it was not enough to maintain the volume of business needed to make a profit. In 1922 Cox & Co., unable to sustain the rapid growth of the previous years and suffering a downturn in business, took over the firm of Henry S. King, who had strong links with India and was the London agent for many Indian-based traders. The bank was

John Ligonier, 1st Earl Ligonier, appointed Richard Cox as his Secretary in 1746

renamed Cox and Kings. However, despite the merger, Cox's business was losing more than £1 million a year, with no more in either its capital or reserve accounts. With reassurances from the Bank of England, and no objections from the Treasury, Air Ministry or War Office, Lloyds Bank took over the firm. Henry Bell of Lloyds stated that it was through a sense of public duty and with a marked lack of enthusiasm that Lloyds would agree to take over the business of Cox & Co.; as for Cox's partners they had no alternative but to sell.

The trust that customers had in Cox's is immortalised by Sir Arthur Conan Doyle in 'The Problem of Thor Bridge', in which Dr John H. Watson, a retired Indian Army doctor, says:

> Somewhere in the vaults of the bank Cox and Co., at Charing Cross, there is a travel-worn and battered tin dispatch-box with my name John H. Watson, MD, Late Indian Army, painted on the lid. It is crammed with papers, nearly all of which are records of cases to illustrate the curious problems which Mr. Sherlock Holmes had at various times to examine.

'British Expeditionary Force', *The Times*, March 1917

Kindly manager of Cox,
I am sadly on the rocks,
For a time my warring ceases,
My patella is in pieces;
Though in hospital I lie;
I am not about to die;
Therefore let me overdraw
Just a very little more.
If you stick to your red tape
I must go without my grape,
And my life must sadly fret
With a cheaper cigarette,
So pray be not hard upon
A poor dejected subaltern.
This is all I have to say,
'Impecunious' R.F.A.

The alleged response from Cox's was:

Sir, the kindly heart of Cox
Cannot leave you on the rocks,
And he could not sleep in bed
Thinking you were underfed;
So if you will let us know
Just how far you want to go,
Your request will not be in vain,
Written from your bed of pain,
We will make but one request –
Keep this locked within your breast,
For if others know, they'll say
'Good old Cox is sure to pay
Only take him the right way'.

This humorous poem appeared in an edition of *The B. E. F. Times* in 1917. Published by soldiers of the 12th Battalion, Sherwood Foresters (Royal Field Artillery) 24th Division, fighting in France on the front line during the First World War, the trench magazine consisted of poems, in-jokes, spoof advertisements and comment satirising the men's military position

Dulcibella Eden (1833–1903),
wife of Hugh Hammersley

THE INQUIRY INTO THE PURCHASE OF COMMISSIONS

The purchasing of commissions perpetuated the non-selective process of officer appointments to those who could afford it – mainly the landed gentry – but who were not necessarily the best for the job. Officers were also known to raise money through their right of exchange of their commissions through Cox's. Instead of approaching the Commander-in-Chief or the Secretary of War for a transfer from one regiment to another where the price of commission was perhaps greater, officers would approach Cox's, ask for a posting, and borrow any difference in cost using the existing commission value as a guarantee of repayment.

Army agents had to prepare quarterly returns which detailed all officers prepared to purchase promotions, and in 1844 there was an attempt to set a regulation price for each type of commission. But every commission, except an officer's first entry-level appointment, had a dual value: its official cost (regulation price) and its over-regulation cost, or regimental value. Prices also varied depending on supply and demand; military appointments in time of peace were an expensive luxury due to limited vacancies, but in wartime, as soldiers were killed and injured, they were more readily available.

However, the wind of change was coming. The Army had been severely unprepared for the large-scale war that broke out in Europe in 1854 on the Crimean Peninsula. Casualties were enormous, the conditions deplorable and reports soon followed of military mismanagement and criticism of the aristocrats in power who had sent these men to war without sufficient intelligence or proper preparation. In 1856, the Prime Minister, Lord Palmerston, agreed to the establishment of a Royal Commission to investigate and recommend changes to the British Army, including the system of purchasing commissions.

Hugh Hammersley, representing Cox & Co., the expert witness, appeared before the Royal Commission. He readily admitted, as reported in *The Times* newspaper, that it was 'a matter of general notoriety that large sums over and above regulation were habitually given throughout the service for promotion', and that 'without any betrayal of private confidence', he could put the Commission in 'possession of exact prices current for all grades'. He went on to inform the Commissioners that in the Cavalry anything under double regulation price was considered reasonable, for example the regulation price for a lieutenant colonel was £6,175, while the actual price paid was £12,000, and in peacetime when there were fewer vacancies the

The Crimean War. Above: Ordnance Wharf, Balaclava, c.1855. The Army had been severely unprepared for the large-scale war that broke out on the Crimean Peninsula. Opposite: Nine-pounder gun of the Royal Artillery, 1855–6. Photograph by Roger Fenton

price would be higher still, £14,000 to £16,000. In the Guards, the regulation price for the same rank was £4,800, with men actually paying £8,200 or £9,000 in peacetime. Infantry prices were less: the rank of lieutenant colonel was £4,500 officially, although men paid £7,000 for it, and a captaincy was £1,800 but the actual price paid was £2,400. Hammersley told the Commission that he believed fixed regulation prices should continue, in spite of the inflated amounts that were actually being paid. He argued that a regulated price would ensure that when soldiers or their families were forced to sell their commissions – either because the soldier had been killed or because he had been so badly injured in battle that he was no longer fit to serve, or merely because he had reached the age of retirement – they would receive a guaranteed amount.

If a captain wished to purchase a promotion to become a major, there would first have to be a commission available for sale. The difference in the regulation price for the rank of major and the over-regulation price agreed went to the vendor of the more senior rank. This was because he would need the extra money to cover the additional costs he may have incurred either in purchasing his existing rank or a new higher rank, or for kitting himself out. Pay in the British Army was not incremental with purchase price. Hammersley pointed out that a 'Subaltern in the Cavalry could not serve with comfort or respectability unless besides his pay, he had a private income of at least £300 a year'. Many who supported the system of purchasing commissions believed that officers who joined the Army out of loyalty to King and country rather than for monetary reward were the best men to lead it.

Hammersley was joined in his evidence that week by Prince George, Duke of Cambridge, Commander-in-Chief of the British Army, chief military adviser to the Secretary of State for War. The Duke had responsibility not only for command of soldiers in the field but also for the administration of the Army. The Duke gave evidence to the Royal Commission in support of the system of purchasing commissions. He recommended keeping the old system of recruitment and promotion which relied on an officer's social standing and therefore his ability to pay for his commission, rather than how good a soldier he might be. Hammersley and the Duke had both come to the same conclusion, although their reasoning was quite different, that the purchase of commission system was preferable to any alternative they might wish to consider.

One year later, the mutiny of soldiers of the East India Company army again highlighted the failings within the British Army itself. In 1858 the War Office appointed a Royal Commission into army reform under the auspices of Sir Jonathan Peel, the Secretary of State for War, to abolish the system of purchasing commissions and create a reserve armed force. The Commission's final recommendations were largely ignored by those in command and with influence who were by their very nature resistant to change. Years later in 1883, it was recorded in Hansard that 'there were questions constantly arising upon the payment of over regulation prices and Messrs Cox, the army agents, were examined over and over again, but declined to answer as they were not bound to incriminate themselves – such a system could never have arisen but for the fact that the evidence of what really took place could never be obtained. The House had to regard those illegal sales as established practice, and the country had to pay accordingly.'

On 18 June 1860, shortly after the end of the Inquiry, Hammersley was invited to St James's Palace

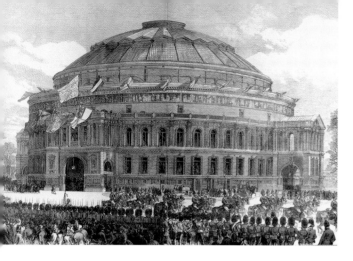

by his co-witness, Prince George, Duke of Cambridge, to attend the 200th anniversary of the formation of the First Grenadier regiment of the Foot Guards, of which the Duke was Colonel. Just as his predecessor Richard Cox, a century before, had won the confidence of the Commander-in-Chief and Colonel of the First Grenadier Guards, Lord Ligonier, so had Hammersley with his successor, the Duke of Cambridge.

THE NEW HOUSE AT COOMBE

At this time Hugh and Dulcibella lived in a very fashionable area of London, at 2 Kensington Gore. They had three young children – Arthur Charles, four, Hugh Greenwood, two, and a baby, Margaret – and employed seven staff including a nurse, a cook, a lady's maid, a housemaid, a nursemaid and a footman. It was an increasingly busy part of the capital because

the whole area had been redeveloped, creating 'Albertopolis' comprising museums and the Royal Albert Hall. This was the brainchild of Prince Albert, who wanted to create a great cultural centre in London, providing the masses with access to educational museums. He had instructed the Commissioners of the 1851 Great Exhibition to use the profits to purchase a block of land south of Hyde Park for this purpose. Prince Albert died in December 1861, just as the project was being completed.

When Charles Hammersley senior died in 1862, he left an estate valued at around £100,000. His son Hugh was a major beneficiary, and soon afterwards he and Dulcibella moved from their home in Kensington Gore, later demolished to make way for the Royal Albert Hall, to fashionable Cromwell Gardens. Their new London town house was opposite Brompton Park House, the location of the South Kensington Museum, later the site of the Aston Webb building which now houses the Victoria and Albert Museum.

In the late 1860s Hugh Hammersley, nearly 50 years old and a member of the emerging Victorian middle class, then made the most significant purchase of his life: land on which to build a country house. Under a lease with certain covenants and conditions of

Above: The burnt brick diapers are a distinctive feature of the oldest walls of Warren House

Right: The crest above the original front entrance to Warren House combines the three gold rams of the Hammersley family with the three garbs or wheatsheafs and three escallops of the Eden family

contract, he bought 14 acres of land on the Duke of Cambridge's Coombe Estate near Kingston upon Thames. Freeholder and leaseholder were associates who had been brought together by the Royal Commission into army reform and also timely good fortune, since one needed to sell the land and the other wanted to build a country house. The Duke of Cambridge was likely to have held an account at Cox's making the purchase straightforward and benefitting both parties. Coincidentally Dulcibella had lived with her family in a large house also known as Warren

House, some three miles to the east, on Wimbledon Common, and so was familiar with the area.

The plot Hugh Hammersley acquired was particularly large compared to other plots in the Coombe area of Kingston Vale, where an increasing number of big houses were being built. These included Galsworthy House, the home of John Galsworthy (the novelist's father) who in turn began to develop property in neighbouring George Road: Coombe Court, Coombe Leigh and Coombe Croft. These large houses attracted only those who could afford to buy or rent them as well as employ the staff needed to run them. These newcomers were characteristic of the era and included merchants dealing in goods from East India and China, army captains, baronets, magistrates, and even a jeweller from Hammersmith.

Right: Cover of James Veitch
and Sons' Rose catalogue, 1868

Below: View of Coombe
Wood Nursery

Above: Sir Harry James Veitch, 1871

Below: The Japanese gardens today

The architect of Warren House was Mr James Pearse St Aubyn. Renowned in London and Devon for his 'rather cheerless early gothic style', J. P. St Aubyn was better known for his churches than his houses, most notably the 1864 restoration of Temple Church in London. Mansfield & Co., builders and decorators of Gray's Inn Lane and Wigmore Street, London, were contracted to build the new house. George Mansfield and his son, Alfred John Mansfield, were partners in trade, employing 180 men in the 1850s. In the early 1860s they worked on the House of Correction at Coldbath Fields Prison, also known as Clerkenwell Gaol, constructing a central building to connect the two outer wings. A second son, George Needham Mansfield, was a highly renowned cabinet-maker and upholsterer, who swiftly rose to prominence after the 1862 International Exhibition.

Under instruction from J. P. St Aubyn, Mansfield commenced construction of a large red-brick, Gothic Revival-style building in the early part of the 1860s, but just as it was reaching completion, disaster struck. On Friday, 28 April 1865, fire engulfed the new building, almost totally destroying it. Very few details of the event survive, but whether insured or not it must have been a devastating blow for Hugh Hammersley. However, over the following five years, like a phoenix from the ashes, Warren House rose from the foundations of its predecessor, and Hugh Hammersley must have been enormously relieved.

He was even more delighted when a number of years later he managed to purchase an additional lease to a piece of land which dissected his land from neighbouring nursery James Veitch and Sons. By the mid-1870s the newly acquired land was laid out as a Japanese water garden, with large ponds, bridges and stepping stones, stone features including lanterns, and a tea house enclosed by a hedge, and planted with rare specimens of Oriental trees, plants and shrubs, which collectors working for Veitch had brought back to England. It was the first garden of its kind in the country, the idea not introduced fully until the early 20th century.

Despite the recommendations of the Royal Commission, it was not until 1870, just as the construction of Warren House was completed, that reform of the Army began to take place in the form of the Army Act. Finally, with the Regularisation of Forces Act of 1871 and the abolition of selling or buying commissions, real and lasting changes began to take effect, as Edward Cardwell, Secretary of State for War in Gladstone's Government, fundamentally restructured

Edward Cardwell, Secretary of State for War, by George Richmond, 1871

the Army introducing promotion by merit rather than by purchase. This was in spite of Hammersley's evidence in which he estimated that the cost to the Government of abolishing the purchase of commissions was £8 million, with £500,000 to £1 million on top of that in retirement costs each year. Money that had once been generated by the officers now had to come from the Exchequer.

Under Gladstone, the abolition of aristocratic privilege had greater support than under Palmerston's premiership, but Gladstone still had to resort to royal prerogative and the support of Queen Victoria to overcome opposition to army reform from the House of Lords and, in particular, the Duke of Cambridge, the Queen's cousin. Following these changes, competition for the more limited army agency work was acute, and many smaller agents were bought out. Fortunately for Cox's, business continued to thrive at Craig's Court. Hugh Hammersley lived in London during the week and was joined in the business by his sons, Arthur Charles and Hugh Greenwood Hammersley. For the most part the family used Warren House as their weekend country retreat.

Despite a heavy work-load, Hugh Hammersley still had time for his family. Dulcibella gave birth to the youngest of their seven children, Sylvia, in 1876, and Hugh seems to have displayed good judgment in order to secure their futures just as his great-uncle Charles Greenwood had done for him and his father. In late 1880, Hugh Hammersley gave his consent for his 18-year-old daughter Dora Edith, still a minor in the eyes of the law, to marry Francis Alexander Campbell, and he provided her with a substantial dowry. Campbell was the fifth son of Louisa Campbell, the daughter of Richard Henry Cox and wife of Colonel George Herbert Frederick Campbell. Hugh's instincts were correct: Sir Francis Campbell went on to become Assistant Under-Secretary at the Foreign Office, and was awarded the KCMG. Indeed marriage between the

two families was to continue when Hugh's son Arthur Charles married Mary Louisa Campbell, the daughter of George Augustus Campbell (a Lancashire cricket player and brother of Francis) and his wife Alice, in the summer of 1882.

Just a month later, tragedy struck. Hugh Hammersley died at Warren House, on 28 September 1882. He was just 63 years old and left a personal estate of £107,852 15s 6d. Cox's legal advisers, Fladgate, Smith and Fladgate, had drawn up his Last Will and Testament just over a year earlier. Solicitor William Mark Fladgate had other notable clients; he represented the Great Exhibition of 1851, Charing Cross Hospital and Drummonds Bank. It was the wish of Hugh Hammersley that 'his dear wife' Dulcibella remained financially secure for the rest of her life and in so doing he bequeathed not only the chattels of a lifetime – all the furniture, pictures, plate, linen, china, glass, jewels, trinkets, books, wines, carriages and horses that they had accumulated – but most importantly his status symbol, Warren House. It is a good indication of the importance he attached to his ownership of the estate that he was most specific in his wishes. The property was intended to be for his wife's own personal use and enjoyment, or if she preferred, to be rented out. Whichever was the case, after her death, he wanted Warren House to be passed on to his eldest surviving son.

Having provided amply for his sons and unmarried daughters, he also included his faithful servants: French governess Aglae Schnaebele received £100 as a sign of his appreciation for her educating his daughters for over ten years. To each of his servants who had, at the time of his death, worked for him for two years or more, one year's wages over and above their usual pay. This would have included Eliza Cuckson, who had been with the Hammersleys as both housekeeper and cook since before 1861, and William Hall, initially a footman and then butler in

HAMMERSLEY'S LEGACY

The Hammersley family's wealth and status continued to flourish after Hugh's death as his siblings were united through marriage and procreation with the great banking and finance families of Cox, Drummond, Eden, Baring, Hambro, Thomson, Bonar, Glyn and Mills.

Hugh's brother, Major General Frederick Hammersley, became known as the father of army gymnastics and was the co-founder of the Amateur Athletic Association.

Julia Hammersley married Captain Edward Joseph Hill Jekyll of the Grenadier Guards. Four sons survived: the Revd Walter Jekyll spent his life in Jamaica and lent his name to his friend Robert Louis Stevenson for his novel, *Jekyll and Hyde*; Colonel Sir Herbert of the Royal Engineers rose to the dizzy heights of private secretary to the Viceroy of India, and assistant secretary to the Board of Trade; Arthur Jekyll joined the Navy but sadly drowned on *HMS Orpheus* in 1863; Edward was a captain in the Foot Guards. Gertrude Jekyll became the famous Victorian landscape gardener. Julia's other daughter, Caroline Jekyll, married her uncle's brother-in-law Frederick Eden and together they established a magical garden in Venice at Palazzo Barbarigo.

Gertrude Jekyll, the niece of Hugh Hammersley, by Sir William Nicholson, 1920

1871, who may still have been with the family, as well as Elizabeth Wilmot, a housemaid who had served ten years at 4 Cromwell Gardens, and perhaps Esther Maynard, the 39-year-old housemaid from Tunbridge Wells, who worked at Warren House.

A year after Hugh Hammersley's death, the partners in Cox's were still family members: his brother Charles Hammersley; eldest son Arthur Charles Hammersley; Henry Richard Cox and Frederick Cox, the brother and son of Richard Henry Cox; and George Augustus Campbell, nephew to the Cox's and father-in-law to Arthur Charles. The role of the business was much the same as it had been earlier that century, but army reforms had taken their toll on the way profits were made. Hugh's brother Charles Hammersley died in 1890, and Hugh Greenwood Hammersley joined the partnership. In 1892, the government fee for disbursements was cancelled, and from then on the firm's profits had to be made

entirely from the banking services offered to officers and their families.

Dulcibella, however, only retained Warren House until the end of 1884. History does not relate why she went against her husband's wishes. Perhaps the tragic death at Warren House of a premature stillborn baby, the child of her eldest son and his wife, in summer 1883, precipitated the sale of Warren House the following year. Whatever her reasons, Dulcibella moved on; she had a family house at Freshwater on the Isle of Wight, and a London home at Sun House on Chelsea Embankment where she died in 1903, aged 70. What seems remarkable at the end of this first chapter in the history of Warren House is that the Hammersleys did not sever all ties with the Coombe Estate when Dulcibella sold Warren House – for, in 1885, Hugh's niece, Rosa Frederica Baring, married Colonel George William Adolphus FitzGeorge, the eldest son of the Duke of Cambridge himself.

2

1884-94

THE TALE OF THE POLITICIAN AND
THE VICAR'S DAUGHTER

GEORGE GRENFELL GLYN, 2ND BARON WOLVERTON (1824-87)
AND LADY GEORGIANA MARIA JULIA WOLVERTON (1826-94)

WARREN **H**OUSE and its 'beautifully timbered pleasure grounds in all nearly 13 acres, including an exceptionally lovely Japanese garden' were put up for auction on 25 March 1884. The successful purchaser was George Grenfell Glyn, 2nd Baron Wolverton, a Liberal member of the House of Lords, and at the time Paymaster-General in Gladstone's second government. He was the eldest of nine sons of the banker George Carr Glyn, 1st Baron Wolverton, from whom he had inherited not only the barony 11 years earlier, but also a large fortune, amassed by his father from the profits of the bank Glyn, Mills, Currie & Co. through shrewd investment in the railways, at home and abroad.

Opposite: Architect George Devey's new east front to Warren House

Above: The eagle and escallop detail from the Wolverton crest from the architrave above the front door of Warren House

It seems that Wolverton was only interested in the house itself, for after occupying it for a short time, an advertisement appeared in the *Morning Post* on 18 August 1884 for an auction of:

> … the contents of the mansion, including the appointments of 23 bedrooms, four reception rooms, and offices, comprising suites of furniture in various woods, duchesse toilet tables, wardrobes, French bedsteads, and bedding, carved oak dining room and library furniture, carpets, batterie de cuisine &c, two Jersey cows, a heifer, donkey, 80 head of poultry and effects.

Almost immediately after purchasing the lease of Warren House, Wolverton engaged the architect George Devey to make substantial alterations to the existing building. Whether Wolverton had met Devey when he had dined with his London neighbour Lord Granville (for whom the architect had worked) at Carlton House Terrace, or had merely made an appointment at the offices of Devey and Williams at their fashionable 123 Bond Street address, he was

Sketch by George Devey of Warren House, 1884

obviously impressed by his judgment and advice, and work on Warren House began in December 1884. Over the next two years, Devey made additions to the east front of the building overlooking the lawns and substantial additions to the offices on the west side of the house, near the staff quarters and kitchens, where he 'added a gable in rough cast, with a curly barge board', the only part of the building whose design is unlike the rest of the house and tucked away at an awkward angle. He was careful to match his work with the original J. P. St Aubyn house, including the coloured bricks which form patterns to resemble timbering, slate roofs and tall chimneys, high lancet windows, bay windows, balconies and balustrades.

Once he had produced the drawings, Devey took a more relaxed approach to building than many architects of his day; he left most of the construction to the expertise of local builders, perhaps together with rafter and chimney plans and details of dragon beams or pendants. He does not seem to have designed fixtures or fittings, but may have advised on plaster-work and panelling detail. He never used window sashes or small panes, which is why all the Devey windows at Warren House are stone mullion. He distrusted the use of modern iron construction, as used in Crystal Palace for the 1851 Exhibition, finding bricks and timber much more to his liking. At Warren House, he was also responsible for the design of some of the garden terraces, walls and steps, to the east of the house. Devey's bill for the works was £1,047; with labour and building materials, one report suggests that the total was in the region of £30,000.

Warren House was one of Devey's last commissions. After simultaneously designing additions to another of Bertram Currie's houses in Hampshire, the Bromley house of another banker, Sir Everard Alexander Hambro, and a large extension to the Dorset home – 'Gaunts' – of Wolverton's cousin Sir Richard George Glyn, which he probably never saw completed, Devey died in November 1886.

Above: George Devey's design for the fireplace and surrounding wall in the dining room at Warren House

Below: the fireplace, unchanged at Warren House today

GEORGE DEVEY ON THE COOMBE ESTATE

The architect George Devey (1820–86). His work at Warren House was to be some of his last

Devey was an architect of high repute, particularly among Liberal Party members and the banking community, and especially on the Coombe Estate. He came with recommendations from two of Wolverton's friends and colleagues, new neighbours at Coombe. Edward 'Ned' Baring of Baring Brothers & Co., financier and former Liberal MP, had employed Devey in the 1860s to build a new stable block and make large additions to his house Coombe Cottage and associated dairy. Baring's neighbour, Bertram Wodehouse Currie, a partner in the Glyn family bank Glyn, Mills, Currie & Co., had employed Devey firstly to make additions to his

newly purchased house Coombe Warren, about a mile from Warren House, between 1868 and 1869, and secondly, after a fire destroyed the newly finished building, he was instructed to construct a new house on the site. Building work was completed on Coombe Warren II in 1872. Devey had also done work in the 1870s for Ferdinand James de Rothschild in Buckinghamshire, Baron Meyer Amschel de Rothschild at his London home, 107 Piccadilly, and the 2nd Earl Granville, Liberal Party leader in the House of Lords, Foreign Secretary and Wolverton's London neighbour at 18 Carlton House Terrace.

THE GLYN FAMILY

Lord Wolverton was 60 and at the height of his political career when he bought the lease on Warren House from Dulcibella Hammersley, later acquiring a further 14 acres of land from the Duke of Cambridge. Born on 10 February 1824, he was the eldest son of George Carr Glyn and his wife Marianne Grenfell, who lived in Stratton Street, London, just off Piccadilly. The Glyn family were bankers, part-owners of the private banking house which had been founded in 1753 at the sign of the Anchor in 70 Lombard Street under the name of Vere Glyn and Halifax. By 1800 the bank had moved round the corner to Birchin Lane, the Glyn and Halifax partnership was joined by Charles Mills, and it became known as Glyn, Mills, Halifax & Co. Then, by 1826, the bank headquarters had moved back to Lombard Street at number 67, near the Bank of

England, in the very heart of the City of London. Bankers based in the City were involved in commercial transactions, rather than mortgage lending to the landed gentry which tended to be the focus of West End-based bankers. Sir Richard Carr Glyn (1755–1838), grandfather of the 2nd Baron Wolverton, was a partner in the bank and one-time Lord Mayor of London like his father before him. He was also an MP for St Ives in Cornwall. The remarkable growth of the business under Richard Carr Glyn can be attributed to the fact that the firm established itself as the London agent to a great number of country banks, whose bank bills were drawn on and made payable at Glyn's.

It was the success of the fourth son, George Carr Glyn (1797–1873), which was to herald the meteoric rise of the Glyn family. From an early age, George Carr Glyn, educated at Westminster, showed great aptitude for banking and had a commercial awareness over and above that of his brothers. This was demonstrated in a letter he wrote to his father just after joining the bank in 1816 at the age of 19, where he stressed the advantage of selling India Bonds and buying Consolidated stock, a form of British government bond, at a time when the British East India Company was facing a lot of resistance from regional rulers. Two years later he became a partner. At the age of 28, George Carr was at the head of a project for the new St Katharine Docks in London, east of the Tower of London. All the great Port of London docks were built in the 25 years following the French Revolution, and some had certain exclusive restrictions. In 1823, just as these were about to expire, a parliamentary commission voted in favour of more open competition between the various dock companies. In the light of this, and the fact that with over 16,000 ships moored on the Thames in 1824 there was an increasing need for warehousing, the promoters of St Katharine Docks stepped in and secured an Act of Parliament to build the new dock. George Glyn, his father and their banking partners were all large subscribers to the capital for the new docks; Glyn's were appointed bankers to the company. Between 1829 and 1831 the bank advanced over £150,000 for the construction of the docks and building of warehouses. Glyn's role as treasurer of the St Katharine Dock Company was to pave the way for what has been described as his chief success – railways finance.

Glyn's interest in railways stemmed from his free trade sympathies, together with the influence of his brother-in-law, Pascoe St Leger Grenfell, a director of the London and Birmingham railway. In 1833 Parliament passed a Bill for the construction of a railway between London and Birmingham; Glyn, Halifax, Mills & Co. became the construction company's London bankers and George Carr Glyn, a member of the London board, was chosen as chairman of the London and Birmingham Railway Company in 1837. As such he became the head of one of the most powerful associations in the world, with capital in excess of £20 million and a line of more than 400 miles, which was opened in 1838. Glyn remained

chairman for 15 years of the London and Birmingham (which became the London and North Western in 1846). He was also a director of Chester and Holyhead Railway, and the Globe Insurance Company. The *London Illustrated News* said of him in 1847: 'As a banker he has the reputation of being one of the most liberal in London in his mode of conducting business. He is very active with energetic habits.' In 1839, when the Whig Party of Lord Melbourne set up the first department to deal with education, George Carr Glyn showed his Whiggish leanings when he proposed that the London and Birmingham Company should build schools for the children of the employees at Wolverton in Buckinghamshire, where the line was yet to be finished.

He was elected to Parliament as MP for Kendall in 1847, where he did much work behind the scenes for Gladstone at the Exchequer. George Carr Glyn was a member of the 1858 Royal Commission into army reform, hearing evidence from the Duke of Cambridge and army agents, such as Hugh Hammersley. Glyn was also responsible for setting up the Railway Clearing House, which opened at Euston in January 1842. It was 'designed to facilitate through bookings for passengers and freight between the various railway companies'. Glyn's services to the London and North Western were honoured by a full-length painting that hung in the boardroom at Euston, and when he was awarded a peerage in 1869, he wrote to the directors at Euston informing them that he had decided to take

An example of a Glyn, Mills, Currie and Co. cheque. The bank continued to flourish, long after George Grenfell Glyn took up his political career

the title of Wolverton to mark 'my connection with the good old honest company, in whose service so much of my life has passed'. It was said that he 'greatly enhanced the reputation of the firm by his industry and ability'. The business that came to Glyn's from investment in the railways was enormous, as they provided the banking facilities for more than 200 of the new railway companies, earning them the reputation as 'the railway bank'. In 1840 Glyn's came second only to Barclays in the amount of money passed through the clearing house, namely £105 million. In 1849, the *Banker's Magazine* said: 'The Bank of Glyn has probably the largest business of any of the London Banks, the [numbers of] staff and clerks in town and country departments are we believe second only to the Bank of England.'

THE LURE OF POLITICS

George Grenfell Glyn was his father's natural successor at the bank. Author Roger Fulford writes of him: '[He] had all the training and all the attributes for success in Lombard Street. While he may have lacked the judgment and balance of his father and grandfather, he had a drive and energy which were remarkable and which might have carried the Bank to fresh triumphs in the difficult decades which closed the nineteenth century.' He was educated at Rugby and University College Oxford, where he particularly enjoyed hunting. In 1848 he married Georgiana Maria Julia

Tufnell, the eldest daughter of the Revd George Tufnell, Vicar of Uffington in Berkshire, to whom he must have seemed a good prospect as he was already a partner in the bank.

However, George Grenfell Glyn preferred the lure of the Palace of Westminster to that of Lombard Street. Perhaps he was responding to the principles instilled in him by Rugby School's great headmaster, Dr Arnold, who believed in the preparation for power: 'first religious and moral principle, second gentlemanly conduct, third academic ability'. In 1857 he was elected to the House of Commons as MP for Shaftesbury, Dorset, initially as a Whig and then in 1859, as a member of the newly formed Liberal Party under the leadership of Lord Palmerston. George Grenfell Glyn's wealth, derived from the successful investments of his father and the growth of their bank, coupled with his own determination, gained him immediate influence within the party. In the past bankers had held seats in Parliament, but by the 1860s the wealth of the bankers had enabled them to purchase a completely different career in public life. For George Grenfell Glyn, however, conflicting interests meant that his dual role as both an active banker and public servant would not last for long. In 1866, just eight months after the death of the Prime Minister Lord Palmerston, Gladstone, then Chancellor of the Exchequer, approached George Grenfell Glyn to fill the post of Chief Whip of the Liberal Party. Glyn declined, making it clear that he could not accept unless he was allowed to remain a partner, albeit an inactive one, in his bank. The problem was that if the Liberal Party was returned to power in the coming election, Glyn as Chief Whip would also have been appointed Parliamentary Secretary to the Treasury, and a professional banker in the Treasury was not above suspicion.

George Grenfell Glyn was Chief Whip during Prime Minister Gladstone's first premiership

Glyn held his ground and, despite objections from within the Liberal Party, in 1866 was appointed to the post of Chief Whip, and was permitted to remain a partner at the bank. The following year saw the passing of the Second Reform Act, which doubled the number of adult men eligible to vote to over three million. However, party leaders did not know how they were going to organise and control new voters, and furthermore with little redistribution of seats, the Liberal Party were at a disadvantage compared to their Tory rivals. George Grenfell Glyn warned Gladstone that the next general election would be an 'incalculable business … all is new and changed and large and I fear I must say in some respects, dark'. Ultimately the effects of the Second Reform Act aided the rise of the Liberals and helped Gladstone to victory, and by 1868, Glyn was rarely seen at the bank. One of the partners, Bertram Currie, explained: 'He was quick, lively and intelligent and able to inspire personal regard, a valuable attribute in the qualification of a banker, but he was too fond of change and excitement to be content with the daily round and common tasks of City life. It was, I think, to please his father that he remained so long a worker in Lombard Street.'

George Grenfell Glyn remained Liberal Chief Whip right through Gladstone's first premiership, ensuring that Liberal MPs attended the Commons and voted as the Prime Minister desired. Furthermore, he and Gladstone were next-door neighbours at Carlton House Terrace, the preferred residence of prime ministers, statesmen and ambassadors. It was a period of Liberal reform: the Cardwell reforms in the British Army had abolished the sale of commissions, new restrictions on individual advancement in the civil service and local government were introduced, as were the first attempts to achieve fairness in Ireland by the disestablishment of the Irish Church and reform of the Irish system of land tenure. Gladstone's Government also changed the nature of English elections through the introduction of secret voting ballots.

On the death of his father, the 1st Baron Wolverton, in 1873, George Grenfell Glyn inherited a large amount of money along with the title, and took up his seat in the House of Lords. It was something that he had looked forward to since an encounter with

TO THE

ELECTORS

OF THE BOROUGH OF

SHAFTESBURY.

GENTLEMEN,

The death of my dear Father, LORD WOLVERTON, has called me to the House of Lords, and has caused a vacancy in the Representation of your Borough

In returning to your hands the trust which you have for seventeen years confided to me, I beg to thank you for the kindness which I have ever received from you.

I look back with pleasure to the period during which I have had the honor of representing you in Parliament. I tender to you my acknowledgments for the opportunities your confidence has afforded me of promoting to the best of my ability, in public and in private, those liberal principles which I have ever professed, and I hope consistently adhered to.

I recognise your indulgence on many occasions, and thank you for the opportunity you have given me, as your Member, of placing my services, however humble, at the disposal of my great leader, MR. GLADSTONE, and the Liberal Party, during an eventful period in the House of Commons.

Our political connection is at an end, but I hope I may trust that I have your sympathy in the great sorrow which now overshadows me, and that the mutual feelings of esteem and regard which I believe to exist between us may long continue.

With the renewed expression of my warmest gratitude and thanks,

I have the honor to be

Your most faithful servant,

GEORGE G. GLYN.

12, Carlton House Terrace, London.
July 30th, 1873.

BASTABLE, Printer, Stationer, Bookseller, &c., Stamp Office, SHAFTESBURY.

George Grenfell Glyn resigned his seat in the Houses of Parliament in 1873 after the death of his father. This poster, informing them of his decision, was displayed in his local Dorset constituency

Gladstone and Lord Granville at the Treasury back in 1869. While drawing up honours for submission to the Queen, Gladstone had asked him if he thought his father would like to be a peer. Glyn had laughed and declared that he supposed that such an idea had never entered the old gentleman's head, but that he would like to have the peerage in his turn and that, therefore, he would accept on his behalf. Lord Wolverton was succeeded as whip by Arthur Peel, youngest son of Sir Robert Peel. Despite his absence from the Commons, the friendship that had developed between Wolverton and Gladstone was to last until his death. The Liberal Party lost the next election of 1874 to Disraeli's Tories and Gladstone retired, albeit temporarily, as party leader.

WOLVERTON'S SPORTING PASTIMES

Perhaps because the Liberals were no longer in power and the Lords did not require so much of his time, the 2nd Baron Wolverton purchased a 2,000-acre estate at Iwerne in North Dorset, not far from his old constituency and the Glyn family seat at Gaunts, near Wimborne. In 1876 he employed Alfred Waterhouse, architect of the Natural History Museum, to design a new mansion in the fashionable Tudor-Gothic style. Wolverton rebuilt and improved the entire parish, building cottages for his employees. He gave up some of his estate to test out the practicality of the allotment system, 'three acres and a cow', and was well liked by local people. But above all, it was ideal for a man who had enjoyed country pursuits since his Oxford days. He owned a famous pack of black and tan St Hubert bloodhounds, bred in Ireland, a few of which he exhibited in 1875 at Crystal Palace. As Master of the Ranston Hunt he and his huntsman, John Boore, hunted carted deer (captive-bred deer released for the chase, then recaptured) in the Vale of Blackmore for

Lord Wolverton owned a famous pack of black and tan St Hubert bloodhounds, with which he hunted carted deer in the Vale of Blackmore in Dorset

eight seasons. Lady Theodora Guest remembers: 'April 8th – 12 o'clock, Lord Wolverton did not keep us waiting, it was a lovely spring day. The Master in his green coat with gilt buttons, embroidered on it a coronet with the letter W.' Another huntsman remembers Wolverton on a milk-white horse, amid golden daffodils, beneath a blue sky. Whyte-Melville, a Scottish novelist and poet of the sporting-field, and a regular at the hunts wrote:

A spirited and truly artistic oil painting, 14 foot long, of these hounds in chase, sweeping like a whirlwind over the downs, by Mr [George Bouverie] Goddard, the well-known painter, hangs on Lord Wolverton's staircase in London, and conveys to his guests, particularly after dinner, so vivid an idea of their picturesque and even sporting qualities as I cannot hope to represent with humble pen and ink. If I were sure of a fine morning and a safe mount I would ask for no keener pleasure than an hour's gallop with Lord Wolverton's bloodhounds over the Blackmore Vale.

Lord Wolverton remained Master of the Hunt until 1880; his patience with the bloodhounds, which do not pack naturally because each likes to follow the scent on its

Tattersall's racehorse auction at
Newmarket, *Vanity Fair*, 1887

own, was commented on by Sir Reginald Henry
Graham in *Fox Hunting Recollections*: 'The 15 couple
big black and tan hounds had a reputation of going
great pace over the Dorsetshire downs. Lord Wolverton
cried out to a young sportsman who popped his whip
"For heaven's sake, don't crack your whip or every one
of them will go straight home".'

In addition to his fondness for hunting and in the
true style of a wealthy country gentleman, Wolverton
also bred cattle and gaming birds at his Iwerne Estate.
But it was his stud farm and thoroughbred racehorses
in which he invested a huge amount of money. He
made most of his money from sales of yearlings bred at
his stud. He purchased the good, thoroughbred brood
mares he needed at enormous cost; for example, at a
sale of the Marden Stud at Tattersalls in 1885, Lord
Wolverton spent £4,260 guineas in one day, his
purchases making up just over 20 per cent of the total
auction sale for that day. Lord Wolverton had mighty
deep pockets when it came to racehorses, but in true

banker's style his expenses and losses were always
offset by his sales. In 1884 he took 1,600 guineas for
a sister of The Bard, the Prince of Wales paid 1,100
guineas for Calistos, 800 guineas for a filly named
The Falcon, and a colt, Madrida, fetched 910 guineas.
In 1886, the sale of 11 yearlings raised 3,665 guineas,
an average of 333 guineas each. These kinds of results
put him among the top ten breeders in the country.

The third and most costly of all Lord Wolverton's
sporting pastimes was yachting. In 1882 he bought
an iron-screw schooner, designed and built by
Robert Steele & Co. on the Clyde at Greenock.
Palatine weighed 305 tons, was 159 feet long with
a 25-foot beam, and was handsomely rigged as a
three-masted, topsail schooner. The waters of the
Solent and the Channel are the favourite choice of
sailors and the Royal Yacht Squadron (RYS) based
out of Cowes on the Isle of Wight was to yachtsmen
what Queen Victoria was to England. Membership of
the RYS, however, was highly exclusive and even the
wealthiest could not buy their way in. Indeed Lord
Wolverton was blackballed in 1882, and was only
elected when proposed by the Earl of Normanton

WOLVERTON'S RACEHORSES

Wolverton employed one of the most successful trainers of the day, Arthur Yates, who after a career as a jockey had become a trainer at his family home in Hampshire. Yates had ridden more than 450 winners over fences in his early slimmer days, including both the 1870 and 1872 Grand Nationals. However, he had much more success as a trainer, saddling nearly 3,000 winners. With an aptitude for maintaining fit and healthy horses, he introduced the use of water for pain relief and treatment of racehorses with leg problems, when he built a box over a stream in which a horse with leg problems could be stood. So long as they were fit and well, Wolverton's horses raced at Sandown Park in Esher (opened in April 1875) and Kempton Park in Sunbury (opened in July 1878), where winners included Ancient Pistols, who won the Sunbury Handicap Steeplechase by three lengths in 1884, earning him a return on this investment.

He and his stud farm manager became experts in identifying the physical and athletic attributes, or desirable ancestry, necessary in a mare for successful thoroughbred breeding. While it was not unusual for him to make an offer on a horse that took his attention during the hunt, most of Wolverton's thoroughbred brood mares were of very sound pedigree. One of their greatest breeding successes, sold at Newmarket in 1884, was The Bard. He was a small chestnut colt with a blade and white hind sock and although he grew to barely 15 hands, he has been called a pocket Hercules, 'no better legs and feet were ever seen, his legs like bars of iron, altogether truly shaped with action, beautifully true ... He had the courage of a lion and the dash of a true race horse', and he went on to win 23 out of 25 races and earn £9,188 for his owner.

Arthur Yates (1841–1922), former jockey and racehorse trainer

The Bard – Wolverton's greatest breeding success

Below: *Palatine*, rigged as a
three-masted topsail schooner,
bought by Wolverton in 1882

and Lord Colville the following year. At the Cowes
Week Regatta that summer, he entered *Palatine* in a
supplementary event against two other of the largest
auxiliary steam yachts, *Czarina* and *Chazalie*, belonging
to the squadron. The course was around the Isle of
Wight under sail, but without the use of her two-
cylinder, 70HP engine, *Palatine* was no match for
Czarina and *Chazalie*. While she may not have won
the race, *Palatine* gave Wolverton status, mobility and
advantage over others. Montague Guest, a Liberal MP
for Wareham in Dorset and fellow RYS member,
criticised Wolverton for using *Palatine* to 'steam from
one Dorset port to another with the Chancellor of the
Exchequer, Sir William Harcourt', in order that he
might address meetings in various parts of the country
at election time. Guest even went so far as to accuse
Wolverton of rigging the vote on polling day by
collecting a Conservative-voting crew from Weymouth
and sailing with them to the Isle of Wight where they
were not able to vote, while putting ashore one hand
who was a Liberal voter!

Wolverton did not deny these accusations, and must
have relished the manner in which *Palatine* strengthened
his relationship with the Liberal Party and Gladstone
in particular, even if the Grand Old Man found it hard
at times to locate his sea legs as his diaries (Vol. 10)
attest: 'The Palatine 1882 16/19 August: Wolverton's
Yacht. On Saturday after staying at Osborne House –
sailed to Portland, four hours with much motion,
which I did not stand well, being fresh from hard brain
work, which makes a great difference in the power of
resisting sea sickness.' Lord Wolverton had the great
man's full attention when yachting off the south coast
or perhaps in a more relaxed state of mind in the
warmer waters off the French Riviera in 1883, when
they stayed together in February at Chateau Scott with
their wives and Gladstone's son Stephen, with *Palatine*
in the harbour with its crew: 'Chateau Scott Cannes
1883 18 January: One of the finest Houses in Cannes.
Nobly situated, admirably planned and the kindness
(of the Wolvertons) even exceeded the beauty and the
comfort' (Gladstone's Diaries, Vol. 10).

FRIENDSHIP WITH GLADSTONE

The two families had become firm friends and
Gladstone's daughter wrote fondly of her father's
escapades with Wolverton and 'his good spirits, keen
pugnacity, singularly practical and un-philosophical
views of politics'. These were better times, as the
Liberals had won the 1880 general election.
Wolverton was long remembered by those at the
Reform Club when he strolled in to hear the
first day's pollings wearing evening dress, an
Inverness cape hanging from his shoulders,
and a Jehu's hat (presumably resembling
the hats worn by 'Jehus' or stagecoach
drivers in America) jauntily cocked over his
eyes. He stood by the noticeboard waving
this unbecoming head gear, as he led the
cheering of an excited, triumphant, united
Liberal Party, filling the hall staircase and gallery,
while news of the Liberal victory came flooding in.
On Gladstone's return to office, Lord Wolverton was
appointed Paymaster-General, a post highly relevant
to his banking experience. He was, however, quite
aggrieved, thinking he had been passed over for
political office, and remarked to Sir Edward Hamilton,
private secretary to Gladstone, that he ought to have
had at least such an office as the Chancellorship of the
Duchy of Lancaster, with a seat in the Cabinet! Despite
this, he held office through the course of the ministry
until 1885, and his loyalty to Gladstone did not
waiver. The hours he worked were long, and he
regularly left Downing Street, or his club Brooks's in
St James's, after late night meetings over dinner and
walked back to his home in Carlton House Terrace. At
weekends, when Parliament was in session, he needed
somewhere closer than his Dorset seat to be able to
commute to Westminster and continue his work,
which may be one of the reasons why he bought
Warren House.

Portraits of Gladstone (top) and George Grenfell
Glyn (above). *Illustrated London News*, 1869

'When he was a boy at Oxford he had set his heart
on three things – to marry a beautiful wife, to be Whip
of the Liberal party, and to be master of the hounds.
All three wishes were fulfilled.' This was according to
Algernon West, one of Gladstone's private secretaries.
West went on to say of Wolverton:

He was a strange character; and he possessed in almost
equal portions the qualifications which a Whip should
have and the disqualifications a Whip should not have.
Among the former were his energy, his fidelity and his
blunt admiration of and devotion to his master, his
entire absorption in his work, and his sharpness and
ability. On the other hand his devotion made him
blind and obstinate, and he was overbearing to those
who even ventured to differ from anything Mr.
Gladstone thought right. He was perhaps tactless and
apt to be tyrannical, very fidgety, and possessing none

of that calm which enables a man to weather the political storm. But take him all in all, he was a joyous companion and a sincere friend and his wife's beauty and reposeful yet enthusiastic temperament compensated for many of his faults.

Although Warren House was within easy commuting distance of Westminster, Wolverton's purchase of the Coombe property in 1884 was probably made for the same reason as the purchase of his yacht, *Palatine* – because he could afford it. Unlike his yacht, which it is said his wife could not bear, Warren House was a place where she could entertain on a splendid scale. And Lord and Lady Wolverton did indeed entertain, seemingly oblivious to the alterations and extensions that Devey was making to Warren House. On Sundays, they kept an open house, and anyone who had received a general invitation was welcome. According to the *New York Times*, which kept a close eye on the social scene in London, there were seldom fewer than 30 at dinner. His guests were mainly his Liberal Party colleagues: Lord Granville, three times Secretary of State for Foreign Affairs; Lord Grosvenor, 1st Duke of Westminster and Master of the Horse in Gladstone's 1880–5 government; Bertram Wodehouse Currie, Wolverton's close friend, neighbour and partner at Glyn, Mills, Currie & Co.; Sir William Vernon Harcourt, Home Secretary throughout Gladstone's second government (1880–5), later leader of the Liberal Party himself; and the 5th Earl Spencer, John Poyntz, who served in Gladstone's administration as Lord Lieutenant of Ireland in the early 1870s, and again in 1882–5. Their leader, William Ewart Gladstone, was also a regular guest at Warren House between 1884 and 1886.

According to Gladstone's personal diaries, he came not only to discuss the issues facing his Government but to enjoy the kindness of his hosts, and to read in the tranquil setting of Warren House, perhaps under a tree in the peace of the garden on a sunny day.

Interestingly he notes down the titles of books he read while at Warren House, their subject matter vividly conveying the interests and thoughts of the statesman; some of them might even have been books that Wolverton had purchased en bloc from Gladstone when he had been forced to sell in a moment of financial stress and difficulty. On 12 July 1884, Gladstone wrote: 'Wolverton's House at Coombe, read G Gemunder, Francesco Cenci, finished the Apostles' Creed.' Gemunder wrote about the arts and its critics in general, Antonio Bertolotti's book on Cenci, written in Italian in 1877, tells of a notorious libertine whose family conspired to murder him, and the Apostles' Creed is a religious text. On later visits to Warren House, it is interesting to follow the wide range of titles, both light and serious, that Gladstone enjoyed. He read Edward O'Dell's *Merciful or Merciless*, a novel; *La Mort Edifiante, or the last hours of Mlle de la Musse*; 'Letters of the Duchess d'Orleans', Elizabeth Charlotte, Princess Palatine, about the court of Louis XIV; Edward Bellamy, American author and socialist; Heraclides, the Greek astronomer, who was the first to propose that the sun was the centre of the universe; several books on religion and also politics, such as G. J. Holyoake's *Deliberate Liberalism*; a biography of Erasmus Darwin; and the correspondence of Edmund Burke, an 18th-century Whig, considered today to be the philosophical founder of modern conservatism.

Wolverton's moral and financial support for Gladstone never faltered. Lord Randolph Churchill said of the two men: 'Mr Gladstone is without exception one of the richest men in England, Lord Wolverton one of the senior partners, I believe, in one of the greatest banks in the City; and he, I am informed on the most reliable authority, has given many thousands of pounds to Mr Gladstone's fund, and is at this present moment engaged in buying up all the horses in Dorsetshire in order to prevent the Conservative voters from going to the polls.'

THE IRISH QUESTION

Gladstone's second ministry, like his first, was highly concerned with Irish affairs: 'My mission is to pacify Ireland.' Gladstone was an Anglican with an evangelical upbringing. He was a man moved by religion and saw politics and political issues in terms of ethics, and Irish affairs were no exception. He believed that England had wronged Ireland, and that he had a moral duty to right those wrongs.

He believed that the grievances of the Irish tenant farmers were due to the dominance of the Protestant elite over the rural Roman Catholics, and in 1869 he succeeded in disestablishing the Irish Protestant Church and passed the Irish Land Act to rein in unfair landlords. However, in 1878 an agricultural depression hit Ireland. The Irish National Land League under Charles Stewart Parnell, leader of the Irish Home Rule Party, argued that Ireland could 'not be cultivated unless the people of the country owned it'. The 'land war' was in full swing when Gladstone came back to power in 1880, and Parnell and many others were arrested. In 1881 the Second Irish Land Act was passed granting fair rent, free sale and fixity of tenure. An agreement was eventually reached between the British Government and the Irish nationalists, and Parnell was set to be released. But in May 1882, the murder by Irish nationalists of the Under-Secretary, T. H. Burke, and the Chief Secretary for Ireland, Lord Frederick Cavendish, Gladstone's nephew and friend, in Dublin's Phoenix Park, set negotiations back months. Gladstone became convinced that England could no longer govern Ireland except by coercion, but the rule of law could only be restored under an Irish parliament. He began to believe that Irish Home Rule was the solution, even though he knew it would divide his own Cabinet. Gladstone's second ministry was brought to an abrupt end in June 1885: he resigned because of the combination of a huge budget deficit

due to the wars in Afghanistan and Sudan, and little development on the Irish issues, and this gave him time to think.

Thinking time and undoubtedly further discussions on Ireland must have taken place at Warren House between Gladstone and his fellow Liberal Party members during his visits in the summer of 1885.

Irish National Invincibles assassinate Lord Frederick Cavendish and Thomas H. Burke, Under-Secretary at the Irish office, in Phoenix Park, Dublin, 1882

Feeling totally at home there, he began to write his Irish policy and read avidly:

11th July – Went to Wolverton's Villa. Saw Lord Grosvenor, Mr McColl, Lord Granville, Lord Spencer, Mr Currie. Read 'Fortnightly on Ireland – an Oxford Professorship' [an academic pamphlet], the Radical Programme's National Council's proposal [a campaign handbook of British political history prefaced by Joseph Chamberlain, detailing his proposals for National Councils in England, Scotland and Ireland].

18th July – Drove to Lord Wolverton's, only the Harcourts there. Dr S came, treatment number 3, read Smyth on 'Old Faiths in New Light' (1879) – Reville's 'History of Religion', and Waksman's 'History of Religion in England'.

19th July – Sunday church in the evening. Saw Lord Wolverton, Sir W Harcourt (Irish affairs).

The Liberal Party won the election of 1885, and was returned to power in January 1886. According to the recollections of Algernon West, Gladstone's private secretary, who dined with Lord Wolverton at the London Whig club, Brooks's, on 15 December, the peer was apparently made a serious offer of the Lord Lieutenancy of Ireland, but it was decided that the position of Postmaster-General suited him much better. Algernon West also describes his visit to Warren House in March 1886: 'On Saturday we went to Coombe Wood in which Lord Wolverton had bought a house and made it very pretty under the artistic guidance of Mr Devey, the famous architect, with whom our youngest son was working. Arnold Morley and Lord Spencer came down and discussed the Irish question from every point of view.'

Gladstone stayed at Warren House during the weekend of 3–5 April 1886. In his entry for Sunday 5 April, he writes, 'Fourth Sunday in Lent. Four hours at Coombe on the matter of my speech.' In Parliament on Wednesday 8 April, this very same speech introduced the first Irish Home Rule Bill, 'The Government of Ireland Bill 1886'. It was Gladstone's first official attempt to create a devolved assembly for Ireland which would govern in specified areas, although Britain would retain control over issues of war, defence, treaties with foreign states, trade and coinage. Wolverton had dinner with Algernon West afterwards, and then they went to the General Post Office to see how Gladstone's speech had been sent off to the provinces. West was amazed to find that by the time they got there at ten o'clock, the text had already been received verbatim in New York and every capital in Europe for, as Wolverton explained, there were over 1,000 miles of telegraph wires laid under the building.

They returned to Warren House together on 9 April 1886, with Wolverton calculating in his usual 'sanguine temperament' that the Government might get a majority of 25 on the second reading, and for the following two months as the Bill was debated in Parliament, Wolverton remained fiercely loyal to Gladstone, at one point calling anti-Home Rule Liberal Unionist Joseph Chamberlain a traitor, likening him to Judas Iscariot as one who had betrayed his master. A vote on the Bill took place on 8 June, and Gladstone's party lost, 341 votes to 311. On 9 June the Government suffered a further defeat on the budget and Gladstone resigned once more. On 12 June Algernon West drove his daughter to see Lady Wolverton at Warren House:

Mr Gladstone who was staying there, had been occupied in writing his Address, but came to tea and shortly after he asked me to go with him for a walk; taking his Address, he feared it might be too long, but it was not as long as Mr Chamberlain's whose name he had not even mentioned. He had driven home the comparison between Lord Salisbury's [Conservative Party leader] and his mode of governing Ireland, the only two alternatives, and sorrowfully admitted that he had lost in this division [of the Liberal Party] a great deal of talent. We walked in the lovely wood above the garden for some time, enjoying the splendid view as if politics were not, but we soon drifted again into discussing the elections.

IN OPPOSITION

Gladstone was successfully returned as MP for Midlothian, but now as leader of the Opposition he sought out the peace and tranquillity of Warren House at the end of July. Having just vacated Downing Street for the third time, he needed time to think and talk with Wolverton and Granville, who had also retreated to Warren House to recuperate after an illness. But even at Coombe, Gladstone's peace could be spoilt by

Granville Leveson-Gower, 2nd Earl Granville (1815–91), Secretary of State for Foreign Affairs

other guests. One such occasion was when Baroness Louisa Knightley, wife of Conservative MP Baronet Rainald Knightley, and her mother Emilia Bowater called on Lady Wolverton. The Baroness wrote in her journal:

> Mother, Rainald and I had a long pretty drive all round by Wimbledon Common and Coombe, where we proceeded to call on Lady Wolverton, and were much taken aback at finding, seated by the tea table, Mr and Mrs Gladstone. But as Rainald remarked, the Grand Old Man was sulky and after asking Rainald if he thought there would be an autumn session, disappeared upstairs, skipping up two steps at a time with provoking activity. I had only time to note once more the marvellous sonorousness of his voice.

Later that summer, having already entertained Sir William Harcourt on a cruise around Guernsey on *Palatine*, Wolverton invited Gladstone to spend time on the yacht, sailing off the coast of Ireland and west coast of Scotland. Wolverton was also joined for a time by Lord Granville, who had by then fully recovered from his illness and retired from public life, and his daughter on *Palatine* as they sailed from Penzance to Plymouth to watch the races. Calm seemed to have returned to the Liberal supporters of Gladstone, at least for a while.

Wolverton resigned his position of Postmaster-General at the end of the summer. It was said the only appreciable contribution he made to his department was solving a mystery which had puzzled all other members of the postal service. It related to the non-delivery of a package to 'Mr Jennings, the Trainer at Newmarket'. His simple explanation was that there were two Mr Jennings' at Newmarket, both of racing fame. Lord Wolverton did, however, write a graceful letter to his successor, devoting the sum of public money he had received as his salary for a use of a charity connected to the department, the first wealthy peer to return an official income to the nation.

Above: Racing in Sussex was at its height in the late 1880s, with Lewes, Plumpton and Brighton (above) racecourses attracting many visitors

Below: Lord Wolverton's funeral was held at St Mary Abbots, Kensington

THE DEATH OF WOLVERTON

It was to be the last public office Lord Wolverton held, for he died suddenly a year later in 1887. He was only 63 years old. True to form, and in spite of very bad weather, Wolverton had been visiting the Lewes races and the Plumpton steeplechases that weekend. He died in his room at the Bedford Hotel, Brighton, on the morning of Sunday 6 November. His body was discovered by his valet, who had taken up his shaving water only a few hours beforehand. Cause of death was given as 'syncope of the heart'. His body was taken from Brighton to the family's central London home at 7 Stratton Street. The funeral service at St Mary Abbots in Kensington was given by his brother, the Revd Edward Carr Glyn, Vicar of Kensington; the coffin was hidden by wreaths and crosses, exquisite flowers and ferns, and his epitaph was 'The strife is over, the battle is done'. His body was interred at the parish church in Ham, on the other side of Richmond Park from Warren House. There was a very large gathering at the graveside and besides political and charitable representatives and members of the departments of the Post Office, there were his true friends and fellow Liberals Mr Gladstone, Lord Granville, Lord Spencer, Lord Northbrook (Thomas George Baring), Mr Arnold Morley and Sir William Harcourt. Also present was the Duke of Teck, brother-in-law to the Duke of Cambridge, and neighbour at White Lodge in Richmond Park.

The *New York Times* wrote on 4 December 1887:

Lord Wolverton's death is a most serious blow to the Gladstonian Party. His expenditure for political purposes was practically limitless and great as was his outlay last year it would have been even more lavish at the next election. Lord Wolverton lived and died in full faith of Gladstonianism, worshipping his leader and believing that ultimately the constituencies would repeat the triumphs of 1868 and 1880. There are not many men of money among the Gladstonians, and Lord Wolverton was one of the band that was prepared to give freely whenever he was asked.

Lady Wolverton and her niece had a close relationship and Gian (as the niece was known) had spent much time at Warren House. To every servant 'whether indoor or outdoor', who had worked for him for at least one year, he bequeathed an extra year's wages.

Lord Henry Richard, 3rd Baron Wolverton, was only 26 when he inherited the title, yet on the day his uncle died, he had an attack of peritonitis. He had inherited not only the title but also the 2nd Baron's interest and shares on trust in the bank Glyn, Mills, Currie & Co. On a visit to Monte Carlo in the summer of 1888, Henry suffered a pulmonary haemorrhage. He returned to Warren House where he received medical treatment, but died there on 2 July 1888, unmarried. He was buried in the churchyard at Iwerne Minster, and his younger brother, Frederick Glyn, became the 4th Baron Wolverton. It was the third death in a year at Warren House, for Giana's sister-in-law, widow of St Leger Glyn, the Hon Florence Elizabeth, had passed away while staying with the Wolvertons on 14 September 1887.

WOLVERTON'S WILL

Lady Giana Wolverton, as she was known, was 61 when her husband died. They had not had any children of their own and so the barony passed to Henry Richard, the eldest son of Glyn's deceased brother, Vice Admiral Henry Carr Glyn. Lady Wolverton, however, was well provided for by her husband as he bequeathed her the lease of Warren House, the manor and estate at Iwerne Minster and everything that he owned, a personal estate in excess of £1,820,000, as well as an annuity of £10,000 for the rest of her life. He left his mother, who survived him, £4,000 a year and his house in Lancaster Gate, and his niece, Georgiana Mary Tufnell, daughter of Giana's older brother Robert Tufnell, a one-off sum of £10,000.

Lord Wolverton's house at Iwerne Minister

Despite Lord Wolverton's obvious attempts to
provide fairly for all of his family, there was a mistake
in his will which was strongly contested as a result of
Baron Henry Wolverton's premature death. The will
clearly stated that on the unexpected death of his
successor, the 2nd Baron's vast wealth passed away
from the 3rd Baron, to the daughters of the testator's
next brother, the late Mr St Leger Glyn. Lady Wolverton
declared that it would have been her husband's wish
for his fortune to remain with the Barony. After much
amiable controversy, the two sides of the family settled
on a compromise. The young ladies retained £100,000
a piece, and £1,000 every year to be paid to them by
Lady Wolverton from the money her husband left her,
and the whole residue, on Lady Giana Wolverton's
death, was to go to the holder of the Barony.

Lady Wolverton lost no time in selling some of her
husband's most prized possessions. Lord Wolverton
had already sold his pack of black and tan St Hubert
bloodhounds to the French Count Couteulx de
Canteleu, who hunted not only wild deer but also wild
boar. His wife sold the yacht *Palatine* before the end of
1887 to Mrs Blanche Watney, wealthy widow of James
Watney, the brewer and one-time Liberal MP.
Wolverton's stud at Iwerne Minster might have been
sold privately for £8,400 but the deal was declined by
those to whom it was offered, including the Prince of
Wales. Fortunately for Lady Wolverton, the price quoted
was preposterously inadequate as was discovered at
auction once the decision was made to break up the
stud and sell the mares and yearlings separately. At the
blood stock sale at Newmarket, 21 broodmares fetched
13,875 guineas; Mon Droit, the joint property of
Wolverton and trainer John Porter, was sold for 2,900
guineas; and 12 foals made 2,815 guineas.

Perhaps because of the publicity which followed
the sudden death of Lord Wolverton, the details of the
will, the size of the estate and the enormous sums of
money involved in contesting the will, let alone the

sale of the yacht and the stud, Warren House became
the target for a 'daring' burglary as reported in *The Times*:

On 27 December 1888 a daring attempt was made to
ransack Warren House, Coombe Wood, the residence of
Lady Wolverton, but the intruder was disturbed before
he made away with anything. All the best bedrooms of
Warren House are in the rear portion of the building
(looking out towards Coombe-wood) and adjoining
which is the lawn. Lady Wolverton's first footman –
William Cosben – was passing upstairs from the ground
floor to the first floor when he saw a man leave her
ladyship's bedroom and pass to the left and into her
dressing room. The man slammed the door and locked
it inside. Cosben raised the alarm and a gentleman
visitor went for the Police. He met Police-constables
Marlow and Kent (of the V division) near the gate. They
could not affect an entrance from the lawn, so they went

in through the front door and proceeded upstairs. The dressing room door had been broken open and it was found that the burglar had made off by way of the window. This was where he had entered, for there was a hole through the window, and the glass remaining had been pasted over with brown paper to prevent any noise being made by the falling of the glass … All the doors on the ground floor leading to the lawn had been made secure on the outside by means of screws having been fixed to the frame and bound to the door handle by stout wire … Two small ladders tied together had been left on the lawn, but had not been used, access to the window of the dressing room having been easily gained by means of some iron skeleton work and wire work. Had the footman burst the door in as the man locked it he could at any rate have assailed him, and perhaps prevented his escape. The intruder was a man of short stature, young and wearing a check coat. His face was not seen as he was turning it away as the footman saw him. Since the recent burglary at White Lodge, Richmond Park, the residence of her Royal Highness the Duchess of Teck, double patrol constables have been especially employed in this neighbourhood.

LADY GEORGIANA WOLVERTON

Lady Wolverton did not live a frivolous life as many of her wealth and title might have done. The Wolvertons did own some beautiful objects, silver plate and silver ornaments, and Lady Wolverton had some expensive jewellery, including large diamond and pearl necklaces. Her homes, such as Warren House, were hung with works of art, and she herself was the subject of at least three paintings.

THE PORTRAITS OF LADY WOLVERTON

As Mrs Georgiana Maria Julia Glyn, she was immortalised by Robert Thorburn (1818–85), the Scottish-born artist famous for his paintings of Queen Victoria and the royal family. Painted in 1855 and exhibited at the Royal Academy, it is a full-length miniature portrait, in which she wears a brown dress over a white chemise, with a gathered neckline and lace cuffs, framed in tortoiseshell veneer and originally in a wooden travelling case. (Sold in 2006 for 2,963 euros.) Shortly after, Lord Wolverton commissioned the well-known artist George Frederic Watts OM RA (1817–1904) to paint

two portraits of his wife. The surviving portrait is a half-length oil of her sitting in a plain red dress, with white lace detail. In July 1860 he wrote asking Watts to give the neck a little additional roundness, but added, 'I am more delighted every day by both pictures.' (Sold in 1995 for £5,980.) Another painting, this time by British artist Edward Clifford (1844–1907), a watercolour painted in 1876, perhaps on the occasion of her 50th birthday, shows her older but no less beautiful, and, like the Thorburn picture, with a stem of white lilies, the sign of purity and modesty.

Mrs Georgiana Maria Julia Glyn,
by Robert Thorburn, 1855

Lady Wolverton, née Georgiana Tufnell,
by George Fredrick Watts, 1860

Giana, Lady Wolverton, by Edward Clifford, 1876

London Telegraph Boys waiting in their 'kitchen' to be sent out to deliver telegrams. *London Illustrated News*, 1871

Lady Wolverton continued her husband's work for the Liberal Party even after he died. On 2 September 1891, she hosted a garden party in the grounds of Warren House for the Kingston and District Liberal Association. The afternoon was given up to music on the lawn and in a large marquee. In the evening the marquee was filled to overflowing with a political meeting chaired by Bertram Currie, their neighbour and her late husband's partner in the bank. After a resolution pledging the meeting to the principle of Home Rule in Ireland and for a speedy dissolution of Parliament was carried, a vote of thanks and cheers were given to Lady Wolverton and Mr Gladstone. Dancing followed and the grounds were illuminated – it must have been a wonderful sight.

CHARITABLE WORKS

For most of the time, Giana Wolverton devoted herself to the good of others, as one newspaper put it 'preventing suffering or wiping away tears'. It may well have been under her influence that Lord Wolverton had decided to return the official income he received as Postmaster-General. During his time in office Lady Wolverton had set up the Telegraph Boys' Institute. This charitable initiative provided 'space for recreation, and a means for moral and mental improvement' for boys, some as young as 13, working for the Post Office, presumably in an attempt to avert strike action as discontent over poor wages and working conditions increased. Spaces were found for the boys to use – a sitting room, a dining room, a locker, somewhere to hang their capes – and teachers and libraries were provided, as well as games in the winter months; prizes were awarded for work and, in some cases, for swimming achievements. Concerts were given to raise money, and Institutes set up around the country. On 3 August 1886, Gladstone visited Warren House, where Lord and Lady Wolverton were entertaining 300 telegraph messengers in the grounds. Gladstone was vociferously cheered as he appeared among the boys.

Lady Wolverton's work with the Telegraph Boys was based on a very successful scheme she had established for orphan or destitute boys. As Mrs George Grenfell Glyn, she had set up the House-Boys' Brigade in 1870 in Chelsea; she was President, her husband Treasurer. Originally called the Door-Step Brigade, it was established for the purpose of training boys for domestic service and the printing trade. It changed its name because over time the boys became available for hire by households in the morning, attending school in the afternoons, thereby con-tributing to around two-thirds of the cost of running the Brigades themselves. By 1883 there were three establishments in London with an average of 165 boys each, and over the following years Brigades were set up in the country as well. The boys were taken in, fed, lodged and educated, and trained for various useful occupations; many of them found good permanent occupations, mostly as servants in the houses of wealthy families, but some as artisans or clerks in offices or the Army. Encouraged to stay in touch with the Brigade, they returned once a year to a celebration dinner and there was an annual magazine called *Our Old Boys Post Bag*, which contained news and letters from the boys, some in far-flung corners of the Empire. A humorous article appeared in the *New York Times* in 1903, some 30 years after the Brigade was formed:

As help for servants you can have the boys of the young brigade to polish furniture, wash dogs, wash up and carry up, clean boots and knives, and carry coals. If you have a party you can have a boy in plain clothes to open and close carriage doors for sixpence an hour. For one shilling an hour he will come in livery. You can have a careful boy to wheel a bath chair for eight pence, and if you feel depressed you can have the boys' brass band play for you in your garden.

Lord and Lady Wolverton also fully supported an orphanage on the outskirts of Iwerne Minster, their Dorset home. Although country-based, many of the boys came from London and there, in association with the House-Boys' Brigade, many boys were brought up and trained for a better position in life. It was on one of her many visits to the orphanage that Lady Wolverton was inspired to set up her most successful creation, The Needlework Guild.

THE NEEDLEWORK GUILD

In 1882 Lady Wolverton was asked by the Matron of the Iwerne Orphanage if she could provide an extra 24 pairs of hand-knitted socks and 12 jerseys for the children within the month. Although she could easily have afforded to buy these additional items herself, as indeed she and her husband had already provided extra food and bedding, she looked for the solution elsewhere. 'If only a little bridge could be thrown from the Island of Waste to the Island of Want, how both would benefit!' she wrote in an article in which she called upon her friends: 'I am asking each of you for two new articles of clothing. They must be new. They must be exactly alike. They must not be expensive. They will be better for the children for whom they are intended, and even better for you, if you make them yourselves. As the work of your own hands they are part of you.' When asked why two

Illustration from the July 1890 issue of the magazine *English Illustrated*, which published articles on the Needlework Guild written by Lady Wolverton and HRH Princess Mary Adelaide, Duchess of Teck

garments each, Lady Wolverton replied, 'What does the child wear while what he has been wearing is being laundered?' Burke MacArthur, an American author, suggests that Lady Wolverton must have known that the response from her friends, who were often 'aimlessly busy, seeking only to pass time without being bored, without the need to think', would be generous. It was fashionable to do something for the poor, yet MacArthur suggests that the ladies of the Needlework Guild felt that they were really doing something for those in need, and not for their own personal gain. Lady Wolverton wrote: 'I have one ambition, to see the Needlework Guild recommended as a panacea to the listless, unhappy, idle heroines of the three-volume novel.'

To encourage others to join her growing Guild, Lady Wolverton put a brief item in her local newspaper; the London press picked up the story and within a year the Guild had attracted 460 members. By 1885 the Guild had established branches throughout the United Kingdom, and the idea had been duplicated in America. As in the rest of Victorian society, there was a hierarchy within the organisation. Each Guild was sub-divided into groups, each containing one president, usually a member of the aristocracy or the wife of a statesman, who had suitable connections and would be in a position to encourage new members to join. For instance the wife of Liberal statesman William Vernon Harcourt, Home Secretary in Gladstone's third administration, was the President of one of the London branches of the Guild. There were several vice-presidents and at least 50 associates. Indeed its structure, which enabled all classes, from all religious backgrounds, regardless of age to work together with one common aim, each to produce two or more items of clothing a year, may have been the reason the Guild continues to this day.

Lady Wolverton made 300 items herself in one year alone. In 1890, she wrote from Warren House:

> We are the plain members of a large family of beautiful needleworks. We write no 'art' or 'fancy' before our name, we fill our needles with no lovely silks in all the 'newest' or 'oldest' shades, which ever chances to be the fashion, our material is not furnished by the looms of Lyons or Spitalfields: we use only Horrocks's stoutest calico and the roughest Welsh homespun, and thread our needles with Coates's 'No 40 best six cord'; we are unpoetical and inartistic, but like the plain member of the family, we are essentially useful – indeed I think to many we have become indispensable. Some have never worked with an objective before – oh how dull that work must be! – some have only filled what I call the 'white elephant' drawers and cupboards existing in most houses. Now they can fill cupboards always, like Oliver Twist 'asking for more', and can work on and on all the year and every year with the same delightful certainty that the best use will be found for the article, whatever it be.

Royal patronage in the formidable form of Mary Adelaide, Duchess of Teck, friend and neighbour of Lady Wolverton, gave real momentum to the London Needlework Guild. The Duchess even used her charms

In 1866 Prince Francis, Duke of Teck (above), married Princess Mary Adelaide (right), daughter of Prince Adolphus, Duke of Cambridge, the youngest son of George III

to persuade the Prince of Wales to lend two rooms at the Imperial Institute for collection, exhibition and packing of articles made by the ladies. These clothes included shawls, petticoats, socks, stockings and pullovers. Ladies were instructed to make the strongest, plainest, largest articles of underclothing they could for man, woman or child, and there was always a shortage of well-made coats for men. Real care was taken to ensure that only those in real need were helped, and in order to avoid favouritism, the articles of clothing were not distributed by the Guild, but by community leaders who knew the specific needs in each area. In 1890, some 200,000 articles of good, useful clothing were distributed to the poorest parishes, homes, hospitals and missions in England. Emergencies, whether big or small, were also catered for; during the cholera epidemic in Birmingham in the late 1880s, the Guild supplied 2,000 items to the

hospitals within a fortnight. In some of the 203 London parishes where the articles went, there were 10,000 to 20,000 people, and the donation of clothing very often meant the children were able to go to school, and mothers to venture out as they now had sufficient clothes to wear. In 1891, over 39,000 articles of clothing were received by the Guild from 96 groups, an increase of 4,000 on the previous year. In 1892, nearly 43,000 items were made, 5,000 of which came from the London Guild to which the Duchess of Teck had recruited her daughter, Princess May.

Mary Adelaide, Duchess of Teck, lived about a mile from Warren House, in White Lodge, Richmond Park. She was sister to the Duke of Cambridge, on whose land Warren House was built, and cousin to Queen Victoria. Her father Adolphus, Duke of Cambridge, was the seventh son of George III. She had married Prince Francis of Teck in 1866 and they had four

children, three boys and a girl, Princess May Victoria, born in 1867. Lady Wolverton was no newcomer to royalty, and royalty no newcomer to Coombe. In 1858, the teenage Prince of Wales had been a virtual prisoner at White Lodge so as to be, as his father Prince Albert put it, 'away from the world and devote himself exclusively to study'. In 1885, the year that Mary Adelaide became patron of the London Needlework Guild, the Prince of Wales and his family had been present at the wedding breakfast given by Lord and Lady Wolverton at Warren House for the marriage of their niece Miss Rose Glyn to Lord Norreys. Not long after, the Duchess of Teck, Princess Victoria of Teck, the Duchess of Albany, Princess Helena and the young Duke of Albany were among the guests at a luncheon party at Warren House.

FUNDRAISING AT WARREN HOUSE

For almost a decade, Lady Wolverton and the Duchess of Teck worked tirelessly together for the benefit of others in the local Kingston community, laying foundation stones and building churches and schools. They also raised funds for the 'Boarding-Out-Fund', an initiative which provided houses on the estate at Coombe to the poor female workers from the East End of London in which to enjoy a brief holiday in the fresh air. Together they were formidable. The two ladies used their position in society to rally other titled and wealthy ladies into fundraising events at Warren House; for example the Countess Spencer agreed to open a bazaar at Warren House for Lady Wolverton to raise funds for the building of a church at St Luke's mission in Kingston. Her presence was to attract many distinguished visitors. The Duchess of Teck joined forces and wrote to Lady Dunraven on 4 April 1890:

> I was charmed to hear that you have kindly consented to take a stall at our Coombe Bazaar (to include any number of entertainments all bespoken by me, and promising to be very first rate.) Dear Lady Wolverton will lend her house for it so that we shall have plenty of space and be able to make quite a thing of it. Lady Wolverton and I propose to have a combined flower and basket stall, and I am longing to know what yours is to be. I am bent on making this affair a grand success because I mean to have a fair share of the profits, in order to start a fund wherewith to lodge and feed a succession of poor worn-out London workers through the summer as we have done these two years past.

In a letter to Lady Salisbury two months later, the Duchess was much more direct: 'I am organising a fete at Coombe for which Lady Wolverton kindly lends her charming house and grounds on 10th and 11th June in aid of our parish needs. I want you very much to help us by coming down one of the days, and further by sending me a contribution of flowers for my stall.'

Lady Wolverton's charitable events had become highly successful social occasions not to be missed. Visitors to Warren House that day read like a who's who of British royalty and aristocracy and naturally attracted the attention of the newspapers. Unfortunately the weather was not good: 'The stalls were arranged partly within the house and in the grounds under tents. Mr and Mrs Charles Wyndham assisted with musical and dramatic entertainments in the house, which were well attended due to the dreadful weather, whilst outside the band of the Grenadier Guards played in the afternoon.'

The enterprising Lady Wolverton on another occasion sold tickets to a lecture given at Warren House by the Vicar of Finley entitled 'My Walk to Rome – a five week tramp of 800 miles' to raise money

for St Luke's. Enough money was raised to build the church, and a further donation from Lady Wolverton ensured that a spire was added to the structure. The two women also raised money for worthy causes outside their local parish, for instance the Duchess of Teck opened an Institute and Gymnasium, possibly the Trinity College Mission, which Lady Wolverton had given to the parish of Camberwell.

Open-air theatrical production of *The Faithfull Shepherdesse* at Coombe House attended by the Prince of Wales after he had visited Warren House, from *The Graphic*, 1885

Inspired by Gladstonian Liberal ideals, Lady Wolverton gave her support to the Barmaids' Guild. There were difficulties in starting the scheme because the founders had called it a union and a number of employers, wary of the implications, threatened to dismiss all girls who had made enquiries. Finally in 1891, the term 'Guild' was adopted, even though the organisation served all the purposes of an early trade union. Working on behalf of over 120,000 young women, who worked from 15 to over 18 hours a day and nine hours on Sundays with one Sunday off a month, the Guild made weekly allowances to members out of employment. Girls illegally and unjustly discharged were defended and the 'grievances of barmaids were vented on their behalf, and their reasonable and just demands enforced'. The Guild also worked to improve wages, which ranged from 4s to 14s a week, from which many of the girls had to pay for glasses broken in the establishments. There were strong protests from the Licensed Victuallers' Society, who even claimed that the business could not be carried on if the hours of barmaids were restricted to 74 hours a week! In 1891 Lady Wolverton invited several groups of barmaids to spend a pleasant day away at Warren House. Her support continued and the newspapers of 1892 reported that Lady Wolverton 'is doing her best to assist barmaids of London and a Home of Rest for barmaids is soon to be opened at Hartley House, 172 Buckingham Palace Road – they are a class of girls who are exposed to much temptation'. Frederick, 4th Baron Wolverton, agreed to act as Honourable Treasurer of the fund which was raised to help members of the Guild, and Lady Wolverton held a series of Sunday afternoons at an address in Mayfair for barmaids and women employees connected with restaurants. By 1893, the barmaids' lot had been much improved by the Guild and other organisations like the Young Women's Christian Association, with whom the Duchess of Teck was closely associated. The Duchess

had even formed a barmaids' branch of the London Needlework Guild for girls with spare time.

ROYAL ROMANCE

The friendship between the two ladies extended beyond their charitable activities. Princess May remembers in her diary: 'Went to Ly Wolverton's where Mama read and I sang to some poor men from Westminster.' This was one Whit Sunday in 1889 when the choir of a London church had been invited by Lady Wolverton to spend the day at Warren House. Mary Adelaide had promised to drive over from White Lodge in the afternoon with Princess May. The weather was so bad that the afternoon proceedings went on longer than expected. The group begged the Duchess to read some things to the men; she did and then chatted to them for over an hour, which more than compensated for the wet day. In September and October 1891, while extensive alterations were being made to White Lodge, the Duke and Duchess of Teck and their family stayed with Lady Wolverton at the Foley Arms Hotel at Malvern. The group which included Princess May and Gian Tufnell, the niece of Lady Wolverton, made sightseeing expeditions to cathedrals, churches and local beauty spots. When they finally returned to Surrey, the Tecks were guests of Lady Wolverton's at Warren House for a further two weeks, as the work at White Lodge had still not been completed.

Earlier that year the Tecks had been to stay at Sandringham for six days. Queen Victoria regarded Mary Adelaide with some caution, but she was very fond of her daughter Princess May who, the Queen believed, had a strong character and sense of duty. Since childhood, May and her brothers had played with their second cousins, Prince Albert Victor 'Eddy' and Prince George, the children of the Prince of Wales, who were of a similar age. In October, just after the

Portrait of King Edward VII and Queen Alexandra and their children, before 1892. Back l–r: George V; Maud, Queen of Norway; Albert Victor, Duke of Clarence, heir to the throne; Louise, Duchess of Fife; front l–r: Queen Alexandra, Princess Victoria, Edward VII; taken before Edward came to throne

Tecks had returned from a three-day visit to Easton to see the Prince of Wales and his family, a letter arrived at Warren House from Queen Victoria, addressed to the Duchess of Teck. The 24-year-old Princess May and her brother Prince Adolphus were commanded to 'proceed northwards to Balmoral Castle, without delay'. Neither the Duke or Duchess had said a word to Princess May about their hopes and her chances of marriage to Prince Eddy, but their excitement was obvious as Mary Adelaide replied to Queen Victoria from Warren House: 'Only a line not to keep the messenger waiting too long to thank you for your very dear letter to say with what joy my children will obey your gracious and more than kind summons, though I must own that I feel inclined to be rather envious! And not a little jealous at being left out in the cold and not invited to accompany them! Albeit very much gratified at your most kind wish to have them with you for a little while.'

In December 1891, following the visit to Balmoral, Princess May became engaged to Prince Eddy, the eldest son of the Prince of Wales. However, their joy was short-lived for the prince died on 14 January 1892, during the worldwide influenza pandemic that engulfed Britain that winter. Princess May and the rest of his family, including his younger brother, Prince George, were at the bedside in Sandringham when Prince Eddy died. At the funeral, May laid a wreath of orange blossom on the coffin, the same flowers she had intended to have in her wedding bouquet. Stunned, and undoubtedly disappointed, the Tecks returned to White Lodge.

The death of Prince Albert Victor ('Eddy') had brought the issue of succession to the forefront of the minds of the royal family. Prince George, now the heir presumptive, and himself recovering from typhoid fever, was unmarried. If George was to die before producing an heir, his sister Princess Louise would become heir presumptive to the British throne, and Louise was not considered a suitable candidate. It was essential that, with some urgency, Prince George was found a suitable wife and had a family.

Presumably with this in mind, the Tecks were invited to Osborne on the Isle of Wight in February 1892, a stay that coincided with what would have been Princess May's wedding day. The significance of this invitation was not missed by Mary Adelaide, who was as determined as ever to promote her daughter's suitability to the Wales's. On their return to Coombe in March, the Duchess of Teck asked her friend Lady Wolverton if she would mind taking them to the South of France so that Princess May could recuperate after the sad turn of events of the previous months. Lady Wolverton agreed to rent a villa on the Riviera, as she had often done before when her husband was alive. However, it was not the sunshine and sea breezes that Mary Adelaide had in mind for her daughter, but the chance to be near the Prince of Wales and his family. As indiscreet as ever, she told Lady Wolverton that she wished to be in Menton, just a couple of miles from the hotel at Cap Martin where the royal party were staying. The Prince of Wales, while consenting to the idea of his younger son becoming betrothed to Princess May, had just spent time with them at Osborne, had his own grief to deal with and wanted to be some distance from the Tecks for a while. He, therefore, called upon the Duchess's brother, the Duke of Cambridge, to intervene on his behalf. Mrs Vyner, a former girlfriend of the Duke and resident of the Coombe Estate, had a villa in Cannes, about 40 miles south of Cap Martin, and was happy to entertain the Duke's sister while staying in the town. But Mary Adelaide declined by telling her brother that the Prince of Wales wanted her and her family at Menton. On

learning this was not the case, the Duke went to visit Lady Wolverton to enlist her help. Lady Wolverton agreed to contact her neighbour Mrs Vyner, and then go to Cannes to find a suitable villa. The Duke saw Lady Wolverton off on the train, safe in the knowledge that even his sister could not take advantage of the situation and the generosity of her friend while she was out of the country.

Lady Wolverton rented Villa Clementine from the Spencer-Churchill family. Lady Wolverton, by now 66 years old, was accompanied by her niece Miss Gian Tufnell. The Tecks took two friends and four domestics, and once again the Duke of Cambridge came to the station to see them all off on 9 March 1892. 'We were most fortunate in the charming Villa

Lady Wolverton had been able to secure, much the nicest for all I have seen at Cannes,' wrote the Duchess to Queen Victoria, 'for it is fitted up in English tastes with all home comforts.' The absence of contact from the Wales's for the first three weeks must have agitated Mary Adelaide. She need not have worried, for by April the Prince of Wales and his son visited daily and they were in turn invited to Cap Martin.

Lady Wolverton and Gian returned to Warren House on 30 April, as the Tecks continued on their European tour. The events that followed are well documented: Prince George did eventually propose to Princess May, and they were married on 6 July 1893. On the death of his father in 1910, George V was crowned King-Emperor of the British Empire, and his wife May (Mary of Teck) became Queen Consort.

LADY WOLVERTON'S LAST DAYS

On 4 December 1893, Warren House was broken into again. This time several pieces of jewellery were taken from the dressing rooms. 'Mrs George Peck [the housekeeper] was in her bedroom when one of the burglars made his appearance, and was thus able to prevent any further plunder.' Just as in 1888, the careful ways in which the doors and windows were wired clearly showed that the burglary was planned so that the thieves were able to get away without being chased out of the ground-floor exits. Sadly they ransacked the rooms quite badly and had obviously been there for a while before being noticed. Fortunately a party that had been arranged for that evening had been postponed, or far more valuables would have been stolen.

Following her return from the South of France, Lady Wolverton spent most of her time quietly in London. It seems that something had troubled her. It may have been her health or perhaps she did not like

the behaviour of her royal friend and neighbour, Mary Adelaide, and the overt ambitions for Princess May, nor the way in which the Duke of Cambridge had involved her in the affair. Whatever the reasons, Lady Wolverton had not lived in Warren House for over a year when in June 1893 some newspapers announced that she had decided to give Warren House, Coombe-Wood, to Princess May as a wedding gift. The house and estate was still held on a long lease by Lady Wolverton, while the Duke of Cambridge owned the freehold and he was going to make over the lease of the property to the royal couple. Another newspaper, however, the *Daily News*, threw doubt upon the authenticity of the story. Perhaps the *Daily News* was right for shortly after her death the following story appeared. On 21 January 1894, a correspondent of the *Liverpool Daily Post* wrote:

A curious circumstance in connection with the charming and charitable late Lady Wolverton is the feeling of strong disapproval she entertained to the engagement between the Duke of York and Princess May. Up to that time Lady Wolverton had been a close friend of the Tecks, and especially Princess May. Living at Warren House, she was their near neighbour and was in intimate companionship with the Princess during her short engagement to the Duke of Clarence. But when the Princess became betrothed of the younger brother, her Ladyship showed her disapproval by closing her house at Coombe Warren, cutting off all association with the Teck family, and it is even said ceasing to be on speaking terms with the Princess. These strained relations continued until her death.

Warren House did not pass to the Duke and Duchess of York, either because it was not promised or because it was not possible to reassign the lease as was also suggested at the time. Lady Giana Wolverton died at 73 South Audley Street on 10 January 1894. Her funeral service, like that of her husband, took place at St Mary Abbots' Church, Kensington, and was presided over by her brother-in-law, the Hon Revd Edward Carr Glyn. She was buried in Iwerne Minster, where her husband's remains had been reinterred some years previously. Among the congregation were 100 boys from the House-Boys' Brigade and a deputation from the Eastern Central Institution of the Telegraph Boys. Both sides of her family attended the funeral, as did the Duchess of Albany, Lady Frederick Cavendish, and Lord and Lady Henry Grosvenor. Those who sent floral tributes to Iwerne Minster included the Queen, the Duchess of York, the Princes Adolphus, Frederick and Alexander of Teck, and Lord and Lady Portman. Notable by her absence was Mary Adelaide, Duchess of Teck, who, on the day of the funeral, left White Lodge for the Queen's residence at Osborne on the Isle of Wight.

Lady Wolverton's will, dated 17 June 1893, sheds some light on her feelings. It stipulated that if she had not managed to sell Warren House and the lands at Coombe Wood, including all the furniture, in her lifetime, which was her intention, then it was to be sold after her death. The mistake in her husband's will and the amount of money that she had given to his two nieces meant that she had been unable to put money aside to provide gifts and legacies to her own family; the sale of Warren House would provide enough money for her wishes to be granted. To her niece Gian Tufnell she left £10,000, as well as the painting by Watts and her jewellery, silver and other ornaments and all her belongings at any other house she may be using at her death, except Warren House. She bequeathed £5,000 apiece to each of her brothers, George, Arthur and Vincent, her brother-in-law, the Hon Revd Edward Carr Glyn, and two nephews. The rest of her husband's legacy, including the London house and the manor at Iwerne Minster, passed on to the 4th Baron Wolverton.

In order to fulfil her wishes, the auction of all the contents of Warren House were advertised in *The Times* on 31 May 1894:

> … comprising a pair of Chinese porcelain Mandarin vases, and covers with red and gold decoration, famille verte and whole coloured vases with or-moulu mounts, and a large folding screen of old Chinese lace from Lady Carrington's collection; also fine marble and porphyry vases with or-moulu mounts, a Louis XIV boulle bracket clock, Louis XVI or-moulu andirons, wall lights and candelabra, an Italian casket of inlaid ebony, a marble bust of the Right Hon. W. E. Gladstone by Baron Marochetti, a marble figure of cupid, and other objects of art. French decorative furniture comprising numerous grand marquetry and other cabinets, secretaries and commodes … in the style of Louis XV and Louis XVI, suites of carved and gilt sofas, fauteuils and chairs covered with silk and satin damask. Also a suite of carved mahogany Chippendale armchairs and settee, Chippendale and Sheraton inlaid satinwood and mahogany cabinets … and other English decorative furniture, etc.

Lady Wolverton's niece Gian Tufnell remained at Warren House, treating it as her own until it was sold. In June 1895 she entertained mother and daughter, Lady Sefton and Lady Gertrude Molyneux, for a week. Her good relationship with the Tecks continued after the death of her aunt. She became the Duchess of Teck's second lady-in-waiting in 1895, and remained a close friend and confidante to Princess May for the rest of her life, including helping her collect small objets d'art for which she was so famous. Gian married Lord George Mount Stephen, a Scots-Quebecker, who had made a fortune investing in the Canadian Pacific Railway, and whose original financing had been provided by Edward Baring of Coombe Cottage and Barings Bank. He was much older than Gian, who was his second wife, and they lived at Brocket Hall in Hertfordshire where they regularly entertained Queen Mary. Lady Gian Mount Stephen was awarded the DBE in 1919 for her work with what had by then become 'Queen Mary's Needlework Guild'.

3

1895–1907

THE TALE OF THE INTERNATIONAL SPECULATOR

MR GEORGE CAWSTON (1851–1918)

THE EXECUTORS OF Lady Wolverton's estate first advertised Warren House for sale in *The Times* on 3 February 1894, but it took three more appearances in the newspaper over 18 months before it was finally sold in 1895. The new owner was Mr George Cawston, a barrister, a member of the Stock Exchange, and a founder member and director of the British South Africa Company.

According to *The Times* he had purchased '… one of the largest and most picturesque palatial residences in this charming locality [comprising] a superior mansion of Elizabethan Gothic design standing in beautifully arranged pleasure grounds and having varied and lovely views'. Its 'magnificent suite of four

Opposite and right: The 'grand staircase of Oak with beautifully carved balustrades' as described by *The Times* in 1895, photographed in the late 1890s. In Cawston's time it was painted white

Above: Detail from stained-glass window, depicting Aesop's Fox and Stork

Warren House photographed by Bedford Lemere
for George Cawston

THE CAWSTON FAMILY

reception rooms of lofty height and spacious
dimension designed with great artistic taste' included
one with 'a lofty fireplace with carved Algerian marble
archway and deeply recessed inglenook, having oak
benches on either side'. Other delights were 'an
Oriental smoking room and pitch pine billiard room
with lavatories ... a grand staircase of Oak with
beautifully carved balustrades ... 27 bed and dressing
rooms' and 'charming pleasure grounds' with a
summer house, two small ornamental lakes and a
wilderness. Like many grand houses of the day it had its
own vegetable and fruit gardens with vineries and
greenhouses. The estate occupied 27 acres and the lease
offered by HRH Duke of Cambridge was for 67 years.

George Cawston was a Londoner, born in Brixton in
1851, the second son of stockbroker Samuel William
Cawston and his wife Elizabeth. George was educated
at Dames School in Streatham. In 1873 he married
Mary Ellen Haworth, the daughter of a Manchester
calico printer. Their first son, George Haworth, was
born in 1876, and two years later Cawston was
admitted to Inner Temple as a student, based for a
time in chambers at 6 Crown Office Row, Temple.
Shortly after the birth of a second son, Cecil Faulkner,
in 1879, he became a member of the Stock Exchange,
working for the family stockbroking firm at
Throgmorton Street, just round the corner from the
Bank of England. Four years later, after being called to
the Bar, his eldest daughter, Ellen Winifred, was born.

Above: The Billiard Room photographed by Bedford Lemere. Right: The room as it is today

George Cawston's display of hunting trophies, fur rugs and African spears once covered the walls and floors of the entrance hall at Warren House

George Cawston's three brothers were also high achievers. Samuel, the eldest, was a broker who took over the family business when his father died in 1881. Arthur was an architect, renowned not only for his design of churches, such as St Philip's Church in Stepney and the British Home and Hospital for Incurables in Streatham, but also for his controversial *Comprehensive Scheme for Street Improvements in London*, published by Edward Stanford in 1893. In it, Arthur advocated more artistic elements in street architecture and the construction of five great boulevards across central London, opening up space and easing passage through the capital. Unfortunately neither he nor his idea survived long, for in 1894, at just 38, he died in a shocking shooting accident at his home in Queen Anne's Gate, London. The youngest brother, Edwin Cawston, was educated at Charterhouse; in 1885 he chartered a ship to Africa, bought 50 ostriches and set up an ostrich farm in Pasadena, California, supplying feathers to the hat industry. Ridiculed for years and referred to as 'that crank Cawston', he finally made a large amount of money and returned to England a rich man.

Blessed with intelligence, an entrepreneurial streak and a certain degree of luck, George Cawston soon became very wealthy, and he and his family reaped the rewards. But as the fortunes of the Empire changed and the effects of colonisation eventually took their toll in the early 20th century, so the hopes and fortunes of George Cawston also faded.

EXPLORATION COMPANIES IN AFRICA

During the 1870s, competition for raw materials and markets increased as the Industrial Revolution spread across the globe, and Britain's share of world trade fell. The country was kept afloat by its invisible exports: banking, insurance and shipping. The abandonment of free trade with Germany and France led merchant adventurers to go in search of cheaper raw materials, travelling east to China and India, and south to Africa. These countries also became the new export markets for British-made goods. European governments adopted the policy of colonial expansion, not just for trade but for power and wealth, to rule, impose law, morality and religion on 'fortunate peoples under imperial rule, so that they might enjoy peace, order and justice' (John S. Galbraith, *Crown and Charter – The Early Years of the British South Africa Company*). Imperialism and colonialism eventually cost Britain money and the colonised peoples their lives and lands. George Cawston acquired Warren House at the height of his fortune which was made from the primary target of this imperial expansion: Africa.

Cawston explained how Africa had become a target for expansionism when invited by Sir Charles Mills to give a lecture on early chartered companies to the Imperial Institute, London, in November 1893. He described four periods in history:

> The first period covered some 400 years, and dated from the first discovery of South Africa to the end of the 15th century, when the Portuguese made settlements along the coast and engaged themselves in endeavouring to discover the rich mines of the 'Land of Ophir'. The second phase comprised 400 months, which dated from 1851 to 1884 …. [That phase was] the most interesting because it was that in which missionaries, hunters and explorers played the most prominent part. During that period Livingstone started his first journey to the Zambezi and the southeast part of the vast continent became known to the civilised world. Those 400 months produced such men as Livingstone, Kirk and Mackenzie, Moffat, Baines and Selous. The third period covered the 400 weeks following upon the year 1867; it marked the discovery of the two principal products of South Africa, diamonds and gold, and also of the famous 'star of

South Africa' [a 47.69-carat pear-shaped diamond, cut from a crystal of 83.50 carats that turned the tides of fortune in South Africa].

With ambitions of his own and a growing family to provide for, George Cawston seized the opportunity for his very own slice of this rich pie. In 1888 his friend Lord Edric Gifford, a former soldier who had been Colonial Secretary in both Western Australia and Gibraltar, convinced Cawston of the prospects for the discovery of gold deposits in the newly acquired Matabeleland, which lay between the Limpopo and Zambezi rivers (now southwest Zimbabwe). In March 1888, this 'formidable financial combination', Cawston and Gifford, registered the Bechuanaland

Exploration Company, followed shortly afterwards by the purchase of the gold mining rights to an area in the Ngwato kingdom (now part of Botswana) from a French group who had been granted them by the Chief, Kgama. Cawston used his City connections to fund the project and the first subscribers were Baron Henry de Rothschild and Henry Oppenheim. For a payment of 5 shillings a month they were granted the right to prospect and for £1 per square mile at a royalty of just 2.5 per cent they were allowed to select up to 400 square miles. Spurred on by their success, Cawston and Gifford then revived an existing concession in the gold-rich Mazoe Valley, an area of Mashonaland, with the establishment of another company, the Exploring Company.

Exploration and mining finance companies were important mining finance intermediaries and their business in the city of London was a complex one. Although well informed men made large amounts of money in the 1890s in the gold share booms, more British capital was lost in these mines than won. Investors expected a higher rate of return from mines as they were 'wasting assets' and the risk investment was greater than in any other industry. However, where

Edric Frederick Gifford, 3rd Baron Gifford, in *Vanity Fair*

The main reef workings at Witwatersrand gold mine, controlled by Rhodes and Rudd

there was high risk, there was also speculation; investors attempting to reap gains through correct interpretation of price and future events. The London Stock Exchange was renowned for its lack of restrictions on speculation. At the same time as increased speculation there was an increase in the number of joint stock mining companies, known as exploration or trust companies which made money out of the issue of new mining concessions. (R. V. Turrell and Jean-Jacques Van Helten, *The Rothschilds, the Exploration Company and Mining Finance*)

Cawston was a master at raising capital but even he failed on some occasions. In the late 1880s he gave a supper at Willis's Rooms in St James's, London, in honour of a South African millionaire. A number of eminent people were invited to meet him – politicians, soldiers, authors, actors, artists and others in the public eye, most of whom knew each other. The millionaire was shamelessly late, so Cawston decided to begin without him. The people sat down at various tables and enjoyed a magnificent supper, and finally went away, not knowing or caring whether the millionaire had been there or not, as most of them had never heard of him.

The Cawston-Gifford partnership later extended further into Matabeleland and Mashonaland (now Zimbabwe), north of the Transvaal, over which they constructed a railway from the Cape border through Bechuanaland, where they owned mining rights. With the backing of the City of London and British businessmen, they managed to secure Colonial Office support, an essential component in maintaining the rights and legitimacy of the concession. However, competition for mineral rights and land in Africa was strong. The major contenders were Cecil Rhodes, the English-born South African businessman and politician, and his partner, Charles D. Rudd. Rhodes and Rudd had established the company Gold Fields of South Africa Ltd in 1887, having discovered gold at Witwatersrand. Rudd was interested in gold in the Transvaal, while Rhodes's interests lay in diamonds; he had amassed a fortune in Kimberley diamonds and established De Beers Consolidated Mines. But Rhodes's dream was to unite Africa from Cape Town to Egypt under British imperial rule. He started with Matabeleland.

Rudd deceitfully secured an important mining concession from King Lobengula of Matabeleland in 1888, giving him the impression that they were only interested in gold deposits. He told Lobengula that no more than ten white men would mine in his territory, a stipulation which was left out of the

Right: George Cawston, pictured bottom right, and the first board of the British South Africa Company, 1889. Top row: Horace Farquhar, Albert Grey, Alfred Beit; middle row: The Duke of Fife, Cecil Rhodes (Founder and Managing Director in South Africa), the Duke of Abercorn; bottom row: Lord Gifford, Herbert Canning (Secretary)

document. Included, however, was a clause that the mining companies could do anything that was necessary to their operations. When a rival agent working for Cawston and Gifford told Lobengula of Rudd's trickery, the King sent the agent and two of his men to London to protest. However, without the Rudd Concession, the result for both partnerships was stalemate. Neither Cawston and Gifford nor Rhodes and Rudd could expand their interests in the area any further.

THE BRITISH SOUTH AFRICA COMPANY

Rhodes bought off Cawston and Gifford with shares in the new Central Search Company and soon afterward their concessions were merged to form a chartered company with the rights and means to exploit the concessions. The British Government agreed, since they were keen to keep rival European powers out of Matabeleland, and the British South Africa Company (BSAC), registered with £700,000 capital, received its Royal Charter in October 1889.

The first Board of Directors consisted of Cawston, Lord Gifford, Rhodes and his avid supporter, Alfred Beit. The great and good of Victorian society made up the remainder: James, Duke of Abercorn, an Irish peer, was appointed chairman; among the rest were the Duke of Fife, married to the daughter of the Prince of Wales, and Albert Henry George, 4th Earl Grey. While the BSAC was a vehicle for the 'soaring ambition' of Rhodes, who hoped it would enable further colonisation and exploitation of the southern part of Africa, for Cawston it was something more profound, as he explained:

Chartered companies are based on the joint stock principle, where noblemen, gentlemen, shopkeepers, widows and orphans can all become traders and investors. Thus the great chartered companies acquired their enormous expansion and transferred the mere commercial associations of adventurers into powerful political associations. Through the agency of companies founded by these great merchant adventurers, they secured the fairest lands of the earth for our race, laying the foundations of our great colonial empire, and thus have secured an undeniable claim to the gratitude of all succeeding generations of Englishmen. (G. Cawston and A. F. Keane, *Early Chartered Companies*, 1896)

AN INTERVIEW WITH THE MATABELE

A COMMON OCCURRENCE ON THE ROAD

THE PIONEER CORPS OF THE BRITISH SOUTH AFRICA COMPANY ON THE WAY TO MASHONALAND

The British South Africa Company pioneer corps as depicted by *The Graphic*, October 1890

Cawston avoided being drawn into an argument about the rights or wrongs of the administration of the territories by the agency of a chartered company, but he emphasised that 'most of the Colonial possessions of the British Empire were in the first place settled through their agency and that the larger part of Britain's foreign trade and commerce originated in the same manner'.

The British South Africa Company was based on the principles of the British East India Company, and did not exist to trade, mine or farm. Instead it gave concessions to others and made profits from their work. The Company set out to explore and exploit the resources for the benefit of Britain, and in doing so built roads, railways and telegraphs. The British Prime Minister, Lord Salisbury, believed that control by a private company would relieve the Exchequer of any costs. All chartered companies' activities were overseen by the Colonial Office, which tended not to intervene in local affairs unless really necessary. In reality the BSAC was a huge concessionaire, establishing and authorising banking, awarding land grants and negotiating treaties. It needed substantial share capital to be successful; the bulk of investment in the BSAC came from Rhodes, De Beers and Gold Fields of South Africa. Shares were not open to public subscription but offered to friends, such as Beit, Starr Jameson and Rudd.

Caricature from the December 1892 issue of *Punch* showing Cecil Rhodes, 'The Colossus' astride the continent of Africa

In his lecture to the Imperial Institute, Cawston highlighted just how much was achieved during the 400 days which elapsed after the granting of the Charter to the British South Africa Company – from 29 October 1889 to 3 December 1890: 'In those 400 days an English colony settled, three townships were laid out, 400 miles of road cut, 400 miles of telegraph laid and 126 miles of railway completed and opened for traffic.' Another director, the Duke of Fife, promised steam locomotion on the Zambezi and a monthly postal service.

However, when the British Government had approved the BSAC's bid for a royal charter, which ultimately legitimised the Rudd concession, it was not aware that the mining rights within the concession were not vested in the BSAC but in a concern of Rhodes, Rudd, Cawston, Beit and others called the Central Search Association, which had been formed in 1889 (renamed the United Concessions Company in 1890). During the first two years the BSAC leased the concession, paying for all costs and development and passing 50 per cent of the profit back to the Central Search Association. In 1891 the Rudd concession was sold to the Chartered company for one million shares. The deception was discovered by the Colonial Office in 1891, but no action was ever taken against those involved.

RISE IN SOCIETY

Cawston was by now living in South Kensington, London. His sons were at Eton, and he had formed his own brokerage, George Cawston & Co., in Holborn. He was well known in late-Victorian London for working with MPs and civil servants to allocate BSAC shares. His connections brought him membership of the Conservative Carlton Club, and the City of London and the Wellington Clubs. His confidence and

success were so great that he was one of those who accompanied the explorer Mr Henry Morton Stanley from the Continent on his triumphal return to England in 1890.

He became a fellow of the Zoological Society of London in 1893, and a governor of the Royal Agricultural Society. He was perhaps not surprisingly also a member of the Royal Geographical Society, and the Society for African Exploration. Like James Rennell, the founder of the latter, Cawston was a highly skilled cartographer. In 1889, Cawston's *Map of Matabili, Mashona and Bamangwato, the territories of Chief Karma and King Lobengula within the British Sphere of influence* was issued by London map specialist Edward Stanford of Cockspur Street. With British colonial expansion, the demand for maps was increasing. Cawston's carefully prepared submission was advertised in the press, and showed the position of goldfields between the Limpopo and Zambezi rivers on a big scale, 16 miles to one inch.

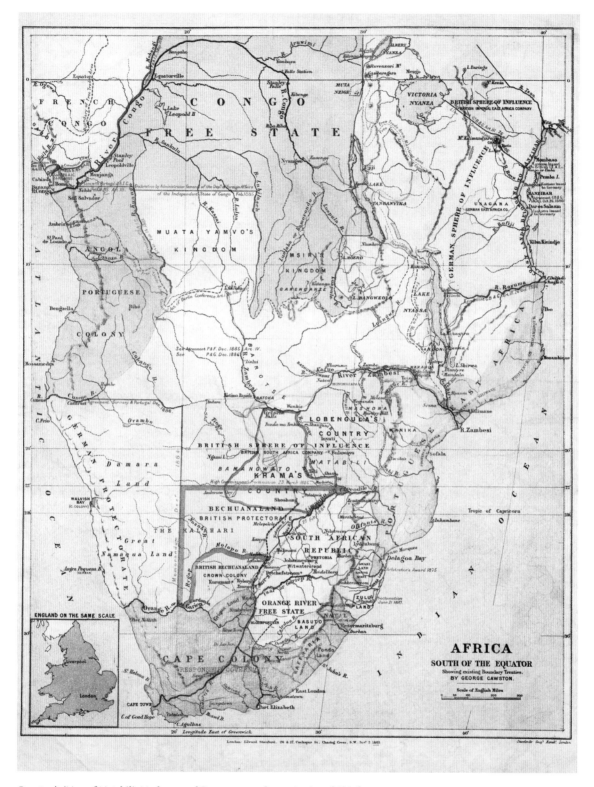

Cawston's 'Map of Matabili, Mashona and Bamangwato, the territories of Chief Karma and King Lobengula within the British Sphere of influence', 1889

As his profile rose, he attended official diplomatic banquets, and was a guest when Petrus Jacobus Joubert, the Commandant General of the South African Boer Republic, came to London in 1890. The Boers, descendants of the original Dutch settlers who had come to Africa as employees of the Dutch East India Company in 1652, occupied the Transvaal and Orange Free State, and resented British dominance in Africa. When, in 1886, gold deposits were discovered at Witwatersrand, not far from the Boer capital of Johannesburg in the Transvaal, the huge migration of foreign prospectors or Uitlanders only served to increase the Boers' resentment and tensions with the British.

During the next five years, Cawston was the 'most active of the Chartered Company's London-based Directors'. The directors of the BSAC wished the general public, and humanitarians in particular, to see the company not merely as a trade association, but, in the words of the Duke of Fife, 'working for elevation of the aborigines of that long neglected country, where I feel these people have been too long the prey of unscrupulous European traders and brutal Arab man-stealers'. To prove the point, Cawston attended the Anti-Slavery Conference organised by King Leopold II of Belgium in 1889–90, which sought not only to suppress the slave trade but also to reduce the traffic of alcohol and guns to the Africans. In 1890, he negotiated with Leopold II over Katanga and the Congo Free State boundary agreements and, on the invitation of Lord Nathan Rothschild, held talks with the Portuguese charge d'affaires, de Soveral, over commercial union between the BSAC and the Mozambique Company in 1890–1.

In the same year, the British Government discovered the secret behind the Rudd concession. Furious that they had been misled, the cabinet declared that if it had known that the BSAC did not own the concession back in 1889, it would not have granted the Charter.

They insisted that the concession was handed over to the BSAC, and exchanged its £4 million shares for £1 million chartered shares. Queen Victoria apologised to King Lobengula for the trouble caused, but even as she did so, Rhodes was planning further territorial expansion, by force if necessary.

Cawston's relationship with Cecil Rhodes was not harmonious. 'While Cawston had been promoting a commercial union, Rhodes's energies had been directed to seizing by force what Cawston would have acquired by money' (John S. Galbraith). So Cawston spread his wings and thus distanced himself from Rhodes. In 1893 he became a director of the South West Africa Company Ltd, which needed an investment of British capital. It had been granted a concession the year before by the Imperial German Government with important rights and privileges in the South West African protectorate, including mineral rights over a selected 14 million acres, freehold rights to 3 million acres and the right to construct railways

from the coast through the northern portion of the protectorate to the frontier of Bechuanaland, a distance of about 350 miles. The company now needed extra financing to enlarge the exploitation of copper, as well as lead and silver. In 1894 Cawston visited Germany where 'he so favourably impressed the German Colonial Department that the Reichstag was subsequently assured of the company's loyalty to the Imperial Government' (*Oxford Dictionary of National Biography*).

Through 1893 and 1894 local uprisings of African indigenous tribes threatened the stability of the concessions, and when fighting broke out between the Ndebele people of King Lobengula and British South Africa Company police forces over territorial claims in Southern Zambezia, outright war was only narrowly averted. The warriors submitted to the British after King Lobengula's death. Rhodes, who may well have provoked the conflict, was honoured for the part he played, and the company's territory was officially renamed 'Rhodesia'.

In 1895, Lord Salisbury won the general election for the Conservative Party. George Cawston, who had resigned his position as Conservative candidate for West Cambridgeshire in 1894 because he was unable

to devote enough time to campaigning, reached the height of his business career and social standing. He was even invited to present a prize to Lord Dudley for his win at a regatta held at the Royal Albert Yacht Club in Portsmouth. His wealth and position in society, with presumably a share of his late father's estate, as well as proceeds from the sale of properties in Streatham, enabled him to move to Upper Brook Street just off Park Lane. Like most wealthy Victorian gentlemen who lived and worked in the polluted atmosphere of industrial London, he needed a residence in the clean air of the country. His architect brother Arthur had been responsible for the design and building of Ascot Wood House in Sunninghill, just outside Windsor, which was occupied by George Cawston's family during the early 1890s before Arthur's tragic death. Ascot Wood was well staffed and conveniently near Eton, but when his eldest son George Haworth left Eton in 1894 and went up to Cambridge, a weekend retreat closer to Cawston's work in London may have been the priority. Ascot Wood was leased to Henry George Liddell, former Dean of Christ College, Oxford, and grandfather to Alice, Lewis Carroll's inspiration for *Alice in Wonderland*. For the Cawstons and their new daughter, Sylvia Phyllis, Warren House fitted the bill perfectly.

THE JAMESON RAID

It is not known to what extent George Cawston, with his political and City contacts, foresaw the events that were to follow in Africa, but they were to change the course of his family's life forever. In November 1895, when the British Government gave control of the southern portion of Bechuanaland to the Cape Colony and the northern to the Chartered Company, Rhodes and Beit, ever eager to bring the whole of South Africa under British control, hatched a plot to

Above: The Jameson Raid, Johannesburg, Transvaal, 1896

Right: Dr Leander Starr Jameson

liberate Johannesburg from the control of the Boer Transvaal Government. Dr Leander Starr Jameson and the private army of the British South Africa Company hoped to incite an uprising of Uitlanders or non-Boers, within the Boer state. They planned to use the outbreak of violence as an excuse to invade the Transvaal and annex the territory. Although no insurrection took place, Jameson crossed the border and on his way to Johannesburg was forced to surrender to the Boer Commander. The plot, known as the Jameson Raid, had failed. Repercussions soared throughout Europe: the German Kaiser congratulated Boer president Paul Kruger on his success; the telegram was leaked to the British press thereby stirring up a lot of anti-German feeling. Telegrams sent by Rhodes and his other plotters were also discovered, causing Joseph Chamberlain, the Colonial Secretary, quickly to condemn the raid, although he had previously approved armed action.

Rhodes, who had lied and attempted to bribe at least one if not two political parties, was forced to resign as Prime Minister of the Cape, and in April 1896, Cawston and Gifford pushed successfully for his resignation as a director of the chartered British South Africa Company. However, when Rhodes was returned unopposed to the Board in April 1898, Cawston, writing from Warren House, resigned:

> Coombe Wood, Kingston upon Thames, June 27th 1898
>
> Dear Duke of Abercorn – As the Directors of the British South Africa Company have now met their shareholders and their policy of strengthening the financial resources of the company has been approved and the reconstitution of the Board has now been complete, I feel that I need no longer defer taking the step which I have had in contemplation for some time, viz, placing the resignation of my directorship in your hands. It is with great regret that I thus separate myself from the Board of the Company of which I have the honour to have been one of the founders, and I shall be at all times, glad to be of any assistance in promoting its success – believe me &c.
>
> George Cawston

In the intervening years between the Jameson Raid and his own resignation, Cawston was as active as ever. While his wife Mary Ellen recuperated from a serious illness at Warren House in the summer of 1896, George Cawston's book *Early Chartered Companies* was

Warren House, late 1890s

published by Edward Arnold and on sale for 10s 6d. It was a work based on his Imperial Institute lecture of 1893, and, Cawston said, 'was projected long before the unfortunate position created by recent events in the South'.

A year after purchasing Warren House, George Cawston bought the Manor of Cawston in Norfolk, and commissioned a new house to be built. Not only did it share his name, but it was larger than the estate at Coombe and perhaps as such, it gave him a greater sense of identity and achievement. He had been associated with the area when in 1894 he had planned to stand as a Conservative candidate for West Cambridgeshire, and may have bought Warren House as a stop gap while negotiations took place in Norfolk and the manor was under construction. Indeed he may have intended to sell Warren House in 1896, for he

commissioned Bedford Lemere to take some of the earliest surviving photographs of the exterior and interior. Whatever the reason, in 1897, the year of Queen Victoria's Jubilee, it was in Norfolk and not Surrey that Mrs Cawston gave parties and handed out medals to the children.

Cawston remained in London and at Warren House during the British Government's South Africa Inquiry into the Jameson Raid in 1897, where Cawston and his fellow directors denied any knowledge of dishonest intention against the South African Boer Republic. Nonetheless they were ordered to pay the Transvaal Government £1 million in compensation for the Jameson Raid. During this time Cawston's social life continued unabated. He attended Royal Colonial Institute dinners, and meetings of the British Empire League. When his wife was fully recovered, they entertained Lord Gifford, His Highness the Thakore Saheb and Her Highness the Maharanee Gondal (descendants of leaders of the British colonial state of Rajkot), Belgian and Chinese ministers, the Earl and Countess of Orford, and the Speaker, Lord Harris, among others at their London home in Upper Brook Street.

LOOKING EAST

In May 1898, there was a second revolt of the Ndbele and the Shona against European settlers, and Cawston, in search of alternative investment, turned his interests east to China. By the late 1890s China represented the most notorious example of the scramble for concessions in the era of Western imperialism. For five years, following their defeat in the 1894–5 war with Japan, China was reduced to chaos, and investors took their chances.

Cawston was approached by Italian Marquis Carlo di Rudini, who had visited Shanghai in May 1896, to form a powerful financial syndicate for the mineral exploitation of the province of Shansi, the richest coal basin in the world, and Honan, where there were vast oilfields. In this area of 21,000 square miles, the syndicate would also be responsible for organising waterways and building railways, connecting the province with the sea. The Pekin Syndicate was incorporated in 1897. It was essential for British political supremacy in China, and was given active diplomatic support in Peking and by the Foreign Office in London. It was a highly valuable resource, as demonstrated in July 1898 when a new issue of Shansi shares looked to raise £1,520,000.

On 19 July 1898 the *Morning Post* reported the story and in true imperialist tones, Cawston described how the Government in facilitating the acquisition had been exercising one of its most important functions, that of encouraging British industry. 'There are British heads wanting work and British money wanting to be used. Work had been found for them in bringing the coal of Shansi to the people in China, and elsewhere ... [But] as a result of the investment the subjects of a European power working in oriental countries must expect the Government to protect the concession, by means of its influence over the potentate.'

Cawston was concerned to protect the syndicate against competing European countries, such as France and Germany, as well as the neighbouring countries of Russia and Japan, but also potentially hostile factions from within China. For their part the concessions were advised to keep within the geographical regions in which Government could assert and maintain its political influence. Cawston's words were particularly poignant as the following day his resignation from the Board of the British South Africa Company appeared in the press.

Ten days later, with high hopes for a new government scheme for development in Equatorial Africa, a letter from Cawston appeared in the *Morning Post*. He emphasised the importance of agreeing policy and finance five years in advance since 'this will give members a chance of some success without feeling themselves liable to be thwarted by any change in Government or by the private views of a Secretary of State'. He warned against relying on money from the existing three African chartered companies: 'The British government must learn to find money itself for the development of its own Colonies.' The single most important element for success, in his ten years of experience, was that 'Railways must in the first place be made from the coast or from the head of the nearest navigable waterway through the fever belt which exists generally all around Africa, thus putting the head of administration under healthy conditions ... without railways and without slave labour almost the only products which can be brought any distance

to the Coast are ivory and rubber.' Cawston advocated 'a continuous policy' and issued a warning by comparing the well-defined and successful British policy in Egypt, with 'our changeable policy on the northwest frontier of India and our government of South Africa in the middle of the present century'. He concluded that with a 'free hand and a vigorous railway policy, I am sure these colonies will become of great value to the Empire'.

In September 1899, the Cawstons held one of their first and last garden parties at Warren House. It was on behalf of the Conservative Primrose League, one of the first mass political party organisations in Britain which, by the end of the 19th century, had over a million and a half members. The League was a means of spreading the Conservative message to obtain support and had been founded in 1883 by admirers of the late Conservative Prime Minister Benjamin Disraeli, namely Sir Henry Drummond Wolff, High Commissioner to Egypt, and Lord Randolph Churchill, father of Winston. The primrose had been adopted as their symbol because it had been Disraeli's favourite flower. George Cawston and his wife were active members, devoting themselves to 'the maintenance of the imperial ascendancy of the British Empire'.

The Times reported the event on 19 September 1899, describing Warren House as once 'the residence of Lord Wolverton, and for many years a rallying point for the followers of the late Mr Gladstone'. Allegiances had obviously changed since Gladstone was Disraeli's rival. Apparently, due to 'the showery weather, the attendance was not as large as expected', but the guests enjoyed some musical entertainment, among them Lady Ellis and Mr Thomas Skewes-Cox, MP for Kingston.

THE BOER WAR

Back in Africa, political tensions had risen after the uprising of the Ndebele and Shona people. Negotiations for the rights of the Uitlanders within the Boer republics failed, and finally Paul Kruger, President of the South African Republic (Transvaal), issued an ultimatum giving the British 48 hours to withdraw their troops from his borders, otherwise he and the Orange Free State would declare war. The Second Boer War started on 11 October 1899.

There was huge support for British soldiers fighting in Africa. Cawston and Lord Pirbright represented the Soldiers and Sailors Help Society at a relief fund for the Boer War organised by the Lord Mayor of London. Through the words of his poem 'The Absent-minded Beggar' written in 1899, the author Rudyard Kipling drummed up public support:

> When you've shouted 'Rule Britannia' when you've
> sung 'God Save the Queen',
> When you've finished killing Kruger with your mouth,
> Will you kindly drop a shilling in my little
> tambourine?
> For a gentleman in Khaki ordered south?

Throughout the whole of the Boer War, George Cawston, filled with confidence from his first-hand experience of Africa, wrote letters to the newspapers, voicing his opinions; for example, in June 1900 he wrote to *The Times* about his views on taxation in the Transvaal. He also took part in discussions at the Colonial Institute, stressing that peace in South Africa would only come if proper consideration was taken of all the factors affecting the region: politics, language and finance.

Above: British troops retreating into Ladysmith after their defeat at Nicholson's Nek, October 1899. Cecil Cawston was at Ladysmith during its five-month siege

Right: Soldiers of the 18th Hussars – Cecil Cawston's regiment – on the train to Pretoria in South Africa during the Boer War, 1900

Cawston's involvement in South Africa had now become personal. In 1899, his younger son Cecil, who had joined the Cavalry's 18th Hussars after leaving Eton, was with his regiment surveying the country of Natal when war broke out. The 23 year old fought in the first battle of the war at Talana Hill, and was at Ladysmith throughout the five-month siege. Finally Cecil was invalided back to England with dysentery on the troop ship, *American*, in May 1900. George Cawston had arrived in Africa just before his son's departure and, as he returned separately on the *Carisbrooke Castle*, his reasons for going may not have been just to see his son safely home, but also to ascertain what was happening on the continent in which he had so much invested. Once back in England, Cecil recovered, but was recalled to Africa by

The political situation was no better to the East, in Peking. In the autumn of 1899, the Boxer Rebellion against foreign imperialism and Christianity demolished confidence in the viability and future of the region. The effect on the Pekin Syndicate was disastrous. A new issue of Shansi shares was reported 'not to make Mr George Cawston look any happier', which was unsurprising since only about 7.5 per cent were sold to investors like Messrs N. M. Rothschild, Mr J. P. Morgan, Sir E. Cassell, Messrs C. J. Hambro, and Lord Charles Beresford, and all of those at a huge discount, but it was not enough and the underwriters were left with enormous blocks of shares.

Despite the warning signs, Cawston remained optimistic, even indicating to a merchant adventurer Mr Herbert W. L. Way, author of *Round the World for Gold*, that he would consider taking up another syndicate in West Africa if Mr Way would go out for him. Even though the German Government continued to support the South West Africa Company and Cawston as part of their effort to promote the development of the protectorate, Cawston was under increasing financial pressure and needed to release some capital, so he put Warren House on the market.

The auction took place on 24 June 1900, but unfortunately for him Warren House was not sold. Cawston continued to keep a small number of staff at Coombe. On the evening of the 31 March 1901 census, Esther Jones, a 52-year-old housemaid from Swansea, South Wales, together with her daughter Jennie, a schoolroom maid, and Bessie Large, a 21-year-old maid from Stoke Newington, London, were at Warren House. On that same night, William Belcher, the groom, occupied the room over the stables; he was 18 and from Farringdon in Berkshire. William Lane, also 18, lived in the gardener's cottage; he described himself to the enumerators as a stationary engine driver, looking after the private electric plant, presumably maintaining the supply to the house.

his regiment. On 8 August his parents gave him a going-away party at Cawston in Norfolk, to which they invited the whole village. Tragically, Cecil died on 2 February 1901 of wounds received in battle at Roodepoort. By the end of the Boer War over 20,000 British troops were buried in the heat and dust of the South African plains, twice as many dying of disease than in action or as a result of their wounds. Britain won the war, but at a price.

The Cawstons put a notice in *The Times* on 12 February 1901: 'Mr and Mrs George Cawston wish to thank kind friends for letters and messages of sympathy during the past week although they do not feel able at present to answer them individually; they hope to do so in the course of a few weeks.' Cecil was commemorated by a large stained-glass window in Norwich Cathedral.

Right: Lady Aberdeen with her
dogs at Dublin Castle in 1910

Below: Lord Aberdeen, Governor
General of Canada, 1893–8, in 1898

Cawston had advertised the previous year for a
gardener – 'a steady single man to tend the lawn and
kitchen garden' – at 18 shillings a week and it is not
clear if he had found one or whether one or both of
these two young men had a dual role.

LORD AND LADY ABERDEEN

Although Warren House was not sold, it was let. The
area was known to Liberals: the house had once
belonged to Liberal Chief Whip and avid Gladstone
supporter Lord Wolverton, and living at neighbouring
Coombe Court was another Liberal politician, the 2nd
Marquess of Ripon, Earl de Grey. It was for this reason
that yet another Liberal family was drawn to the

locality: Lady Ishbel, Marchioness of Aberdeen and
Temair, her husband Lord Aberdeen and their
daughter Lady Marjorie Gordon rented Warren House
during 1902. As one newspaper explained: 'Lady
Aberdeen, originally Miss Ishbel Marjoribanks, when
quite a child, formed an ardent admiration for Mr
Gladstone, who at that time was a frequent guest at
her father's houses.' She had married John Campbell
Hamilton-Gordon, Lord Aberdeen, in 1877. A Scottish
Liberal politician, he had served briefly as Viceroy to
Ireland in 1886 and was Governor General of Canada
from 1893 to 1898.

Lady Aberdeen was known for her philanthropic
works, but was also 'a social power to be reckoned
with. At Haddo House in Aberdeenshire, at her town
residence in Grosvenor Street and more recently at
Warren House, Kingston on Thames, she entertains
not only the Liberal Party, but much that is bright and
distinguished in the London world, and not a few of
the rising representatives of Science, Art and Literature.
Middle-aged people declare that the late Mr Gladstone
was never seen to such social advantage as under the

roof of this hospitable hostess.' She was a lady of many talents, with a great fondness for spinning, and a writer and editor, having written *Through Canada with Kodak* and edited a Sunday School magazine and a book on the International Congress of Women. She possessed 'some wonderful jewels', in particular a tiara given to her by her father, Lord Tweedmouth, which contained five of the largest emeralds in the world.

The appeal of Warren House in 1902 was helped by the advent of the motor car, which enabled Lord and Lady Aberdeen to live out of London while keeping engagements in town. Their tenure brought Warren House back to life again: their parties, with their warm welcome to guests of the highest social standing, were reminiscent of those given by Lord and Lady Wolverton 15 years previously. During the short time that the Aberdeens occupied Warren House, the most important court and social engagement since the death and funeral of Queen Victoria was the coronation of Edward VII. The ceremony had been scheduled for 26 June 1902, but when Edward fell ill with appendicitis on 24 June, his coronation was postponed until 9 August 1902. This may explain why so many foreign dignitaries were able to attend a garden party given by the Aberdeens at Warren House in July.

The *Sheffield Daily Telegraph* recorded that:

> On Saturday 12 July 1902, by carriage, by motor, by train and four in hand, Colonial guests, members of Parliament, Liberal Federation Ladies, and members of the Bermondsey Guild of Play and the Guild of the Brave Poor Things, went down this afternoon to a delightful garden party given by Lady Aberdeen in the grounds of The Warren, Coombe Wood.

Among the guests were Sir Edmund and Lady Barton, Lord and Lady Balfour of Burleigh, Mrs Elspeth Campbell, who came over from Coombe Hill Farm, and Mrs Cornelia Sorabji, a lady barrister who wore Indian dress. Lady Aberdeen herself displayed her famed jewels, 'some lovely turquoise and emeralds with her gown of black lace over white chiffon and shady hat with pink roses', while her daughter Lady Marjorie, 'looked delightfully cool and dainty in cream lace and lace net with pink roses and a bunch of pink malmaisons in her silver waist belt'. *The Times* picked up the story:

> Canadian friends especially received a warm welcome as the Earl of Aberdeen was Governor General of the Dominion from 1893–8. Lady Aberdeen received by the garden entrance and close by the band of the Scots Guards, under the direction of Mr F. W. Wood. The children of the Bermondsey Guild, in brightly coloured costumes, gave representations of their games, which were followed with much interest by the assembled company. There were present, the United States Ambassador, the Spanish Ambassador and the Duchesse de Mandas, the Greek Minister and Mme and Mlle Metaxas.

On 5 August 1902, four days before the coronation of Edward VII, Lord and Lady Aberdeen left Warren House for Scotland and Haddo House, perhaps to prepare for the Coronation. There is no record of them at Warren House after that. In 1905 Lord Aberdeen was appointed Viceroy of Ireland, a post he held until 1915.

The British victory at the end of the Boer War coincided with a period of relative peace for Cawston. Cecil Rhodes, whom the *Guardian* called a 'materialistic patriot', had died on 26 March 1902. Cawston suspended work for the day while he and his wife went to the memorial service at St Paul's Cathedral, which was attended by royalty and a great many foreign ambassadors, politicians, aristocrats, businessmen and family. Rhodes's position as chairman of the BSAC was now occupied by Earl Grey, who had been on the board since 1889, and who later became the Governor General of Canada. Cawston returned to the usual events of a Victorian gentleman's social calendar: dinners given by the committee of the Stock Exchange, the Royal Eye Hospital in the Whitehall rooms, and functions at Inner Temple where he had qualified. He was a member of the China Association and the London Society, and also the City of London Free Trade Association, for he believed that the prosperity of London and the empire was based on the principle of free trade, and that it alone was responsible for the development of industry and the huge growth in exports over the previous 50 years.

One happy event was the marriage of his elder daughter Ellen or 'Queenie' in November 1904 to Captain Montague Percy Oakes of the Irish Lancers. In 1902, at her coming-out ball in London, she had entered the ballroom on a 'quaint old sedan chair, of the kind most affected by our fashionable grandmothers, decorated inside and out with superb white flowers, which she distributed to the guests as mementos of the occasion'. It was suggested at the time that some of the cotillion presents, which consisted of dainty work bags made from expensive brocade, had been looted from the royal palace at Peking.

FINANCIAL FAILURE

Cawston increased the number of companies and syndicates in which he was involved, his holdings showing investments throughout the world: Gearless Motor Omnibus Company Ltd, the Spanish Copper Company Ltd, British South Africa Townships Ltd, the Rosario Western Railway Company in the Argentine, Korean Waterworks Ltd, the Siam Company and the Prah, Opinto and Sun Syndicates. However, many of these were risky: the returns dwindled over the next few years and several of them were liquidated. Unable to sell Warren House, Cawston managed to reduce his liability in 1906 through a number of conveyances

and conditions agreed between himself and the heirs of the Duke of Cambridge, who had himself died in 1904. Finally in 1907 he sold Warren House to Lady Mary Paget, the American wife of British soldier, General Arthur Paget, for £20,000.

This must have gone some way towards helping his financial situation. By now the offices of George Cawston & Co., Stockbroker had moved, perhaps in an attempt to reduce rent. But Cawston does not seem to have economised completely for, after Warren House, he and his family moved to another large house, Netley Court near Netley Abbey, just outside Portsmouth, where he had presented the yachting prizes some years before. In 1911, two months after his daughter Sylvia was presented at court, the company Charterland Goldfields went into liquidation: Cawston and his shady Australian business associate, Edmund Davis, were directors, and the liquidator complained that there was 'an absence of regard by the directors for the interests of the shareholders', an accusation roundly denied by Cawston. However, in that same year, his father's firm of stockbrokers Samuel Cawston & Co., in which George was a partner, was dissolved, and he lost control of the Bechuanaland Exploration Company and the South West Africa Company to Davis. The Pekin Syndicate could not fully exploit their concession as the Boxer Rebellion was followed by the 1904–5 war between Japan and Russia, and action was further hampered by the Chinese Revolution of 1911. The steady decline of this once successful man continued. Cawston moved out of Upper Brook Street, where he had lived for over 15 years, to the less expensive Queen's Gate. There is no record of him at Cawston Manor in Norfolk after 1913, the year his elder brother Samuel died.

Whether an optimist or a fool, Cawston continued to look to the future. In January 1914, he attended a dinner given by the London Society, where architect Sir Aston Webb spoke of his 'Dream of 2014'. In his

An Agreement

made the twelfth day of June One — thousand, nine, hundred and seven **Between** George Cawston of Warren House Coombe Warren in the Parish of Coombe Kingston-on-Thames in the County of Surrey (hereinafter called "the Vendor" of the one part) and Mary Paget the wife of Lieutenant General Sir Arthur Henry Fitzroy Paget of 35 Belgrave Square in the County of London K.C.V.O.C.B

Whereby it is agreed, as follows:

1. The Vendor shall sell, and the Purchaser shall purchase **All** those piece or parcels of land messuage and premises described in the first, and second parts of the first Schedule hereto but, subject to the stipulations, and restrictions hereinafter mentioned

2. **The** consideration for the said sale, shall be the sum of Twenty thousand pounds The Purchaser shall pay to the Vendor on the twenty fourth day of June next the sum of Three thousand pounds and, the amount of the valuation for certain fixtures, and fittings hereinafter mentioned On such payment, and on giving to the Vendors Solicitors a written acceptance of the Vendors title the Purchaser shall be entitled forthwith to enter into possession of the said property but pending the completion of her purchase, she shall not take or remove from the property, any gravel clay bricks, stone or other substance from or make any structural or other alterations on the said premises without the consent in writing of the Vendor The rent and outgoings payable in respect of the property up to the said twenty fourth day of June, shall be discharged by the Vendor or an allowance made to the purchaser in respect thereof, as from which day all rents, and outgoings including rates, or charges made but not demanded till after that day shall be discharged by the purchaser such outgoings if necessary, being apportioned for the purpose of this condition

3. The Purchaser shall also purchase, at a valuation to be made as hereinafter provided certain fixtures, and fittings specified in a list prepared by Messrs Toffs & Warner, and signed by or on behalf of the Vendors, and the Purchaser

4. **The** balance of the said purchase money namely Seventeen thousand pounds together with the sum of One hundred and ninety one pounds five shillings being three months interest thereon at the rate of Four pounds ten shillings per cent per annum computed from the said twenty fourth day of June next and shall be paid and the purchase shall be completed on the thirtieth day of September next at the offices No 30 Mincing Lane London E.C. of Messrs Hollams Sons Coward & Hawksley the Vendors Solicitors, and if from any cause

[margin note:] Possession given & title accepted subject to outlawry re: quiritrs Hollams Son Coward & Hawksley

prescient vision of London in 2014, smoke and dirt
had been banished and the waters of the Thames were
so clean that fishing for salmon and trout was possible;
St Paul's Cathedral was still standing and was safe for
centuries, and a law was passed that no sewers or
tunnels should pass within 150 feet of it; parties no
longer entered into municipal politics so the south side
of the river was embanked and along this south
embankment were picturesque warehouses; the county
council buildings by Westminster Bridge were used as
government offices, while close alongside were the
Imperial Parliament buildings where the parliament
of the Empire met and thought imperially every three
years; South Kensington had gone rather out of fashion
and houses down Exhibition Road and Queen's Gate
had been turned into hostels for students; Southwark
had been rebuilt and the roofs of the houses were flat,
and here people sat on a summer's evening on their
roof gardens; aeroplanes had been forbidden over
London, because they were apt to drop unpleasant
things and they became a nuisance; besides railway
tracks, there were great arterial roads stretching out of
London in all directions; they were 120 feet wide with
two divisions, one for slow traffic and one for faster
moving vehicles; the people had wireless telegraphy,
wireless telephones and wireless electric light; and a
belt of green encircled London, a sylvan glade formed
out of various town planning schemes. Another
member spoke of a time when in our houses there
would be hot air in winter and cold air in summer, laid
on by municipal enterprise. George Cawston may have
laughed along with the other 150 guests, but nine
months later, he would certainly have wished that he
too had had the power of such foresight.

Shortly after the beginning of the First World War
when German Colonial forces in South West Africa
attacked South African troops, a paragraph in *The
Times* entitled 'Mr George Cawston's Affairs' brought
more bad news: 'The creditors of Mr George Cawston
Stockbroker and director of public companies, of
Salisbury House, London Wall EC, met yesterday at
bankruptcy buildings and accepted an offer of a
composition of 5s in the pound.' He had gross
liabilities of £27,987 11s 9d of which £17,775 8s 1d
were expected to rank for dividend, and assets valued
only at £1,862 9s 7d. Five months later on 9 February
1915, George Cawston made an application for
discharge of the bankruptcy but because the courts
believed that he had contributed to his bankruptcy by
an 'unjustifiable extravagance in living', and his assets
were not of a value equal to 10 shillings in the pound
on the amount of his unsecured liabilities, the
discharge was suspended for a further two years and
six months until 3 September 1917.

George Cawston's battle ended six weeks after
Armistice Day. He died on 27 December 1918 at the
Great Eastern Hotel in Liverpool Street, and was
buried in Norfolk. The Pekin Syndicate paid nothing
until 1936, when shareholders received just a half-
year dividend.

4

THE TALE OF THE GENERAL AND
THE DOLLAR PRINCESS

GENERAL SIR ARTHUR HENRY FITZROY PAGET GCB KCVO (1851–1928)
AND LADY MARY 'MINNIE' FISKE PAGET (1853–1919)

We Britons born beneath a duller star,
Knew that her wit could blaze exceeding bright,
But scarcely fancied it would reach so far
As literally make the house alight.

Lord Crewe for Lady Paget, 1896
(Source: *Personal Letters of King Edward VII,*
edited by J. P. C. Sewell, 1931)

THE NEW MISTRESS of Warren House, Lady Mary Paget, was a wealthy American heiress. In the years before the First World War, she and her British aristocratic husband, General Sir Arthur Paget, made Warren House their home for a quintessential upper-class family life and weekend house parties that epitomised Edwardian high society.

Opposite: Detail of a Persian tile from the fireplace surround in the former Persian Smoking Room at Warren House, currently the dining room

Above: Ornate garden ornaments were introduced by the Pagets

Already in her fifties, Lady Paget was still an attractive, fashionable woman of 'medium height with dark hair growing rather low on a broad forehead, dark brows above particularly brilliant grey-blue eyes and a mouth which displayed determination and power without losing its mobility. She had an almost imperceptible American accent, looked English and dressed like a French woman' (J. P. C. Sewell). Although she was from New York, Lady Paget was very suited to the English upper-class way of life. With her remarkable organisational flair, she brought life back to Warren House, inviting royalty, aristocrats and politicians as her guests to eat, drink and play under her watchful eye. When the ravages of war took hold, generals were added to her guest list.

A few years before her purchase of Warren House, Lady Paget had been interviewed by a fellow American, Kate Carew. Famed for her caricatures, Carew was commissioned by Pulitzer in 1901 to conduct interviews in Europe for his *New York World*.

'Oh, it's the simplest, easiest thing in the world,' she said. 'All you have to do is throw open doors and simply stand there. When the people come in you hold out your hand, that's all. You don't have to introduce people; you don't have to do anything to entertain them; it is all most beautifully simple.'

'But there must be something else,' I protested, 'because some hostesses are failures.'

'Oh, well, a little tact,' confessed Mrs Paget. 'Just a little tact – that's the whole secret.'

Since her marriage to the young Captain Paget, 30 years before, Mary Paget had worked tirelessly to achieve and maintain this social status. It had not been an easy task, but one made a lot easier by her longstanding friendship with Edward VII.

During the latter half of the 19th century, the Prince of Wales, later Edward VII, was the leader of a fashionable elite who travelled around Continental Europe, soaking up the atmosphere of optimism during the belle epoque that preceded the Great War. Invitations to state dinners given by royalty were extended to the upper classes, champagne was perfected, haute couture was embraced and burlesque became popular. Across the Atlantic, the United States was in the process of developing a modern industrial economy. During what Mark Twain called 'the Gilded Age', super-rich families emerged, and with their money from railways, shipping, steel and oil, they lived a life of a hitherto unseen opulence.

THE STEVENS OF NEW YORK

Born Mary Fiske Stevens, and known as the Belle of Newport, Lady Paget was educated in New York and Paris. Her father, Paran Stevens, was a wealthy entrepreneur and self-made man 'with refined tastes', well known on the East Coast. After the death of his

In an article about herself in *Pearson's Magazine*, December 1904, Carew recounted her meeting with the then Mrs Paget:

> She compared society in a monarchy with society in a republic, English with American husbands, and American with English women. She discussed the importance of not being sentimental in society, the philosophy of international marriages, the sort of cleverness necessary to a woman who would please the King, and other absorbing topics. Would you know Mrs Paget's recipe for the making of a successful hostess?

Lady Mary Paget, by Edward Hughes of the Swan Electric Engraving Company

The New York City residence of Mrs Paran Stevens, who owned one unit in Marble Row, 244 5th Avenue, photographed c.1894

first wife Eliza, he married a young woman, Marietta Reed, 25 years his junior. Marietta was a grocer's daughter who had become a teacher, but she was socially very ambitious. They had two children: Mary Fiske, born in 1853, and Henry Leiden, born in 1858.

In 1848 Paran Stevens bought land between Fifth Avenue and 27th Street, New York, for $5,000, on which he intended to build a hotel. In the meantime the family moved from Boston, where he managed the Revere and Tremont Hotels, to Mobile, Alabama, moving back again in the late 1850s. Paran Stevens then completed and opened what proved to be the biggest and best hotel New York had ever seen: the Fifth Avenue Hotel. The family lived just around the corner at 244 Fifth Avenue. Paran Stevens became one of the most prosperous hotel proprietors in the United States, at one time controlling the Continental in Philadelphia, and seven hotels in New York. He also founded the Stevens High School at Claremont, endowing it with $50,000.

Initially, the traditional old 'Knickerbocker' families of New York led by Mrs Caroline Astor considered the Stevenses to be 'low-born upstarts'. But Marietta Stevens fought off these criticisms with an extremely strong will and the help of social arbiter Ward McAllister, and it was not long before New York social elite and visiting foreigners craved invitations to her salons. Much of her success was down to the musical prowess of her sister, Fanny Reed. In his memoirs Frederick Townsend Martin, an American writer, recalls, 'Everyone flocked to Mrs Stevens's musicals to hear Miss Fanny sing – indeed she sung her sister into society.' Fanny Reed's voice even attracted the Prince of Wales who, in 1860 on his first tour of America, had stayed as a guest in the Stevenses' Fifth Avenue Hotel in New York.

Paran Stevens, who preferred breeding racehorses to hobnobbing with society, was also considered the best judge of wines in the country. In 1857 he went to Europe to select rare vintages for the Fifth Avenue and Continental Hotels. In addition to a large quantity of Grand Vin Chateau Lafitte of 1841, he purchased sherry, brandy and madeira. In early 1867 he was appointed a United States commissioner to the Paris Exposition, where the family rented a house and entertained many people.

Eager to maintain the associations with the French and European aristocracy, Marietta Stevens and her daughter, Mary, went again to Paris in 1870, during the final months of the Franco-Prussian War and the bloodless coup which followed the capture of Napoleon III at Sedan, and the fall of the Second Empire. With Paris under siege, Marietta and Mary were urged to leave and fled north to the coast. They crossed the channel to Brighton where they stayed for a few days. From there they headed for London with fellow Americans, the mother and three daughters of the Cuban-American Yznaga family, and the wife of Leonard Jerome, a business and horseracing acquaintance of her father's, who also had three daughters.

Travelling in Europe with her mother, Mary was only 19 years old when her father died in New York in April 1872. Paran Stevens had just completed the finest apartment house in New York on Fifth Avenue and 27th Street, which later became the Victoria Hotel. The terms of Paran Stevens's Will and the $10 million fortune he had amassed from property in New York and New England were contested from the moment he died. There was an complete lack of agreement between Marietta and the trustees to whom Paran Stevens left the management of his property. It was a battle that was to last 30 years and one Marietta, who estimated she had spent £250,000 in lawyers' fees, would eventually lose. Paran Stevens was buried in Mount Auburn cemetery near Boston, where his wife erected a huge memorial.

Lord and Lady Randolph
Churchill, *c.*1874, the year of
their marriage

AN IDEAL HUSBAND

As part of the New York social elite, Mary Stevens,
known as Minnie, was a guest at the Delmonico Ball,
a costume party held at the favourite restaurant and
party venue in New York in 1875. However, for
Marietta Stevens, who still did not feel entirely socially
accepted, it was not enough. She decided that it was
essential for her standing in New York society that she
find her daughter a suitable European aristocrat as a
husband. All Minnie's potential American suitors were
dismissed and from then on she and her mother spent
much time in Europe, visiting the distinguished
Europeans who had been guests at their hotels.
Nouveau-riche Americans like the Stevenses could
achieve greater social status in Europe than they could
in the rigid society of New York through association
with and, particularly, marriage into the British and
European elite; this also brought them in contact with
political power and influence. While France had

become a very different place from what it had been
under Napoleon III, upper-class society in England
still offered solid traditional values and an established
aristocracy – and far more opportunities for finding a
suitable husband.

Although many impoverished British aristocratic
families welcomed wealthy American girls with open
arms, love was considered a bonus. Members of the
landed gentry who had growing debts from huge
estates, and whose political or military careers did not
pay well, were often more interested in the dowry than
the bride. It was an arrangement often referred to as
'gilded prostitution'.

Minnie's friend Jennie Jerome had married Lord
Randolph Churchill, and Minnie had been bridesmaid
to another friend, Consuelo Yznaga, when she married
the British peer and MP, George Viscount Mandeville,
later the 8th Duke of Manchester. It was Consuelo who
invited Minnie to join her at the Marlborough House
parties given by the Prince of Wales. Prince Albert
Edward, 'Bertie', welcomed anyone into his social
circle so long as they were amusing, well mannered,
sporting and wealthy. He was particularly fond of
some American women, though not all! Attractive,
intelligent and wealthy, Minnie was an instant success.
She and Consuelo were renowned for both their
popularity and wit, while being quite different
characters – Consuelo was 'all sunshine and glitter for
everyone worthy, Minnie was more cool and calm – it
was the difference between a summer morning and a
moonlit night, each charming in its way and full of
great possibilities', explained the *New York Times*.
Along with 1,400 other guests, Minnie was invited to a
Fancy Dress Ball at Marlborough House on 22 July
1874. Despite dancing well as the Ace of Hearts in the
Card Quadrille, it seemed that Minnie was destined to
be forever the bridesmaid.

It was not on account of her looks or personality
that she spent the next six years looking for a suitable

General Sir Arthur Henry Fitzroy Paget, photographed by Bassano in 1911

husband, for she was described by Lilly Langtry as 'an American of remarkable popularity, besides being very attractive and good looking', and she was one of upper-class society's photographed Professional Beauties (PB for short). Among her potential suitors were Irish Lords Rossmore and Newry, and also Lord William Hay 'who did not suit'. Perhaps the answer to her unmarried state lay in her exaggerated financial status which, when scrutinised by the French Duc de Grammont and his son Guiche, was found to be four times less than Minnie and her mother had claimed. The revelation led to further rejection, the Duc declaring, 'We will proceed no further in this business.' Even the reported theft in London of $50,000 worth of jewels by Mrs Paran Stevens's French maid does not seem to have convinced them of her worth. The rejection prompted Lady Waldergrave to remark that she considered Minnie 'an awful storyteller who never indulges in a word of truth even to her most intimate friends and admirers'.

By the age of 25, Minnie decided that it was better to be married with no title than not married at all. So in July 1878 she accepted the proposal of marriage from a brave soldier and close friend of the Prince of Wales, Captain Arthur Henry Fitzroy Paget. In 1873, when just 22 years old, Arthur had served in the debilitating climate of what is now Ghana, under Sir Garnet Wolseley. It was a battle over the control of coastal Africa, so important for British imperial trade in West Africa, which became known as the Third Anglo-Ashanti war.

CAPTAIN ARTHUR PAGET

Arthur Paget was the eighth child and eldest son of General Lord Alfred Paget, Chief Equerry to Queen Victoria, Clerk Marshall of the Royal Household and MP for Lichfield, and his wife Cecilia Wyndham.

Arthur's grandfather was Field Marshal Henry William Paget, 1st Marquess of Anglesey, who fought as Commanding Officer of the Cavalry Brigade under the Duke of Wellington at the Battle of Waterloo. His great-grandfather, Henry Paget, was the 1st Earl of Uxbridge. In 1861, at the age of ten, Arthur was appointed Page of Honour in the Royal household, a post he held until 1867. He was educated at Wellington, and then purchased a commission into the Scots Fusilier Guards in June 1869 (called the Scots Guards from 1877). He had distinguished himself in battle and, during the years of peace that followed, Arthur Paget led the privileged life of a young officer in the Foot Guards as a close friend of the Prince of Wales and a member of the Marlborough House set.

Paget was interested in racing and became the owner of many racehorses, which he bought and sold under the pseudonym of Captain or Mr Fitzroy. He attended sales at Tattersall's, Newmarket, and Hampton Court,

Dr Fothergill 'Fog' Rowlands, on Bold Navy, *c.*1850. Years later Captain Arthur Paget employed this former jockey turned trainer to manage his team of racehorses

The paddock at the Epsom Derby. Paget not
only owned horses but backed them too

where the Queen held an annual sale of yearlings, or
made his purchases direct from the breeder's stud farm,
such as Eastern Park. Arthur was an avid race-goer and
would watch his horses race over the Croydon Hurdles
or at Sandown Park, at the Grand National, and in
Baden-Baden in Germany. Paget's most expensive
horse was John Day, bought for 2,650 guineas. In
December 1877, the *Glasgow Herald* exposed the
identity of Mr Fitzroy, who had become quite a
celebrity, not only at the sales but in the newspaper
columns with his sporting prophecies, 'Mr Fitzroy's
Selected' and 'Mr Fitzroy's Best': 'Mr Fitzroy, in whose
name John Day runs, is a Captain Paget who is now
one of our principal plungers.' Captain Paget and Lord
Marcus Beresford employed Mr Fothergill 'Fog'
Rowlands of Pitt Place, a former jockey and the pioneer
of National Hunt Steeplechase, to manage their team

of horses until Fog's death in 1878. Arthur paid the best
jockeys, such as John Jones, to ride his thoroughbreds.
But when entering his horses Chilblane and Pilgrim's
Progress in the Military Hunt Cup Races and
Household Brigade Cup, it was his fellow officers that
rode well for him. A number of years later, Paget,
Edward VII, Charles Beresford and Topps Hartopp (Sir
Charles Edward Cradock-Hartopp, 5th Baronet of
Freathby) all used John Jones, who had started in the
stables of Fothergill Rowlands, as a trainer.

Beresford and Paget not only owned horses but
backed them too. It was a lucrative pastime: in 1878
Paget won £772, Beresford £1,040, and with good
wins at the Derby that year it was reported that
Captain Paget made £4,000 in winning bets. These
may not have been all his own, for the young men
were often accompanied by the Prince of Wales. As it
was inappropriate for the Prince to be seen 'backing
his fancy' in public, Arthur Paget would place the
Prince's bets in his own name.

THE ENGAGEMENT AND WEDDING

St Peter's Church, Eaton Square, London. Captain
Arthur Paget and Mary 'Minnie' Stevens were married
here on 27 July 1878

Arthur had asked Minnie to marry him on two separate
occasions, prompted by the Prince of Wales. She turned
him down on the first occasion, and he later attributed
the rejection to the fact that he had asked with his head.
However, when he asked again, this time with his heart, she
accepted. The Prince of Wales wrote, 'Long ago I hoped that
Arthur would find favour in your eyes, and now that all is so
happily settled, I cannot tell you how I rejoice that he is to
be your future husband.'

Although there was no title to inherit, Minnie may have
hoped that one day Arthur would be honoured with a
knighthood for services to his country. Ruth Brandon in
The Dollar Princesses explains Minnie's motives: she 'did
not equate marriage with happiness. It was merely, in this
society, the necessary prelude to self-fulfilment in social
terms'. Her dowry, according to the dowry fund of Craven-
Bradley-Martin alliance, was around £200,000. A pre-nuptial
settlement provided Arthur with an annual allowance of
$20,000 a year.

Captain Arthur Paget and Minnie Stevens were married in
the afternoon of Saturday, 27 July 1878 at St Peter's Church,
Eaton Square. Minnie wore a white satin dress trimmed with
point d'Alençon and a lace veil over a wreath of orange
blossom. The wreath was attached to her train by five
diamond stars, a gift from Arthur. She wore a diamond
necklace, a present from her brother, and a sapphire and
diamond bracelet given to her by the Prince and Princess of
Wales, while her mother had given her diamond earrings. She
was attended by her mother and four bridesmaids who wore
Louis XIV jackets of white satin, and striped Pekin silk and
white Indian muslin skirts trimmed with Valenciennes lace
and tulle veils, each carrying a bouquet of red roses. Each
bridesmaid wore a locket set with black and white pearls in
the form of the initials M. A. Lord Marcus Beresford was Paget's
best man and the Prince of Wales, Prince Louis of Battenberg
and the Duke of Connaught were in the congregation. The
ceremony was performed by the Dean of Windsor, and Minnie
was given away by her brother, Henry, while the celebrated
composer Arthur Sullivan played the organ. The reception
took place at Lord Alfred Paget's house in Queen Anne Street,
where the military band of the Scots Fusiliers played. As
Arthur and Minnie left to spend their honeymoon at The Hatch,
the house of Mr Gerald Paget, Arthur's younger brother, at
Windsor, as well as Lord Alfred Paget's house in Bushy Park,
they were loudly cheered by a large throng that had gathered
on the pavement and were pelted with copious showers of rice
and slippers from the door.

The wedding presents were fabulous: the Prince of Wales
gave a *garniture de cheminée* (mantelpiece ornaments)
consisting of a Louis XIV clock and candelabra purchased at
the Paris Exhibition that year, and the Princess of Wales gave
Minnie a serpent bracelet of gold set with rubies, sapphires
and diamonds. Princess Louise gave a pair of gold pearl
earrings and a massive silver coffee pot, Prince Louis of
Battenberg gave an Egyptian necklace, Prince Edward of
Saxe-Weimar a blue Venetian vase and Lady Mandeville gave
a splendid set of Dresden china. The *New York Times* said that
'the wedding was universally considered as one of the most
brilliant ever seen in London'. Minnie had arrived, and as a
member of the Prince of Wales's set and the daughter-in-law
of a peer, she had the opportunity to create a place for herself
in London society, while her mother returned to New York to
do the same.

Once married, it was thought that Arthur would give up his thoroughbreds and racing, but this was not the case. At least four of his thoroughbreds were still racing in 1884 and Arthur, riding his own hunter Elvino, came fourth in the Military Hunters Steeplechase at Sevenoaks on 1 May 1880. Some 12 years later Arthur was still devoted to the Turf and, employing trainer John Porter of Kingsclere, he continued to be successful. As for Lord Marcus Beresford, he was appointed manager of the Prince of Wales's stables in 1890, winning the Derby and the St Leger in 1896 with Persimmon, and the Derby in 1900 with Persimmon's brother Diamond Jubilee, and then in 1909 with Minoru.

Racehorse trainer John Porter (1838–1922) of Kingsclere, *Vanity Fair*, October 1889

THE EARLY YEARS

While Arthur was occupied as a gentleman soldier, his wife Minnie was fast becoming one of society's greatest hostesses. With steely determination, Minnie took advantage of every social opportunity. She had enough money to please people with lovely dinners, and enough sense, according to writer Hesketh Pearson, to collect a number of amusing guests, thus meeting the demands of entertaining London high society including royalty. Their home at 3 Halkin Street became known as one of the smartest in town.

Minnie did not often join the royal parties out of London, but the Prince of Wales was a regular visitor at her dinners and bridge parties. Since her presentation at court by Lady Suffield, she had befriended many others in royal circles, including the Prince's brothers: Leopold, Duke of Albany, and Arthur, Duke of Connaught. She gave one party in honour of Arthur, where she played charades with him, and Leopold, writing to her after his engagement in 1881, said, 'You are such an old friend of mine that I know you will be glad to hear of my happiness.' Like many wealthy Victorians, she spent her time organising countless bazaars and charitable functions. The *Daily News* on Saturday, 11 June 1881 reported:

> A Royal Bazaar at Bagshot Park, the home of the Duke and Duchess of Connaught, under the immediate patronage of Queen Victoria and in aid of funds for a new Parish church ... The visitors, many of whom had come on special trains from London, enjoyed seats under the park trees listening to the two military bands, whilst in a large marquee, hedged about with potted flowers and shrubs, flags and garlands, there were thirteen stalls. With the names of the Proprietors written in large letters, the Duke of Connaught, Lady Listowel and Mrs Paget ran the American bar selling cocktails of brandy, gin and whisky, sherry cobblers, cream pearl long drinks, and temperance tea nectar, handing the thirsty not only a deliciously cool liquor, but a brace of orthodox straws wherewith to do it justice.

The Pagets' close friendship with the Prince and Princess of Wales was honoured when the royal couple became godparents to their first-born son, later named Albert Edward, in 1879.

> My Dear Arthur,
> Accept my warmest congratulations on the birth of your son – and that Mrs Arthur's confinement is safely over. It was very kind of you writing at once to tell me and I hope she got over her troubles well, and that both are doing well. I can hardly fancy you as a Papa!

> Unless you have any special relation to be a sponsor, may I be godfather to young Arthur?

A daughter, Louise Margaret Leila Wymess Paget, was born three years later in 1882.

The young family travelled regularly between London, New York and Rhode Island, where Minnie's mother spent the summers. It was there in July 1885 that the untimely death from cancer of Mary's 27-year-old brother, Henry Leiden Stevens, took its toll on her health. Minnie, reported one newspaper, was with him but 'stayed so short a time and was so grief stricken that she saw very few of her friends. Those who did were surprised at the ravages that grief and a recent illness had had on her beauty.' In the same month, the newly promoted Lieutenant Colonel Arthur Paget had been ordered to Egypt with the second battalion of the Scots Guards to serve in Sir G. Graham's Suakin Expedition to Sudan. Still grieving for her brother, Minnie Paget and the other wives of the three battalions of Guards walked with them to the station as the pipes played amid the uniforms of scarlet and gold. This prompted a kind letter from the wife of the Prince of Wales, Princess Alexandra.

> My Dear Mrs Paget,
> I was so sorry for you today and you were so brave and plucky in walking by the side of your dear Arthur all the way through the streets. It gave me such a lump in the throat to see you poor wives having to take leave of your husbands. I hope you will come and dine with me tomorrow, quite a small party of the poor disconsolate wives.

During this campaign, the regiment took part in the Battle of Hasheen, made worse by the heat, sand, flies and dysentery, and the skirmishing 'Fuzzies'. Arthur wrote to Minnie: 'They never leave us alone, charging us by day, and firing at us by night. Our casualties have been very severe.' The Prince of Wales and Arthur Paget also exchanged regular correspondence, Arthur not hesitating to give his opinion of the situation and the

generals involved. The Prince passed the letters full of details of the campaign on to the Duke of Cambridge as intelligence. He did, however, warn Arthur to be careful when criticising superior officers, even asking Minnie to return a couple he had forwarded to her in case the contents were made public. The battalion returned home in late 1885, having been away for just nine months. When the British ordered troops out of Sudan, the enemy leader Osman Dinga wrote, 'God struck fear into the hearts of the English and they went away.' Arthur, in contrast, wrote to his wife suggesting what he would like for dinner on his return.

The peace of the summer of 1886 in Newport, Rhode Island, was not relived the following year when Colonel Arthur Paget and his battalion were sent to fight in the Third Anglo-Burmese War in 1887–8. The British were victorious, and with annexation of Burma came the end to the threat of expansion into British

India. Once the fighting was over, Arthur took some time out in India to hunt game. He kept up correspondence with the Prince of Wales who, putting in a few good words on his behalf, duly passed his informative military letters on to the Duke of Cambridge and Field Marshal Lord Garnet Wolseley, who had commanded the expedition to Ashanti and served in Sudan as well as Burma.

Minnie had been pregnant with twins during the whole of Arthur's campaign, and sons Arthur Wyndham and Reginald Scudamore were born in Paris in March 1888. Just five months later, Arthur's father Lord Alfred Paget died, aged 72. Lord Alfred had been Chief Equerry and Clerk Marshall to Queen Victoria while the Prince of Wales was growing up and Bertie was genuinely sympathetic when he heard the news; he wrote in a letter, 'There is no one I have known so long as your poor father, ever since I was born almost, and I shall always regret him as the oldest friend I had ...'

Otto von Bismarck and his son Herbert, State Secretary of the Foreign Office from 1860–90, by Franz Seraph von Lenbach, 1892

KAISER WILHELM II AND THE BISMARCKS

Colonel Arthur Paget accompanied the Prince of Wales to Germany in 1890, on a visit to the Prince's nephew, the new German Emperor, Kaiser Wilhelm II. The timing of the visit was crucial, as the ascendance of Wilhelm marked the beginning of Germany's attempts at world domination which were to culminate in the First World War and the Kaiser's own ignoble escape to Holland. Arthur Paget's letters to his wife from the Berlin palace tell of the pomp and grandeur of the Prussian Guard: 'There was a tremendous show on our arrival in Berlin, the Emperor, all the Princes and Staff were there, Guard of Honour etc. I never saw such magnificent men.' In another he wrote, 'I never dreamt HRH's visit was so important a one – and fancy coming here at this crisis and being entirely behind the scenes and knowing what is going on, besides meeting these men who are, or will shortly be, celebrities in every sense of the word.' On dining with Herbert von Bismarck, the Foreign Secretary of the German Empire, on the eve of his father Otto von Bismarck's dismissal,

Paget wrote, 'Herbert was so pleased to get us all round him, and it was his last dinner whilst in office. Today he is no more, and goes on a year's leave. This is for your private ear.'

Minnie Paget had met and befriended Herbert when he had been sent to England by his father with specific instructions to 'get in touch with the people of prominence and do what he could to overcome their misgivings towards German foreign policy'. Herbert and Minnie had exchanged many letters since. Arthur was therefore very excited to meet Prince Otto von Bismarck, and he told Minnie, 'I have brought away and will give you something of more value than I have ever given you – a photo of himself, signed and dated, and the value of it consists in that it was given on the day he said good-bye to his Sovereign, perhaps forever.'

Otto von Bismarck, the 'Iron Chancellor', had been responsible for unifying Germany and creating the balance of power that kept Europe at peace after 1871. Wilhelm II opposed Bismarck's careful foreign policy, preferring rapid and vigorous expansion. The Kaiser, keen to curry favour with his uncle and British guests, gave Arthur Paget a beautiful cigarette case in silver with the German Emperor's crest in diamonds and a portrait of himself, which he hung in his London home.

Bismarck had accurately foretold that 'one day the great European war will come out of some damn foolish thing in the Balkans'; less than three decades later, his prediction was to prove sadly accurate. This was a time when predictions by seers were fashionable: in 1891 Minnie Paget invited the Prince of Wales to her house in Belgrave Square for a séance by the world-renowned seer Cheiro, who was consulted by famous people, including Mark Twain. His predictions were rumoured to be highly accurate, but history does not relate what Cheiro 'saw' for the Prince of Wales. Perhaps it was the untimely death a year later of his eldest son, Prince Albert Victor, whose engagement to Princess May of Teck had pleased them so much.

THE DOLLAR PRINCESSES

The salary of a British Army officer was not high and with only a modest income from her father's estate, Minnie resorted to arranging more than just entertainments. With her mother in New York and Aunt Fanny Reed at Rue de la Tremoille, Paris, she ran what amounted to an international marriage bureau. It was said that for a substantial fee, they arranged the marriages of two fellow Americans, Anna Gould to Marquis Boni de Castellane in 1895 (who later divorced after Boni had spent $10 million of his wife's family's money) and a Miss Alice Thaw to the Earl of Yarmouth, another marriage that ended in divorce. Elizabeth Eliot in *Heiresses and Coronets* said, 'It is certain that a great deal of money was involved in each case. Minnie is credited with introducing Miss Jeanie Chamberlain in 1889 to husband Sir Herbert Naylor-

Leyland, and rumour had it that many years later she tried to match wealthy American widow, Mrs Nancy Leeds, with Prince Louis Napoleon Bonaparte, the brother of the French pretender.'

Her best-known protégée was Consuelo Vanderbilt, later Duchess of Marlborough, although her marriage too ended in divorce. Minnie first met the 17-year-old

Consuelo Vanderbilt, Duchess of Marlborough (*c*.1900) was Minnie Paget's best-known protégée

THE GILDED AGE IN FICTION

Out of the Gilded Age came great novels, many of them inspired by Minnie Paget and her circle of friends. Consuelo and Marlborough's story and the clash of cultures are fictionalised in Edith Wharton's unfinished book *The Buccaneers*. In it, Nan St George's unhappy marriage to the Duke of Tintagel at Longlands House evokes Consuelo's life at Blenheim, and the characters of Conchita Closson who marries Lord Richard Marabel, a gambler and wastrel, were based on Consuelo Yznaga and the Duke of Manchester. Edith Wharton, née Newbold Jones, part of an old established New York family, had been engaged to Mary's brother Henry Leiden Stevens – but the engagement was broken off, as neither family approved of the other. Mrs Paran Stevens, however, used the press to imply that the marriage had not taken place due to the bride's low intellect. Later, Edith Wharton in her prize-winning book *The*

Edith Wharton at her writing desk

Age of Innocence (1920), used Mrs Paran Stevens as the inspiration for the social climbing 'shoe polish' queen, Mrs Lemuel Struthers, a woman on the fringes of New York society, who eventually attains popularity. Wharton also left a note to herself, 30 years later, to use Stevens for the vulgar greedy mother in *The Buccaneers*.

It is also likely to have been Minnie Paget that author Henry James had in mind in his portrayal of Fanny Assingham in *The Golden Bowl* (1904), who 'pioneered a trail in the London marriage market'.

Consuelo Vanderbilt, god-daughter of her friend Consuelo, Dowager Duchess of Manchester, in 1895. Miss Vanderbilt later described being 'critically appraised by a pair of hard green eyes'. Minnie Paget agreed to bring Consuelo out, but was adamant 'that she must be able to compete, at least as far as clothes are concerned with far better looking girls'. Within a couple of months at a dinner party given by the Pagets, Consuelo was seated next to Charles Spencer-Churchill, 9th Duke of Marlborough. What resulted was a fated, sad marriage, which Consuelo called a heartless business arrangement. The 9th Duke 'Sunny' Marlborough was strapped for cash with a run-down Blenheim Palace to refurbish and he needed the

$2.5 million of stock that marriage to the railroad heiress would bring. Minnie Paget had the connections, for 'Sunny' Churchill's aunt was her friend and fellow American, Jennie Jerome, who had married Lord Randolph Churchill in 1874. Jennie's father was a stock speculator, known as the 'King of Wall Street' and often a partner in the deals of Cornelius Vanderbilt, Consuelo's great-grandfather. Consuelo Vanderbilt's mother, Alba Belmont, was a childhood friend of Consuelo Yznaga, later Duchess of Manchester for whom Minnie Paget had been a bridesmaid in 1874. Minnie had remained friends with Consuelo throughout her unhappy married life as the faithless 9th Duke of Manchester squandered away her money.

HUNTING IN SOMALIA

While his wife was busy matchmaking, Arthur took advantage of the relative peace in Europe and travelled to Africa. Big game hunting in East Africa had become a fashionable pursuit among the arrogant upper classes. In early November 1892, Colonel Arthur Paget and Frederick Glyn, the 4th Baron Wolverton, set off to spend five months in Somaliland 'in search of sport and adventure'. Freddy Wolverton, the rich nephew of George Grenfell Glyn, had been living with Lady Jennie Churchill, a relationship which lasted until late 1894. Jennie had become seriously ill in the autumn of 1892, and perhaps her friend Minnie had encouraged Arthur to remove Wolverton from the scene while her friend recovered.

At the time, Somalia occupied a strategically important position south of the Red Sea and was a British protectorate, garrisoned from Aden and administered from the British India colony in Bombay. Arthur left four days before Freddy, travelling first to Aden, before joining Mr Vine their cartographer who had gone ahead to purchase the 66 camels needed to carry food, water, ammunition and equipment. The expedition of 80 men journeyed inland from Berbera, on the Gulf of Aden, with two Irish terriers, a large herd of sheep, oxen, seven donkeys and eight ponies. Although British influence extended some 100 miles inland, it was a dangerous journey and the pair spent time instructing their guides in the use of muskets. A revolt over the consumption of a camel that was deemed not fat enough to eat threatened the future of the expedition, but once Arthur and Freddy had removed all weapons at gun point, the situation was resolved. With 12 armed men at the front and rear, Arthur on the right of the column, Freddy on the left, and Mr Vine keeping an eye on the animals and men, they rode for six days without meeting anybody. The Somalis welcomed the Englishmen – with their guns and experience – as, to them, lions and panthers were feared man-eaters who also destroyed flocks and herds and, as it transpired, Irish terriers. Wolverton says in *Five Months' Sport in Somali Land* (1894), 'We have now in a small degree begun to restore confidence to a community absolutely terrorised by lions and panthers.' Freddy Wolverton's arrogance is typical of a colonial power's attitude towards the less developed parts of the world it controlled. Most of the animals, including 30 lions, were killed for their skins and their romantic belief that hunting was a sport which they were privileged enough to enjoy; however, some of their prey, such as snakes, Grevy's zebra (a new species) and several newly hatched ostriches, were presented to the British Museum. The Prince of Wales welcomed Arthur's return: 'I think you have done wisely to return to the civilised and attractive life of Cannes, instead of hunting dangerous wild beasts in unknown and inaccessible countries.'

LA BELLE EPOQUE

The Prince of Wales and Arthur Paget, in common with most wealthy and fashionable people, spent much time on the French Riviera. Blessed with fine weather, the cosmopolitan set enjoyed endless dinner parties, carnivals and gambling in Monte Carlo, as well as sports such as golf and yachting. Minnie explains the appeal in an interview by a New York newspaper in London, August 1891:

> Mrs Paget met me with so cordial a handshake accompanied by so bright and genuine a smile I fell at once under the spell of her personality. 'I am very glad to see you,' she said, 'though you find me in dire confusion. I am only just returned to town, and should be on my way to the South of France; we never stay as late in England as this. I cannot endure the dirt and

Edward, Prince of Wales, on his yacht *Britannia* in 1894

dust and the miseries and horrors of the English climate in winter. It is far too depressing for so impressionable a temperament as mine or for one who loves sunshine and brightness and flowers and clean windows and dainty surroundings as much as I do.' Mrs Paget says that golf and fishing are her chief amusements, but she also likes everything else in the way of outdoor sports and in her earlier days was a horsewoman of more than usually daring characteristics.

The Prince of Wales and Paget would often be seen in March and April walking along the Croisette in Cannes. While the Pagets stayed at Arthur's mother's villa, Chateau Garibondy, the Prince lived on his yacht, entrusting its arrival into harbour to Arthur, then moving it to wherever he needed to be with greater ease. Arthur Paget was an experienced yachtsman and had tested the Prince's new cutter *Britannia* in heavy seas just after her launch in 1893. The Prince wanted races and regattas organised at Marseilles, Toulon,

Easton Lodge, home of Daisy, Countess of Warwick, and venue for many shooting parties

Cannes and Monaco so that he could show off his new super yacht against other vessels of a similar class. There were not many of these. His main rival was *Vigilant* owned by the American Mr George Jay Gould whose sister, Anna, had been one of Minnie's protégées. Arthur persuaded Gould to race *Vigilant* against *Britannia*, which they did 13 times in British waters in July 1894, *Britannia* winning 10 races. However, in the course of a match for Lord Wolverton's Cup, *Vigilant* signalled that it had lost its centre-board, and the race was abandoned. Later, when it was revealed that the keel had not been lost but jammed in the trunk, some, including the Prince of Wales, considered her withdrawal an excuse to avoid being beaten again. Paget, who had been on board the American yacht, did not agree, but when he said so he merely incurred more royal anger.

Arthur was often invited to shooting parties at Easton Lodge, the childhood home of Daisy, Countess of Warwick. Daisy had had a torrid affair with Lord Charles Bereford, brother of Marcus Beresford, Arthur's best man. When she discovered that Lady Beresford was pregnant by her husband, Daisy wrote a damning letter to her lover which was intercepted by his wife. Ever resourceful, Daisy found a shoulder to cry on in the form of the Prince of Wales, and she became his unofficial and indiscreet mistress until 1898.

American George Jay Gould (1864–1923), financier and owner of the yacht *Vigilant*, which raced the Prince of Wales's yacht *Britannia* 13 times in British waters in July 1894

On 2 February 1895, the Earl and Countess of Warwick invited 400 guests to a *bal poudré*, a lavish costume ball, a recreation of a ball at the French court in the period of Louis XIV and XV, when powdered wigs were high fashion, and the guests danced in the Cedar drawing room to Stanislas Wurm's famous White Viennese Band. Supper, announced by three trumpeters in the blue and gold of Louis XV's infantry regiment, was served to all 400 guests simultaneously in the Great Hall. Amid the brilliant assembly, its hostess, the mistress of Edward VII, was dressed as Marie Antoinette, and 'reigned the unquestioned queen' in a headdress of pink and white ostrich plumes, with a blue aigrette fastened with diamonds. Minnie as the Duchesse d'Orleans, arrived on the arm of her husband who, reluctant to sacrifice his moustache, was allowed to appear dressed as a musketeer. Other guests included the Austro-Hungarian Ambassador,

Prince Francis of Teck. The ball started very late, around 10.45pm with guests still arriving at midnight, and the revellers stayed up late into the next morning.

MRS PARAN STEVENS'S DEATH

In April 1895 Mary Paget's mother died at her home on Fifth Avenue. Minnie and her maid travelled on the first available steamship, the *Luciana*, while Arthur and their daughter Leila followed in August. Mrs Paran Stevens, with the help of a press agent in her employ, had risen to great social heights on the strength of her daughter's marriage and had finally been accepted by most of New York society. The teacher from Massachusetts had become a philanthropist, art collector and patron – even President Arthur had dined with her in 1882. As the *New York Times* wrote:

> No woman in New York was better known. She was an impulsive woman, never hesitating to give full expression of her opinions about everybody and everything uppermost in her mind for the moment, but her impulsiveness took a charitable turn to an extent that would scarcely be believed by people who did not know her. Her generosity to the poor was not ostentatious, but it was liberal. Her death will be mourned in many houses very remote from the social set with which she had been prominently identified for many years. Probably no woman in New York society has been more talked about than Mrs Stevens, and it was a favourite jest of hers that the public picked out nothing but her faults. She was an ambitious woman, eager for social prestige, and she stamped out everything that stood in the pathway of her ambition.

She was said to have revolutionised staid New York by innovating Sunday evening soirées. On one occasion she held a lunch for her society friends at the Casino at Narragansett Pier, where the maître d'hotel Julius Keller created a dish for the occasion featuring

Ludgate Circus, 1897, decorated for Queen Victoria's Diamond Jubilee

clams on the half-shell baked with bacon called Clams Casino, still available to this day. In her will she left $1.5 million in real estate and personal property to her daughter, $5,000 to her sister Fanny for life, and the same to Arthur Paget.

On 12 November 1895, Arthur's younger brother Almeric Hugh Paget, who had emigrated to America in 1881, married heiress Pauline Payne Whitney, daughter of William Collins Whitney, ex-US Secretary of the Navy and a major investor in thoroughbred horse-racing. President Grover Cleveland attended the wedding. Huge crowds gathered outside the church to see all of New York's finest attend the ceremony. Almeric was a great favourite of Mrs Paran Stevens, who – had she lived long enough – would have been delighted by the union. He was the third member of the Paget family to marry an American girl.

COURT AND SOCIAL ENGAGEMENTS

The year 1897 saw Queen Victoria's Diamond Jubilee, and London was full of important visitors as Britain showed off the might of its new imperialism. Gladstone, with his anti-imperialist views, had resigned, and the situation in Ireland was calmer. On 22 June, Queen Victoria, accompanied by 50,000 troops, paraded through the streets of London to a thanksgiving service outside St Paul's Cathedral, cheered on by thousands. Society hostesses were celebrating by giving even bigger and better parties than usual.

The Devonshire House Ball of 2 July 1897 was hosted by the 8th Duke of Devonshire and his wife, Lady Sophia Murphy; it was described by their grand-daughter as 'the most magnificent entertainment of

Guests of the Devonshire House Ball
gasped 'with wonder and astonishment'
as Mary Paget entered the ballroom
dressed as Cleopatra

the century'. Devonshire House, one of the grandest houses in London, stood on Piccadilly with views over Green Park. The Duchess gave a ball every season, and the Jubilee was the perfect occasion to host an evening that would surpass all others. The 700 guests were invited to come in fancy dress of an allegorical nature or pre-1815 historical costume, and various themes were suggested.

The Duchess of Devonshire led the Oriental procession which included Lady de Grey, Lady Dudley, Lady Randolph Churchill, Miss Muriel Wilson, Margo Asquith and Minnie Paget, dressed as Cleopatra. As they passed in front of the royal family, they salaamed in Eastern fashion which caused great amusement among the crowd.

Arthur Paget came as Edward, the Black Prince; tall and dark, he suited his black armour of chain mail down to his fingers. But the guests gasped 'with wonder and astonishment' when his wife entered the ballroom followed by a 'negro servant' holding a fan of ostrich feathers over her head. The *Daily Mail* oozed praise: '… small, lithe and seductive, a lovely serpent of the old Nile. Mrs Arthur Paget seemed born to play the part of Cleopatra, for she is dark haired, with a low white brow, and scarlet lips, and her beautiful big eyes are like star sapphires so mysteriously blue are they.' The symbolism was not lost on another Cleopatra, her future neighbour at Coombe, Lady de Grey, nor Daisy, Princess of Pless, as the Queen of Sheba, whose own beautiful costumes were no match for the spectacular J. P. Worth creation worn by Mrs Paget. This expensive costume was based on one designed for her in 1891, which was im-mortalised in watercolour on ivory by the French artist Fernand Paillet. The train of black crepe de Chine was embroidered with gold scarabs, while the bodice, encrusted with gold and diamonds, was held upon the shoulders with straps of large emeralds and diamonds. A black and gold striped headdress made

of cloth of gold was 'one mass of real red rubies, emeralds, turquoises, diamonds and pearls', with side pieces studded with diamonds; it was crowned by an ibis with outstretched wings of diamonds and sapphires, and the jewelled crown of Egypt. There was a small diamond asp nestling on her right shoulder that pointed to Cleopatra's fate.

Social occasions that were organised to raise money for charitable causes were just as wonderful and no less imaginative. 'All the world seemed to be driving to the Royal Albert Hall yesterday afternoon in aid of the special appeal fund of the Charing Cross Hospital,' exclaimed the *Daily News*, Thursday, 22 June 1899:

> The stalls within were themed by country and manned by ladies and gentlemen of royalty and the aristocracy. The Duchess of Devonshire ran the Danish Stall, there was an Egyptian stall selling relics of the Omdurman and Bagdad Prayer rugs, an Indian stall run by the Marchioness of Lansdowne aided by Lily, Duchess of Marlborough, an Argentine stall doing trade in leathers and furs … In the centre, a great pagoda, where Mrs Arthur Paget sold flowers, was photographed all afternoon with its group of beautiful women, the Duchess of Marlborough, Lady Westmoreland, Mrs W. Grenfell, Mrs W. James, Mrs King and Lady Juliette Lowther, all wearing cream-coloured gowns and large black hats. In the interests of this stall Lady de Grey and Prince Francis of Teck [later Mrs Paget's neighbours at Coombe] went about the room selling flowers, whilst the Duke of Manchester and other gentlemen dressed as waiters in white jackets served drinks from the American bar. Herbert Beerbohm Tree, actor and London theatre manager, directed the afternoon theatrical entertainment.

A good, if biased, insight into Mrs Paget's reputation as a hostess appeared in an article on American women in *Ainslee's Magazine*, in 1905, which praised Minnie Paget as a social innovator in the American tradition:

She has all the truly American tastes for featuring their entertainments most delightfully. To continue in the commonplace round of quite conventional functions as approved by society is not to be borne by this energetic and novelty loving lady, and a dinner or supper party and dance at Mrs Paget's is sure to develop some unexpected and charming phase … It is to Mrs Paget, for example that we are indebted for the introduction of that purely American festivity, 'The Ladies Luncheon', which is now quite acclimatized here; we have accepted it as we have also accepted 'The Ladies Dinner Party' which was wholly unknown previous to the American invasion … It is safe to say that this tall, vivacious, energetic lady … carries almost more social power in her small right hand than any other untitled woman in London.

Another American newspaper claimed that she had spent $10 million 'in the pursuit of social distinction', yet without her calm, strong and attractive personality, Minnie's money alone would have got her nowhere.

Minnie Paget was not merely an excellent hostess but she was also an arbiter of the avant-garde. She befriended Eulabee Dix, an American artist who specialised in painting oval miniatures in watercolour on ivory. Under the patronage of Mary Paget, she gained prominence by painting portraits of celebrities, including Daisy, Countess of Warwick. Minnie Paget was already a patron of miniaturist Amalia Küssner Coudert, having met her in the late 1890s and sponsored her travels in Europe, where she became known for her portraits of royalty. Portrait miniatures were experiencing a renewed popularity around this time, despite the invention of photography, and it is not surprising that Minnie Paget, with her interest in the decorative arts, wanted to be at the forefront of this revival. She must have felt particularly satisfied when the fortunate Dix returned to New York and in 1909 painted the last portrait of Mark Twain before his death.

The *New York Times* wrote of Minnie Paget: 'She is as enthusiastic about music as she is about books: "I love it, but alas I am not able to devote myself to it exclusively. Of course music has been as the breath of my nostrils to me, brought up as I was in the constant society of my Aunt whose exquisite voice attracted always the best of musical people, perhaps I have inherited the love of it from her."' A few years later Miss Fanny Reed, who was a famous amateur singer, brought out a book of reminiscences based on French celebrities she had known while in Paris, from the composer Liszt to Paul Deschanel, and dedicated the book to her niece. Minnie Paget also became an early patron of Fabergé and Boucheron.

THE SECOND BOER WAR

In October 1899, while the *New York Times* reported that 'Mrs Paget is still busy paying a round of country house visits' and *The Sketch* remarked that 'notwithstanding his brilliant social gifts and military skill, Colonel Arthur Paget has been quite content for

Lieutenant Albert E. Paget, ADC (first left), and his father Major General Arthur Paget (second left) and staff of the Scots Guards in South Africa, pictured in *The Navy and Army Illustrated*, October 1900

Left: A meeting of the committee of the *Maine* Hospital Ship Fund. Lady Randolph Churchill standing centre, Mary Paget to her left. Below: The American Ladies' Hospital Ship *Maine* was chartered and fitted out entirely by the American Ladies' Society

some time to be known as "le marie de Madame"', another war reignited Paget's military career. On the point of retirement he received the command of the 1st Battalion Scots Guards and was sent to South Africa on the outbreak of hostilities against the Boer republics. In October 1899, the Prince of Wales inspected the 1st Battalion of the Scots Guards, under the command of his friend Colonel Paget, before their departure south.

As part of the 20th Brigade, Paget and his men advanced through the Cape Colony. From Modder River, where Lord Methuen and the Guards Brigade under Major-General Sir Henry Edward Colville were attempting to relieve the besieged town of Kimberley in 1899, and from Klip Kraal Drift in 1900, Arthur typed long letters, some eight pages long, to his wife and the Prince of Wales. He kept the Prince informed and continued his criticisms, mainly of the intelligence department whose information was invariably wrong – and Bertie was grateful.

With the outbreak of the Second Boer War, society hostesses turned to fundraising for the injured and their families. It must have been an anxious time for Minnie with both her husband and eldest son away fighting in

South Africa. On 25 October 1899 she joined other American society hostesses in London for what was to be an extraordinary wartime philanthropic project, the American Ladies' Hospital Ship, *Maine*. Chaired by her friend Lady Jennie Churchill, now a widow, and with assistance from the Duchess of Marlborough and other American ladies, the Society raised enough money in two months to convert the *Maine*, a former Atlantic cattle trader, into a hospital ship. The vessel together with its crew had been given to the British Government by Bernard N. Baker, a shipping magnate from Baltimore. The ladies found sponsors, put on concerts and other entertainments, including a tea chantant held in November at Claridges Hotel. The entire floor of the

MRS. CYRIL MARTINEAU (NÉE SAVILE-CLARKE) AS "PROSPERITY."

MRS. CRUTCHLEY AS "GLORY."

LADY FEODOROVNA STURT AS "INDIA."

LADY CLAUD HAMILTON AS "BRITISH COLUMBIA."

hotel was converted into a perfect garden of chrysanthemums and roses, illuminated by multicoloured lights. At the entrance, welcoming the guests, were the Life Guards, in their white and scarlet uniforms, and the drummers and pipers of Arthur Paget's Scots Guard, in tartan. The exquisitely decorated rooms buzzed with the fashionable elite, and the orchestra played while the guests bid at an auction, enjoyed tea or visited the American Bar. The crimson crosses worn on the arms of these fashionable ladies were a poignant reminder, amid the splendour of the occasion, of the grim reality of war. Lady Randolph Churchill only looked in for a few moments; she was deeply distressed because her son, Winston Churchill, was believed at the time to be a prisoner of the Boers. The newspapers reported that the 'absence of the leading spirit in the movement, due to the uncertainty as to the death or capture of her son, gave a tragic tone to the gathering'. However, £1,700 was raised for the *Maine* fund. In New York, Lillie Langtry raised $5,000 by holding a society tea. In total £41,597 was raised and at the end of November, the ship was contracted to the Royal Navy for fitting out. Ten thousand visitors came to see the ship in West India Dock, before it sailed for South Africa in 1899 with Lady Churchill on board. Amid some political friction, *Maine* served the injured soldiers of the Second Boer War until January 1901, when she returned to London and was given to the British Government.

While in South Africa, Arthur contracted typhoid, and the *New York Times* reported on 9 January 1900:

> Mrs Arthur Paget is very much alarmed concerning the condition of her husband who is very ill with typhoid fever in South Africa. At last accounts he was at Modder River. During her anxiety concerning her husband she is occupying her mind with the final touches of the tableaux and theatricals in aid of the Guards Fund. The Duchess of Marlborough, who is so upset by the resolution of the Duke to go to War, will not recite. Lady Feo Sturt and Mrs Hwfa Williams are to lend their aid, and as royalty with a very big 'R' will be present, there is no doubt whatever of a very great success.

So Mary Paget set to work for the widows and orphans of HM Household troops. She held a musical entertainment in the form of a series of tableaux which included a masque of Peace and War at Her Majesty's Theatre, Haymarket, London, on 13 February 1900. In appealing to the patriotic ideals of the late Victorian era, this spectacle was by far the most successful of all Lady Paget's charitable endeavours. These ideals were admirably expressed in a John Davidson poem recited at the Masque by Miss Muriel Wilson:

A *tableau vivant* from the entertainment at Her Majesty's Theatre entitled 'Great Britain and Her Colonies and Dependencies'. Ladies representing Great Britain and Ireland sit in solitary splendour as others, representing countries within the Empire, group themselves around them. *The Graphic*, 17 February 1900

They breathed no slur on her Imperial fame,
No crafty question of her right:
From East and West across the seas they came,
For England's sake rejoicing in the fight.
England at war? To arms! In England's name.
One destiny is ours; one heart; one might.

Inspired by the Arts and Crafts movement and the poems of Alfred Lord Tennyson, the drama was written by Louis N. Parker, with music by Hamish MacCunn, costumes designed by Percy Anderson and directed by Herbert Beerbohm Tree. Many titled women portrayed such roles as Pity and Mercy, acted *tableaux vivants*, and took part in the concluding procession 'The Patriotic Picture of Great Britain and her Colonies' to music by Sir Arthur Sullivan. The performance raised over £7,000 for the widows and orphans of the Household troops and also marked the first appearance of the great tenor Gervase Elwes.

Minnie Paget decided not to delay the 'coming out' of her daughter Leila, although her father and brother were away fighting in South Africa. Leila had already been seen with her mother, taking part in theatricals and selling at bazaars, and she made her formal society debut in the spring of 1900, presented at court to the Princess of Wales, alongside Miss Jeanne Langtry, daughter of Mrs Lillie Langtry, and the daughter of Mr and Mrs Hwfa Williams of Coombe, Kingston. Leila wore white point d'esprit with sprays of white lilac decorating her train of white satin. Her mother, still beautiful in her late forties, wore a dress of the palest green satin, veiled with fine creamy lace, and jewellery of diamonds and emeralds.

In South Africa, Arthur found himself in disagreement with the general in command of Free State operations and relinquished his command. Despite being urged by the Prince of Wales to remain, Arthur refused and returned to England. He disembarked in April 1901 to an England in mourning for the Queen. Edward was finally crowned King on 9 August 1902 and while Arthur did not hold a command that day, his wife was invited to the coronation. She was seated in what was dubiously termed the 'King's Loose Box' – a witticism that Edward, the only king to have won the Derby, would have savoured – together with some of Edward's close friends and paramours, including Countess Daisy

Far left: Major-General Arthur Paget, Commander the 20th Brigade of Methuen's Division, Second Boer War. Near left: His son, Mr Albert E. Paget, ADC, just gazetted into the 11th Hussars. From *The Onlooker*, 20 April 1901

list when he was 17 years old. He fought alongside his father in South Africa and returned safely to the family, subsequently awarded a medal with four clasps.

LADY PAGET'S ACCIDENT

When it seemed that everything in the Pagets' life was peaceful again, disaster struck. On 2 August 1904, Mrs Paget, returning home to Belgrave Square with her twin sons after a dinner party, was seriously injured. She stepped into the empty liftshaft and fell to the basement below, fracturing her thigh and kneecap, and once rescued by servants, was rushed to hospital. She received many letters from around the world expressing concern at such a terrible accident. A close friend, Frederick Townsend Martin, recalls Minnie Paget at this time in his book, *Things I Remember* (1913): 'I remember once going to see her after her accident, and found her reading a number of letters of condolence which had just arrived. Some of them were from crowned heads, but Lady Paget seemed especially charmed with the contents of a dirty little note she had just opened. "Oh, Fred," she said, "this letter has given me such pleasure, it's from my washerwoman, and I don't think anything has delighted me more than that she should have thought of me."'

For Christmas, another friend, the Irish novelist George Moore, sent Minnie a copy of his 1881 *Pagan Poems*, presumably to help while away the time while she recovered. Moore had been introduced to Minnie by American Maude Burke, later Lady Cunard, for whom he had great affection. In one of his letters to Maude, he writes, 'Minnie Paget I saw once again, she sent for me; I am obliged to you for the introduction, for I think I shall always see her with pleasure; she is of our kin and one must keep to one's kin.'

Recovery was not easy, and eventually the King persuaded her to see his own surgeon, Sir Frederick

Warwick, Mrs Alice Keppel, Sarah Bernhardt, Mrs Ronnie Greville, Lady Sarah Wilson, Feo Sturt and Olga de Meyer, possibly his illegitimate daughter, all of whom were not otherwise entitled by status to attend the Abbey. When the Boers finally surrendered in 1902, Arthur's rank of Major-General was made permanent and he was appointed Commanding Officer of the First Division of the First Army Corps at Aldershot, a position he held until 1906. It is safe to presume that Arthur's career from here on was highly influenced by the newly crowned monarch, perhaps as a token of thanks for the war correspondence he had received, and the news of Arthur's next posting was sent direct from the King's yacht *Victoria and Albert*, while on a cruise to Balmoral. The King, however, also offered a few words of advice: 'You have, my dear Arthur, such a good reputation as a fighting soldier that I hope you will become a serious one also. Your future advancement will all depend on your giving your whole heart and mind to your new command.' And again: 'You will I trust prove to them that you are worthy of the important command entrusted to you, and will stick to your work without letting the racecourse and the Turf Club take first place!'

The Prince of Wales had also taken a great interest in his godson, Albert Edward Paget, and personally asked General Sir Dighton Probyn, Comptroller of the Royal Household, to put him down on his own 10th Hussars

122   THE WARREN HOUSE TALES

The King and Queen of Denmark arrived on the royal yacht *Victoria and Albert* during their state visit in 1907. Lieutenant General Sir Arthur Paget was in attendance during their stay. Here, the royal yacht is shown on her last journey in 1939

Treves. Over the next two years she had 15 operations without much success. She finally consulted Professor Albert Hoffa, the Director of the Orthopaedic Polyclinic in Berlin. Queen Alexandra wrote, 'I am sorry I shall not be able to see you before you leave, but trust that on your return I shall find you walking about as well as ever.' Although he did not completely cure her, Hoffa did succeed in making Minnie's condition better. Once again Edward took interest and offered his advice, visiting her regularly once she had returned home. She was to employ nurses to help her for the rest of her life.

In May 1905, the US Supreme Court finally settled the arguments over Paran Stevens's estate. Mrs Paget and her maid travelled on the *Luciana* to hear the verdict. The arguments had lasted 33 years. Hundreds of thousands of dollars had been spent on lawyers' fees, and some of the lawyers who had originally appeared in the case were dead by its end. The two beneficiaries of the estate that was valued at $10 million dollars in 1872 were to be his two daughters, Ellen and Mary.

A COUNTRY RETREAT AT COOMBE

The next year, at the age of 54, General Arthur Paget, vacated his appointment at Aldershot, was promoted to Lieutenant General and invested as a Knight

Commander, Royal Victorian Order (KCVO). Although Arthur was not to have an army posting for the next 18 months, he was not idle. On 8 June 1907, when King Edward VII sent the royal yacht *Victoria and Albert* to welcome the King and Queen of Denmark from Flushing and bring them to Portsmouth for the beginning of their state visit, Lieutenant General Sir Arthur Paget was in attendance at Buckingham Palace and Windsor Castle.

Importantly for Minnie, her title had finally arrived. In January 1907 the *New York Times* reported: 'King Edward VII dined with Lady Paget at 35 Belgrave Square. Lady Paget wore white with lace and a chain of diamonds around her neck and a low all-round tiara in her hair. She went into dinner with the King, still lame and walking with a stick.' Other guests included Mrs George Keppel and the Portuguese Marquis de Soveral. In New York, Minnie's association with the Prince of Wales implied great influence and now that she had her own title, she had gained even more social importance.

In both Victorian and Edwardian times, one of the easiest ways of displaying wealth and social status was to buy a country estate, a few surrounding acres and invite lots of important people to your house parties. This is just what Lady Mary Paget did. The settlement of her father's estate made it possible for her to purchase Warren House, as well as 14 acres, three roods and five perches, a coach house and stables, from Mr George Cawston on 4 October 1907 for £20,000.

In honour of King Edward VII's visit in 1908, a new
ballroom was built at Warren House. The white
ornamental cornicing and mouldings, fashioned in
the style of the Hall of Mirrors in the palace of
Versailles, remain today

It was a perfect country retreat for a family who had become celebrities of their day. Wishing to avoid the crowds and photographers that had become a great nuisance at fashionable London weddings, the Pagets remained in rural Coombe for their daughter's wedding on 28 October 1907. Louise Margaret Leila Wymess Paget married a distant cousin, Ralph Paget, the British Minister and Consul-General in Bangkok, at the church at Kingston Vale. The *New York Times* reported: 'Most guests motored down from London so there were about a score of automobiles outside the church. The bride wore a soft clinging gown of creamy crepe de chine and a beautiful lace veil valued at $2,500, lent for the occasion by her grandmother, Lady Alfred Paget, who was unable to be present. Lady Paget arrived at the church in a motor and wore a smart gown of blue velvet and some nice furs ... There were only a few guests, outside of the immediate family, invited to lunch at Warren House afterwards.'

In celebration of a happy year, Lady Paget gave one of the largest of the London New Year dinners. Guests of significant standing were invited, including the Russian Ambassador, the Spanish Ambassadress Madame de Villa-Urrutia, Count Albert von Mensdorff, Countess Benckendorff, the Duchess of Marlborough and Lord Colebrook. But the event that finally placed Lady Paget at the top of the social ladder, alongside the landed aristocracy of England, took place on 6 July 1908 when she entertained the King, the Queen and Princess Victoria at Warren House.

ROYAL GUESTS

The Pagets had invited about '100 guests to meet their majesties, all well-known society people, among them the American Ambassador and Mrs Whitelaw Reid, and Mrs J. J. Astor, and after dinner they planned a theatrical performance for which the famous soprano Miss Marie Tempest had been engaged'. There was much work to be done in the house before the house party. An extension was reportedly built on to the house to provide accommodation for all the guests and several marquees were erected in the gardens. A new white marble bathroom had been installed for the King, and a new ballroom built with white ornamental cornicing and mouldings fashioned in the style of the Hall of Mirrors in the Palace of Versailles.

Lady Paget would have allocated rooms for her guests and their servants, and decided what entertainments to provide, but for the day-to-day running of the household, she relied on her staff: the butler, housekeeper and housemaids. The Pagets employed servants for each of their homes. At Warren House, the butler was John Richard Holt from Oxfordshire, and three housemaids and a kitchen maid worked alongside the cook, Mabel Stutt from London. At important house parties, Lady Paget may have brought her French chef, Monsieur Saint Mass, from Belgrave Square to give a certain prestige to her dinner parties. Carriages or motor cars entered Warren House through huge ornamental gates – said to rival those at Sandringham – just a short distance from the junction of Warren Road and Kingston Hill, and approached the house from the northwest, passing the coach house and stables on the left. The frontage of the property at the time was almost a quarter of a mile long. The groom Frank Thurlby, originally from Derbyshire, and his wife Annie and son Hubert lived above the stables, with the Paget's chauffeur, Vernon Young, when he was in Coombe. There was also spare accommodation for any visiting servants, such as Sir Arthur's valet, who travelled with him.

The occasion was reported in *The Times*:

The King and Queen paid a visit to Lieutenant-General Sir Arthur and Lady Paget at Warren House, Coombe-wood, Kingston-Hill yesterday. Their Majesties drove down in a motor car from Buckingham Palace in late afternoon and honoured Sir Arthur and Lady Paget by remaining to dinner.

The dinner party included the Russian Ambassador and Countess Benckendorff, the Austro-Hungarian Ambassador, the Portuguese Minister, the Prime Minister and Mrs Asquith, Mr Balfour, the Earl and Countess of Dudley, Earl and Countess de Grey, the Earl and Countess of Crewe and the Earl and Countess of Illchester. Their Majesties, later in the evening returned to London in their motor car.

Perhaps delighted by the hospitality he had received at Warren House, the King had put in another kind word for his friend, for in 1908 Lieutenant General Sir Arthur Paget replaced Lord Methuen as General Officer Commander-in-Chief of Eastern Command. Conveniently based at Horse Guards in London, Arthur held the post until the end of 1911.

While her husband was busy with his work, Lady Paget crossed the Atlantic on the *Adriatic* accompanied by her son and his cousin, Lord Anglesey; she was going to stay in New York, while the men went west on a shooting holiday. The *New York Times* noted that a series of long bridge games took place on almost every day of the voyage and 'among the players said to be most deeply interested' were Lady Paget, Captain Paget and the Marquess of Anglesey.

The frequent absences of the residents of Warren House gave ample opportunities for burglars. In 1909, two Germans, William Uhl, 36, a hosier, and Richard Gilben, 27, a baker, were charged with committing a burglary at Warren House on the night of 30 March and stealing articles, including a quantity of valuable china vases, to the value of £300. In another case Harry Johnson, alias Coles, was also charged with a burglary, this time at the house in Belgrave Square. The thief had been wearing a tie of King Edward VII's racing colours, one of four made on his majesty's order to celebrate a victory of his racehorse Persimmon. Another royal gift stolen from Sir Arthur's bedroom was a large bedside watch.

However, this does not seem to have deterred King Edward VII who, on 22 May 1909, spent the weekend with General Sir Arthur and Lady Paget at Warren House. 'The King,' revealed *The Times*, 'has just taken delivery of his new 65hp four cylinder Mercedes car, supplied by Ducros Mercedes of Long Acre. It is fitted with a limousine landaulette body, seating four, and is of ample dimensions. Folding chairs are fitted to sliding rods on either side behind the doors. The interior is fitted with electric lights, communicators, pockets for papers &c. A Gabriel horn with a deep musical note has been fitted.' A wonderful photograph still survives of that weekend. Lady Paget's guests are posed in front of the Italian loggia, the waters of the fountain just missing the skirt of Lady Johnstone whose attention is neither on the hem of her dress, nor the photographer, but instead given to Mrs Spotswood, with whom she seems to be deep in conversation. The loggia had been newly constructed by James Pulham and Son, who also renovated the gardens at Warren House. The Pagets were particularly fond of their gardens, and there were at least three gardeners employed to maintain the beautiful landscaping, as well as the kitchen garden and greenhouses behind the stables which were an important source of fresh produce. A local man, Sidney Fuller, from Morden, was the chief gardener, assisted by James H. Latimer from Dublin and Edward March from the Weald in Essex, all living in the grounds in the Lodge or small cottage.

On one of his visits King Edward VII planted a cedar tree in the grounds and gave his friends the ornamental lead cranes, said to be part of a set of 12 that he distributed as presents, to adorn the lakes. It was probably around this time that the verse from Dorothy Frances Gurney (1858–1932) was inscribed in stone on the terrace garden wall:

> The kiss of the sun for pardon
> The song of the birds for mirth
> One is nearer God's heart in a garden
> Than anywhere else on earth.

A social gathering at Warren House, 1909

1. Mrs George Keppel: society hostess and long-time mistress of Edward VII

2. Rt Hon John Elliot Burns: MP Battersea, socialist trade unionist turned Liberal, President of the Local Government Board

3. Lady Winifred Hardinge of Penshurst: former Lady-in-waiting to Queen Alexandra, future Vice-Reine of India

4. Luis Pinto de Soveral, Marques de Soveral: Portuguese diplomat and close friend of Edward VII, nicknamed 'the blue monkey'

5. Mrs J. Allen Townsend: American friend of Minnie and daughter of New York lawyer, Dexter Hawkins

6. Mr Ralph Paget: British diplomat, husband of General Paget's daughter, Leila

7. Rt Hon Henry Chaplin: Conservative MP Wimbledon, racehorse owner, and jilted fiancé of Lady Florence Paget, a distant relative of General Paget

8. Captain Albert Edward Paget: eldest son of General Paget, Officer in 11th Hussars

9. Colonel George Lindsay Holford: close friend and former equerry to King Edward VII, owner of Dorchester House, London, and Westonbirt House and Arboretum

10. General Sir Arthur Paget: close friend of King Edward

11. Sir Charles Hardinge of Penshurst: diplomat, permanent Under Secretary at the Foreign Office, later Viceroy of India wounded by a bomb in Delhi

12. Rt Hon Richard Burdon Haldane: Liberal MP Haddingtonshire, Secretary of State for War, future Lord Chancellor

13. Lady Mary Paget: American wife of General Sir Arthur Paget and owner of Warren House

14. HRH King Edward VII: King of the United Kingdom and the British Dominions, and Emperor of India 1901–10

15. Mrs Kitty Spotswood: American, future Baroness Eugene de Rothschild. She gave the King a little green frog for luck in the Derby. When his horse 'Minoru' won, the King sent her a frog encrusted in diamonds in return

16. Lady Alan Vanden-Bempe-Johnstone: American wife of a British diplomat, who made headlines in New York for 'shocking behaviour' when she upset the City fathers by smoking in the restaurant on a cruise liner!

THE GARDENS AT WARREN HOUSE

One of the ornamental pagodas in the Japanese water gardens

Hammersley positioned Warren House on the highest point of his land, where the far-reaching views over the trees to Wimbledon Common were at their best. However, it was his later purchase of an extra strip of land that cut across his own, formerly part of a neighbouring horticultural nursery, which was to be Warren House's crowning glory for over 100 years.

This land, some six acres in total, was laid out as a Japanese water garden and had been part of James Veitch Junior's world-renowned Coombe Wood Nursery. Originally from Exeter and a well-established family horticulturist firm, Veitch had achieved remarkable success at the Great Exhibition of 1851, where he had shown many new varieties of plants collected from South America, India and the Far East. Victorian Londoners, with their romantic ideas of adventure, were eager to buy exotic plants and so Veitch opened a nursery in an old market garden in the King's Road, Chelsea, in 1853. Business boomed, but growing space was limited so three years later, Veitch purchased the lease to 35 acres on the Duke of Cambridge's estate at Coombe Wood. Here the clean air, south-facing slopes, light sandy soil and moist subsoil, together with the option to plant on undulating ground in both shade and sun, all contributed to the success of the new nursery.

Veitch's collectors travelled the world, bringing back plants hardy enough to thrive in England's temperate maritime climate. Propagation of the collections of seeds, cuttings or bulbs was done in the greenhouses at Coombe Wood, which soon became famous for acers and rhododendrons and many other foreign species of herbaceous and woody plants. Plant collecting was financially risky as well as dangerous. Collectors, such as William and Thomas Lobb, and Ernest Wilson, spent months, sometimes years, travelling beyond the realms of the Empire in search of new specimens. Veitch's own son John Gould went as far as Australia, Polynesia, Samoa, Tonga and Fiji to bring back plants to satisfy the Victorian desire for all things exotic. Not all plants survived the journey, or took to British soil, but many flowered for the first time at Coombe.

In 1860, John Gould Veitch was sent to Japan as Botanist to Her Britannic Majesty's Legation at Jeddo. He was among the first group of foreigners permitted to visit Mount Fuji. His notes describe conifers, aucuba, maples, azaleas and magnolias set among 'waterfalls all blended together with exquisite taste and without formal appearance'.

Above: 'Maples, azaleas and magnolias set among waterfalls all blended together with exquisite taste and without formal appearance.' John Gould Veitch, from his notes from Japan, 1860

Right: Pulhamite stone was used to re-landscape parts of the garden by the Pagets

He explained how every house had a small garden with dwarfed (Bonsai) trees, rocks, a mini lake and lawn. His collection of these native Japanese plants, including Japanese ivy, primula and the Golden-rayed lily was the most spectacular of any collector. He returned to Coombe in 1867, and that same year a correspondent from *The Gardeners' Chronicle* described the abundance of Patagonian holly, Japanese holly, junipers, firs, cypresses, cedars and Japanese red pine that were all available to buy in the nursery.

John Gould died suddenly at the age of 31 in 1870, just a year after his father, and the London nurseries were taken over by his younger brother, Harry. Around the same time other members of the Veitch family, Robert T. Veitch and his son Peter, were working with a German rockwork expert, F. W. Meyer, creating rock and water gardens using natural stone. By the late 1870s, as the trend for gardens which imitated natural scenery grew, Veitch and Meyer became leaders in their field. Peter joined his cousin Harry Veitch at

Above: 'A grass vista with herbaceous borders on either side leads to the lake which is one of the finest examples of water gardening I have seen for a long time.' *The Gardeners' Chronicle*, 23 August 1924

Right: The Japanese tea room was rebuilt in the 1980s

Coombe in 1870, so it is likely that he and Meyer created the Japanese water garden at Coombe Wood Nursery, using the naturally occurring springs to create a perfect backdrop for showcasing the huge number of Japanese plants that the nursery had cultivated.

For Hugh Hammersley, ownership of the Japanese water garden demonstrated that he was a landowner not only of wealth and status, but also of good taste and sophistication. The abundance of rare and beautiful plants set amid tranquil streams, waterfalls, ornamental lakes and rockwork gave a real sense of nature and the garden being at one with each other. After Hugh Hammersley's death, there were not many references to the content or structure of the garden at Warren House. However, one gardener and journalist, William Robinson, who worked not only for Veitch but also with Hugh Hammersley's niece Gertrude Jekyll, included a sketch of Warren House and its garden in a review on British gardens in 1892. Known for promoting the idea of the wild garden, and natural-looking planting schemes, he wrote, 'A beautiful house in a fair landscape is the most delightful scene of the cultivated earth.'

After a number of years of neglect the gardens, like the house, were revitalised under the ownership of Sir Arthur and Lady Paget. They commissioned James Pulham and Son to design ornamental seating and the central fountain and the wall fountain in the sunken garden, as well as the balustrades around the formal gardens, which were planted in much the same way as they are today. Another company, Messenger & Co., built a winter garden on to the end of the house adjoining the Billiard Room. The height of fashion, it was covered by a glass roof and heated by a large boiler, whose pipes extended under the Billiard Room floor, heating that area too. Within the winter garden, Pulham's installed a fernery and a stone grotto from a proprietary artificial cement render known as Pulhamite stone. Pulham's also re-landscaped the Japanese water garden with this

Right: Looking from the former Billiard Room towards
the grotto and fernery, once part of the glass-roofed
Winter Garden built by Messenger & Co. for the Pagets

Below: Cherubs set in a garden wall. Bottom: The
ornamental fountain in the sunken garden

artificial stone, installing a large rock wall at the entrance,
new rock-lined streams, and ten stone cascades down
which water from natural springs could fall into the ponds
below. The firm had such a link with the Pagets that they
also manufactured some ornamental pots especially for
them: called Paget Pots, they were advertised for sale in the
Pulham and Son catalogue.

In 1914, the lease on Veitch's nurseries at Coombe Wood
expired. Harry Veitch was an elderly man of 74, and with no
one left to inherit the business, he decided to sell up. After a
ten-day auction, during which all the stock was sold, the
family of the Duke of Cambridge put the land on the market.
To her delight, Lady Paget managed to acquire two acres of
the former nursery which bordered the Japanese water
garden of Warren House. The land lay adjacent to the
bottom pond and stream and was where all Veitch's Chinese
and Japanese trees and shrubs were planted.

The most vivid description of Warren House gardens,
including Lady Paget's 1914 purchase, appears in an edition
of *The Gardeners' Chronicle*, 23 August 1924. It describes
just how beautifully Veitch's water garden had matured over
50 years, and the results of the hard work undertaken by the
Pagets' gardener, Mr W. J. Penton:

> The palm [prize] for size and natural beauty, as well as
> from a garden standpoint, must be given to General
> Paget's estate. The owner moreover is a keen horticulturist
> and has planted the grounds with a wealth of choice of
> trees, shrubs, and beautiful plants of all kinds. The loggia is
> built in the Italian style from stone pillars obtained from
> Pompeii. This ornate building is covered with climbers, and
> between the columns supporting the structures, are old
> flagons, six of them being wine flagons of great historical
> worth, handsomely decorated with floral figures.
> Immediately in front of the loggia is a paved garden with
> two octagonal water pools and a central fountain. The
> water pools are planted with nymphaea, trollius and other
> water-loving plants, while eight pyramidal box trees in
> terra-cotta receptacles are disposed one on either corner
> of the pools. The little border that surrounds this flagged
> garden is gay in summer time with such subjects as Paul
> Crampel Pelargoniums, Ambutilons, Zea Mays etc, with
> Dactylis Glomerata as an edging. On the chief lawn are

'The path leads to an enclosed croquet lawn with a summer house at the back of an ornamental wall.' *The Gardeners' Chronicle*, 1924

'Guarding the entrance to the Japanese Garden are two kylins [now sadly gone] that were brought from Pekin, beautiful examples of oriental art and very valuable.' *The Gardeners' Chronicle*, 1924

several trees planted by royal personages, including two cedars planted by Edward VII and Queen Alexandria respectively and two of Cupressus sempervirens planted by King Manuel and Queen Augusta Victoria of Portugal.

While the dressed portions of the gardens are very interesting, the chief glory of Warren House is the extensive natural woodland with the many beautiful sylvan walks. The place abounds in rhododendrons and azaleas in great variety, these beautiful flowering shrubs forming avenues through many parts of the grounds, and equally as beautiful as the rhododendrons and azaleas are the hollies of which there are many remarkably fine specimens, several of perfect pyramidal shape up to forty feet high. It is rather strange that arborescent subjects should luxuriate as they do at Warren House, for the soil is of a very light sandy nature and dries out quickly in the summer. Doubtless the big trees and shrubs have penetrated to the deeper moister sub-soil from which they obtain the necessary moisture.

A very pleasing walk on the south-west portion of the estate leads through a glade of such shrubs as rhodo-dendrons, Andromeda floribunda and hollies, to a rockery and pool in a garden where Japanese maples, dwarf Abies [firs], Cotoneaster horizontalis and Muchlenbeckia complexa, the last in size like a very big shrub, are included. Here rock roses grow to a large size and as showing how favourable the situation and climate is it may be mentioned that Francoa ramosa remains out of doors all the winter without protection. The path leads to an enclosed croquet lawn with a summer house at the back of an ornamental wall enclosing the croquet lawn. The lake is continuous to the croquet lawn and is one of several fine pieces of water on the estate. Two splendid silver hollies each thirty to forty feet high grow near to where the stream enters the lake. The part of the ground is ablaze in early summer with the bright colours of Azaleas and Rhododendrons and the perfume of these plants is delightful. There are about forty acres of woodland at Warren House, principally of silver birch and oak, and the whole of this large area may be described as a woodland garden. In some parts, where clearings have been made, camellias have been planted and these have grown splendidly and they flower freely each season. There are also almost all of the cultivated species and varieties of magnolia. The rare Magnolia macrophylla has flowered and set seed pods this season. A number of Chinese plants, introduced by Mr E. H. Wilson, are growing in favoured spots.

The Japanese Lily Lake in the upper grounds is another very pretty piece of water almost enclosed by beautiful trees and shrubs ... Whilst this water garden is known as the Japanese Lily Lake, the principal Japanese gardens are in the lower portions of the grounds. The introduction of many beautiful, strong and metal ornaments brought from China and Japan serves to make this Japanese garden of very realistic appearance; guarding the entrance are two kylins that were brought from Pekin, beautiful examples of oriental art and very valuable.

The way through the Japanese garden is traversed by stepping stones placed irregularly and leads over a stone bridge where the water tumbles down several feet to the dell below. I was informed that when the flowering cherries, magnolias, Malus floribunda and similar spring flowering shrubs are in bloom, the scene in this part of the gardens is enchanting. In the depth of the Japanese gardens bamboos grow to a remarkable size, in fact they make bowers with dense growth overhead. One feature that impressed me very much was the blue colour of the hydrangeas, for they are all a real blue shade and as there are large plantings of them, the effect can well be imagined.

There is a new garden formed on a portion of the old Coombe Wood Nursery of Messrs James Veitch and Sons. A stream runs through it and fills a large piece of ornamental water. A grass vista with herbaceous borders on either side leads to the lake which is one of the finest examples of water gardening I have seen for a long time. The soil in the newer part of the estate is of very favourable character and everything seems to grow in perfection. Many plants grow along the narrow stream, pink iris, bamboos, Japanese maples, a weeping mulberry to name but a few. Two imposing golden willows overhang the lake which is planted with a variety of nymphaea and in the vicinity is a whole host of conifers, many of them in small ornamental receptacles. The higher portion of this part of the estate contains a rose garden and a rose border with herbaceous plants in the background, many of which the gardener, Mr Penton, has raised from seeds. As the highest ground is reached, a splendid view of Wimbledon Common and the Coombe Hill Golf course is obtained.

HOME AND ABROAD

An English version of a German comic musical *The Dollar Princess* opened in 1909 and was a great hit, running for 428 performances at Daly's Theatre, just off Leicester Square. One of the original Dollar Princesses, Minnie Paget, during her annual visit to New York a year later, was honoured by Mrs Cornelius Vanderbilt at one of the largest and most brilliant entertainments of the New York season. In a house decorated throughout with red spring flowers, 150 guests dined, and were later joined by 200 other guests to dance to the very popular Nathan Franko's Orchestra. Minnie's mother, Mrs Stevens, would have been very proud, as all the important families of New York society were present.

On her return, Lady Paget attended the Shakespeare Memorial National Theatre Ball at the Royal Albert Hall, dressed as a court lady from *Henry VI*. The ball was organised by her old friend Jennie Jerome, now Mrs George Cornwallis-West, to raise money in support of a national theatre commemorating Shakespeare's achievements on the 300th anniversary of his death. Four thousand guests dressed in Elizabethan costume or as characters from Shakespeare's plays paid for tickets and the ball raised £10,000 towards the fund, which was supplemented by a souvenir album by Frederick Warne & Co., full of photographs, at 5 guineas a copy.

On 6 May 1910, King Edward VII, without whose friendship and influence Minnie would not have achieved such social success, died. He was 68. The Pagets must have joined the mourners at his funeral, which became the largest and one of the last gatherings of European royal families before the First World War. Two years later, Sir Arthur Paget attended King Edward's Memorial in Cannes. The King would have enjoyed the banquet at the Casino in Cannes, and approved wholeheartedly of the statue of himself, in yachtsman's dress, smiling down on the distinguished guests gathered on the esplanade.

Just as she had been present at his father's coronation, so Lady Paget attended the coronation of George V and Queen Mary at Westminster Abbey. Once again an area was set aside for personal friends, perhaps more those of the late King, who included Mrs William James, Mr and Mrs Leopold de Rothschild, Mr and Mrs Arthur Sassoon and Madame Melba, the Australian singer and one-time Coombe resident.

Unfortunately, Lady Paget had a slight fall from grace in March 1912. A gossip columnist in the *New York Times* wrote a damning piece about her, claiming that it was from her social circle that derogatory comments about Queen Mary had originated. Minnie was berated for neglecting her late mother, Mrs Paran Stevens, and accepting invitations to places where her mother was not welcome. There were also claims that the Paget children were

abandoned by their mother in London and often wrote to their grandmother, asking her to send them money. The column, unlike that of 20 years before, praised the generosity of Minnie's mother, claiming that she preferred Arthur to her daughter, and had kindly sent him $10,000 and left him and her grand-children money in her will. Probably most damning of all was the comment that Minnie was no longer in favour with the royal family. It was even suggested that Princess Alexandra had never liked her, but this can be disproved by the kind letters the two women exchanged for over 30 years. Further claims that Lady Paget, unlike her husband and children, was not welcome at Sandringham, are also highly questionable when considering the friendship she had with Edward VII. In stating that she was unable to secure King George at any of her dinner parties, the column revels in her demise, but considering her continued friendship with Alexandra, it is unlikely that Minnie Paget ever endorsed any unkind comments about Queen Mary.

During this time Paget, who had been appointed aide-de-camp to George V, and his other commanders ensured that there were real improvements in peacetime military training. Soldiers were taught the principles of fire power and troop movement with sections attacking each other in company training, learning how to seize the offensive and defeat the enemy. Paget took charge of the Eastern and Southern command, while General Sir John French commanded the Aldershot and London Commands during these regular large-scale mobilisations.

Louis Blériot and his
monoplane on the front
page of the *Daily Graphic*

M. BLERIOT AND HIS MONOPLANE, IN WHICH HE YESTERDAY ACCOMPLISHED THE FIRST 'CROSS CHANNEL FLIGHT BY A "HEAVIER THAN AIR" MACHINE. THE FLIGHT FROM BARAQUES, NEAR CALAIS, TO DOVER OCCUPIED TWENTY THREE MINUTES.

PIONEER ERA OF AVIATION

Arthur Paget was already interested in cars and was a member of both the Automobile Club of Great Britain and Ireland, and the Motor Union, but like so many people at the time he was very excited by the new innovation of flight and its possibilities. As a senior military figure, he was invited by the committee of the Aero Club to act as an honorary observer of flights within various club competitions and trials for records. In early May 1909, in honour of the Wright brothers, Sir Arthur Paget, together with Prince Francis of Teck and 150 distinguished guests, attended the Aero Club's banquet at the Ritz Hotel. The American Wright brothers were responsible for the first successful piloted, powered flight in 1903, bringing about one of the greatest changes the world has ever seen. This started the Army and Navy thinking about the importance of the aeroplane to Great Britain.

In July 1909 another momentous event in the history of aviation took place and once more Sir Arthur Paget was present. Louis Blériot was the first person to fly across the Channel, landing by Dover Castle, and winning the prize of £1,000 offered by the *Daily Mail*. The presentation was at a lunch given by Lord Northcliffe at the Savoy Hotel, and Arthur Paget was there with two recent guests from Warren House: the British Secretary for War, R. B. Haldane, and Mr Hugh Spottiswoode. While Blériot's aeroplane was on display at Selfridges, Haldane, speaking in French, told the aviator that he had 'done it with wonderful ease, because you had great courage'. Another man renowned for his courage, Lieutenant E. H. Shackleton, who had recently returned from an expedition to the Antarctic, was also present.

At the Aeronautical Society in 1911, the first public discussions were held on the issues of armament with regard to the 'military aeroplane'. General Sir Arthur Paget attended along with Vice-Admiral Prince Louis of Battenberg, Colonel Seely, the Under-Secretary for War, Major Sir A. Bannerman, Commandant of the Air Battalion, principal Army officer pilots and most of the leading aeroplane designers and manufacturers. *Flight Global* reported that, 'The meeting was chaired by Major General R. M. Ruck CB, and General Sir Arthur Paget and a member of the general staff of Eastern Command gave a lecture in which they illustrated by means of maps two cases of actual warfare where aeroplanes would have rendered invaluable service in terms of reconnaissance and fighting. They were in no doubt that they were "in the presence of a new and formidable science that would revolutionise warfare", in which the Army and Navy would work hand in hand.' Six months later, the military had a design for a military scouting aeroplane, and the beginnings of a new flying corps. While the soldiers practised tactics on the ground, the Commanders were learning the advantages of the observation tactics of the fledgling

Left: The front and back of the fan-shaped programme from the Fête at Versailles, Royal Albert Hall, 5 June 1913. When closed it formed the shape of a fan and when opened it comprised four circular pages, which contained information on the musical programme, cast list credits and a dance card

Below: The première of Anna Pavlova's film *The Dumb Girl of Portici* was shown at the Philharmonic Hall in aid of Lady Mary Paget's Million Pound Fund for providing permanent homes in France and England for soldiers blinded in the war. *Tatler*, 10 May 1916

Royal Flying Corps. It was a strategy that was to prove highly advantageous to the British Expeditionary Force of 1914.

Lady Paget and her many society friends made a contribution to a military charitable cause which surpassed the splendour of the Shakespeare Ball of the previous year. In July 1912 they held the One Hundred Years Ago Ball, in aid of the Incorporated Soldiers and Sailors Help Society, celebrating the soldiers and sailors of 1812. The boxes and balconies of the Royal Albert Hall were converted to resemble the Regency style of the Brighton Pavilion, and 26 sets of quadrilles were the central feature of the entertainment, as the dance had been introduced into England in 1815. Lady Paget had organised the Waterloo Quadrille, which opened the second set of the evening, well past midnight; it was based on the famous ball given by the Duchess of Richmond in Brussels in 1812 on the eve of the Battle of Waterloo, and Byron's famous poem. Minnie wore a black satin empire gown, with turquoise and diamante trimming and silver epaulettes, and a huge blue bonnet with a pink feather. Unable to dance, she took a box, and the Duchess of Richmond was played by Consuelo Duchess of Marlborough, who led the Waterloo Quadrille with Viscount Hardinge as the Duke of Wellington. The event made a profit of over £5,000 for the Society.

A year later, Lady Paget was still raising money for those injured fighting for their country. She and her fellow organisers were hoping to raise money for the Soldiers and Sailors Help Society by finding 10,000 annual subscribers to the fund at a price of a guinea (or more) a piece. What better way to raise money than to invite distinguished and wealthy guests to a festival? On 5 June 1913 the Royal Albert Hall opened its doors to the Fête at Versailles – the court of the Roi Soleil. *The Times* reported that wisely, in its opinion,

PAVLOVA IN "THE DUMB GIRL OF PORTICI"

The great Pavlova film, the first performance of which will be given this afternoon (May 10) at the Philharmonic Hall in aid of Lady Arthur Paget's Million Pound Fund for providing permanent homes in France and England for soldiers blinded in the war. This colossal undertaking has received the patronage of the King and Queen of England, Queen Alexandra, the King and Queen of Belgium, President Poincaré, and innumerable notable people. Lady Paget started her scheme in America, the land of her birth, and is at the head of the strongest committee ever organised in the United States. This committee is collecting funds, which are coming in freely, one concert in New York alone yielding £5,000. Lady Arthur Paget, prior to her marriage to General Sir Arthur Paget, was Miss Stevens, the daughter of the late Mr. Paran Stevens of New York. Mlle. Pavlova is seen in the right-hand side of the above picture

185

no attempt had been made to 'reproduce any particular part of Versailles in the Albert Hall, a building which no amount of ingenuity could ever make like anything at Versailles'. However, the organ was hidden behind hangings and everything was covered in ivory white and great golden fleurs-de-lys banners, with Louis XIV's favourite orange trees in tubs placed here and there. The year was 1680, and fancy dress was essential. The Russian Ballet of Anna Pavlova and Laurent Novikoff performed stately dances of the period. Lady Paget organised players representing the French court to cross the hall to the music of Lully's gavotte. With 17 royal courts represented, it must have been a magnificent sight.

THE CURRAGH MUTINY

In 1912 Arthur Paget was sworn a Privy Counsellor of Ireland, and sent to Ireland as Commander of the Forces. With his official residence in the Royal Hospital Kilmainham and his Headquarters at Parkgate, Dublin, he commanded two infantry divisions and two cavalry brigades. Half of the troops of the Irish command were based north of an imaginary line between Sligo and Wexford, half to the south. It was an important posting because in 1910, with the return to power of a Liberal government supported by Irish nationalists, came the return of Gladstone's Irish Home Rule Bill. Lady Paget did not join her husband in Ireland and chose instead to remain in London, dividing her time between London and Coombe. With the confidence of a seasoned professional, and the help of her many servants, Lady Paget carried on holding large dinner parties at Warren House, sometimes inviting American singers to entertain.

In January 1913 the Home Rule Bill was passed but, without a majority in the Lords, the position in Ulster was to be delayed until 1914. The Loyalist Ulster

Unionists, led by Edward Carson, did not want to be ruled from Dublin and they pledged to defy the Bill. Carson established a militant arm of the party, the Ulster Volunteers, who were ready to resist any attempt at Home Rule, by force if necessary. In response, the pro-Home Rule Irish Nationalists formed their own military organisation, the Irish Volunteers. With an increasing number of plots to raid army stores of arms and ammunition, opposition to the Bill mounted. The role of the British troops was to maintain law and order and the rule of government. Paget commanded army manoeuvres both in Ireland, and across the Irish Sea back in England, under the command of General Sir John French and alongside General Douglas Haig. In London, Prime Minister Asquith formed a committee to deal with the unrest.

Commensurate with the importance of the posting, and in reward for his loyalty, Paget was awarded the Knight Grand Cross of the Order of the Bath in 1913. His status as a significant military figure was underlined when he attended an important diplomatic banquet at the French Embassy with the President of the French Republic, George V and the

British soldiers from the Suffolk Regiment on parade at the Curragh Camp, near Dublin, during the Curragh Mutiny, 1914

Prince of Wales, government leaders and ambassadors from all over the world. Up to this point General Sir Arthur Paget's time in Ireland had been without incident, but he had always been a man of strong opinions, and he was just about to voice another. At a dinner held at the Corinthian Club, Dublin, in late February 1914, Paget delivered a politically highly charged speech that was heralded as a mistake by shocked journalists in London. Usually aloof from politics, but perhaps with the confidence of his rank, position and popularity in Ireland, his words highlighted the anxiety and distress which prevailed in the Army in Ireland at the time. His speech was printed in *The Times*, just two days later. He explained that he had fought alongside regiments from Ireland in South Africa and previous wars, and that they were 'very distinguished'. In his mind 'it is not thinkable – it is not possible – for me to contemplate even being asked to concentrate my men to move against the forces that are, I believe, in being in the north of Ireland.' At the same time, he reminded his audience 'that in our lives we soldiers have to do things that we do not like …

and if the order [to go north] was not obeyed it would mean that the Army is not in that state of discipline in which you would wish to see it … Although you may condemn us in any act of ours, at the same time you will say to yourselves, "Well, after all, they only did their duty."'

To deal with the increase in Ulster Volunteer raids on British Army depots, General Paget was 'ordered to take special precautions', and was then ordered back to London to explain what he had achieved. He told the War Office Committee, comprising the Secretary of State for War, Jack Seely; First Lord of the Admiralty, Winston Churchill; Chief Secretary for Ireland, Augustine Birrell; Liberal politician and member of Asquith's cabinet, the Marquess of Crewe; Chief of Imperial Staff, Field Marshal John French; the Adjutant General Sir John Spencer Ewart and senior army officer, Major General Sir Cecil Macready, that he was reluctant to order more troops into Ulster 'lest it precipitate a crisis', exactly in line with what he had said at the Corinthian Club a month earlier. Seely reassured him that he had full discretionary powers to deploy forces as he saw fit to safeguard the depots, and Churchill promised Paget the support of the Navy should the railways go on strike. Seely, keen to find a way around the objections, gave him an ultimatum to put to his officers: those who lived in Ulster could apply for permission to be absent from duty during the period of operations and would be reinstated afterwards, and any other officer not prepared to carry out his duty should say so and would be dismissed.

Paget met all his unit commanders at Headquarters in Dublin and implied that they were soon to be engaged in active service against Ulster and so a formal ultimatum, as laid down by Seely, would need to be given to all officers. The officers were furious, in particular General Hubert Gough and 57 officers in his 3rd Cavalry Brigade at Curragh, and most resigned. Paget sent a telegram to the War Office informing them of the crisis and then immediately went to the Curragh base to try to persuade them that he and the Army had no intention of urging a war on Ulster. With cries of mutiny at the Curragh camp, Gough was summoned to the War Office to explain his version of events. After a weekend of high political intrigue, and newspaper panic that read 'A military cabal seeks to dictate to Government the Bills it should carry or not carry into law', Paget, French, Churchill and Seely were all asked to explain themselves to the House of Commons and the King. Paget was initially blamed for his muddled handling of the ultimatum which Seely said was a hypothetical scenario and not an official order. For once it was Arthur Paget and not his wife whose name filled the newspaper columns, as in *The Times*: 'There is much talk about General Arthur Paget's position. It is assumed that in justice to himself he will insist on immediate and authoritative clearing up of the whole mystery. His friends in Dublin feel strongly that only one course is open to him – he must require the government to vindicate his reputation as a soldier and his actions during the three or four critical days in March or resign and claim a free hand to vindicate himself.'

Weeks of debate and discussion followed. Arthur's mother, Lady Alfred Paget, died on 3 May 1914, which added to the General's woes. Gough managed to get a guarantee from Seely that troops would not be called upon to enforce the Home Rule Bill in Ireland, but Asquith rejected it, saying that it was wrong for an officer to demand such an assurance from the Government. This decision forced the resignations of Jack Seely as Secretary for War, Field Marshal John French as Chief of Imperial General Staff and the Adjutant General Sir Spencer Ewart. Gough was heralded a hero.

On 28 March a new Army Order was passed in which 'no officer or soldier should in future be questioned by his superior officer as to the attitude he will adopt in the event of him being required to obey orders dependant on future or hypothetical contingencies.'

There was no mutiny. Paget's views on armed aggression against the Irish were very clear and his somewhat tactless personality must have been well known to his superiors; he sought guidance about his concerns and in turn had received the ultimatum. In carrying out his orders, as he understood them, blame did not lie entirely with him, but also with Seely, Ewart and French who had grossly mismanaged the situation. Whether the Curragh Mutiny was the 'product of accident and confusion on the part of Paget, or conspiracy and collusion' on the part of Asquith's committee, a mutual distrust between politicians and military leaders had emerged which lasted throughout the war that was to follow. The Third Home Rule Bill was passed on 28 May 1914, and in the statute books by September 1914 with the proviso that it would not come into effect until after the war.

J. B. Priestley said that Paget was 'a brave but never a very thoughtful man, but an excellent gardener'.

Oldway Mansion, Paignton, Devon, housed the 250-bed American Women's War Relief Fund Hospital, staffed by American Red Cross Units during the First World War

French, still mistrusting Paget after the Curragh incident, agreed. When war broke out in August 1914, Paget was brought back from Ireland, not to command the Third Army Corps as expected, but in command of the First Army, made up of the territorial force for Home Defence. Paget was furious and managed to have Sir William Pulteney appointed instead. He was then selected as British representative at French headquarters, but Lord French over-ruled that appointment, and a younger man took his place. Paget's chance of seeing any active or influential role during the war then practically disappeared. He was appointed Colonel-in-Chief of the Buffs, East Kent Regiment, a position he held until his death.

HELPING THE WAR EFFORT

Lady Paget was President of the American Women's War Relief Fund ably assisted by Mrs Nancy Astor, Vice President, and Lady Randolph Churchill who was chairman of the hospital committee. Founded at the outbreak of war from 123 Victoria Street, London, and 360 Madison Avenue, New York, the volunteers, composed mainly of American women married to Englishmen, managed to supply six motor ambulances for use at the battlefront, while a seventh was presented to the War Office by supporters in Boston. They also set up five workrooms for unemployed British women where they made socks and other woollen garments. On hearing that an additional American Red Cross unit of four doctors and 12 nurses had been transferred to the 250-bed American Hospital in Paignton to work in the Paget Ward, Lady Paget enthused, 'We will be glad to have this second unit. These American physicians and nurses have done splendid work since they came and have received the highest praise from the English hospital officials. The time will undoubtedly come when we will need more of these doctors and nurses, but we will require more money to enlarge the hospital.' She was also keen to meet fellow American Mrs Harry Payne Witney, née Gertrude Vanderbilt, whose hospital project for northern France was underway. The fund raised more than $600,000 and also provided a 42-bed hospital with a well-equipped operating theatre for officers in Lancaster Gate, London.

In September 1914, in response to Queen Mary's Appeal for 300,000 pairs of socks and a like number of abdominal belts for British soldiers at the Front, Lady Paget cabled the *New York Times*. She asked the women of America 'to knit or send pairs of socks if unable to help with money ... Knowing the generosity of the country that was my birthplace, I feel confident that this appeal will not go unheeded in the United States.' Indeed, just a few months later, a large quantity of woollen underwear and socks was sent for British

King George V (1865–1936), pictured here in 1914, entrusted General Arthur Paget to confer honorary military decorations on the Crown Prince of Serbia

soldiers. Minnie Paget's work was recognised by her old friend, Alexandra, by then the Queen Mother: 'You have never changed since the happy time I first knew you at Court in our youth. How far off those happy days seem now – now all changed into sorrow and terrible anxiety on account of this awful cruel and ghastly war. You have indeed worked hard for the benefit of our brave troops and wounded, and with complete success. I am so glad to have been able to be present at most of your matinees.'

During 1915, General Paget, with no role in France, accepted the role as the head of a British military mission to the neutral Balkan states, where his son-in-law, Ralph Paget, had served as British Minister in Serbia, and his daughter Leila was stationed at Uskub in Serbia, running a Red Cross hospital. General Paget's task was to arouse sympathy in favour of the Allies, and report back to London. Arriving in Rome on 1 March, he believed it was 'not difficult to reconstruct the Balkans if the campaign became completely favourable to the Allies and a settlement was reached between Britain, France and Russia'. From Italy he went on to Greece, where he was met by Ion Brătianu, Prime Minister of Romania. He travelled next to Bulgaria, a country whose geographical location and strong military force made it potentially a very important ally. In Sofia, on 16 March, Arthur was given an audience with King Ferdinand and dined with the Minister of

War, diplomatic representatives and military attachés, as well as ex-premiers Geshov, Danev and Malinov and other prominent statesmen. He wrote to Lord Kitchener, 'All possibilities of Bulgaria attacking any Balkan state that might side with the Entente is now over and there is some reason to think that shortly the Bulgarian army will move against Turkey.'

Following negotiations in Sofia, General Paget went on to Serbia to confer military decorations from King George V on the Crown Prince of Serbia. Paget then travelled with the British military mission to Russia. He was received by Tsar Nicholas II and his wife, who rarely entertained, at Tsarskoe Selo, and Sir George Buchanan, the British Ambassador at Petrograd. He visited the Russian positions outside the Austrian fortress of Przemysl in Galicia in present-day Poland, where he had a narrow escape from a German shell which burst rather too close to his position; his only remark, according to the *Illustrated London News* which featured his visit on the front page, was typical: 'Their shells are bursting well.' But the efforts of both the Russians, who were trying to build a new Balkan League, and Paget's military mission were ultimately unsuccessful, and by the spring of 1915, Bulgaria joined Turkey, allied themselves with the Central Powers, and over-ran Serbia.

One regular visitor to Warren House was an ex-soldier turned journalist, Charles à Court Repington, who used his friendship with the Pagets and others in Government and the War Office to write articles which had increasing influence on military policy as the war progressed. His memoirs were published in 1920. General Paget had been appointed Officer Commanding the Salisbury Training Centre and lived during the week in 'a nice old-fashioned house owned by an official of the Cathedral'. Repington visited him there in November 1915 to see the new 4th Army and commented on how fit this 64-year-old General still was: 'He bounded like a stag over trenches full of

infantry with fixed bayonets; I followed, remembering that he was a crack hurdle racer in the old days.' Arthur Paget was very short of reserves at Salisbury and despaired at not being able to get battery commanders for his divisions. He was as critical as ever of the senior ranks of the Army, believing there were too many Cavalry officers in high command in France. Lady Paget asked Repington to try to stop her husband expressing these views in letters to Asquith, the Prime Minister. Arthur was eventually persuaded to see Lord Kitchener instead, much to the relief of Lady Paget and his staff.

THE WAR YEARS

Arthur returned to Coombe at weekends to join his wife and twin sons, both soldiers in the Irish Guards; his eldest son Bertie was a Captain in the 11th Hussars, General Staff Officer at GHQ in France, and a member of the Cavalry under Haig's patronage. Most weekends Warren House was filled with guests, and regular visitors included the Aga Khan, Lord and Lady Charles Beresford, Lady Drogheda, Robert Vansittart of the Foreign Office, Italian and American diplomats, and General Sir Jack Cowans, Quartermaster General to the Forces and Director-General of the Territorial Forces. The ladies included Mrs Alice Keppel, Mrs Leeds, Mrs Astor, Mrs McCreery and Mrs Duggan. They talked of the war, of the possible capture of Bagdad, the Balkans, how the Bulgarians were bluffing and would never attack Serbia, and how the Romanians were mobilised and would fight if supported by the Allies. The women were as well informed as most of the men, and certainly voiced their opinions. They played bridge and tennis on the red courts behind the stables and walked in the gardens.

They also talked of Lady Paget's charitable work. As determined as ever, she had begged Lloyd George, Minister of Munitions, to speak at a demonstration at the Empire Theatre in aid of the British Red Cross. Her efforts in 1915 were concentrated on the Russians. She held a dinner and concert at the Carlton on Russia Day on behalf of the wounded and prisoners in Germany, and another at the Alhambra, where Russian ballerina, Lydia Kyasht, performed. Lady Paget was tremendously pleased at the success of these events, though 'nearly dead with fatigue'.

The cheery evenings of 1915 culminated in a New Year's Eve party at 35 Belgrave Square where they 'dressed up in hats from crackers, ragged a good deal'. After hearing the chimes in the square at midnight, they returned inside to an excellent punch and a loud rendition of Auld Lang Syne. Just a week later, the House of Commons voted in favour of conscription as the war reached new heights. At Warren House the talk turned to the Ottoman attack and the evacuation at Gallipoli. Sir Arthur, kept on as sector commander in a reorganisation of senior command, bemoaned the lack of ammunition for the Home Defence and the lack of horses for the 18-pound guns, while his wife continued to entertain the likes of Prince and Princess

Sir Arthur Paget, head of the British Military Mission to Russia, on returning from viewing the enemy's position accompanied by Captain R. Glynn and two Russian officers, had a narrow escape from a German shell. From a sketch by the war artist H. C. Seppings-Wright of the *Illustrated London News*, stationed on the Eastern Front, 1915

Victor Napoleon, US President Wilson's confidential emissary Colonel House, and Madame Grouitch, the wife of the Serbian Minister.

Sir Arthur was asked to give up the Salisbury Training Centre and go on another mission to Russia. He was accompanied by Lord Reggie Pembroke (who had married his cousin) and their main task was to present Tsar Nicholas II with a Field Marshal's baton from George V. Sir John Hanbury-Williams in *The Russian Diary of an Englishman* recounts the events of 28 February 1916, after lunch at the British Embassy: 'When the time came for making the ceremonial presentation and the General had begun his speech, it was found that the baton had been left on the piano in the other room, and had to be hastily fetched!' Paget must have been a formidable figure, dressed in a red and blue coat, towering over most people in the room.

He was certainly treated with great honour. At a performance by the ballerina Mathilde Kschessinska, a former mistress of the Tsar, Arthur Paget, seated in the centre of the Imperial Box, while three grand Dukes sat in side boxes, bowed to all those around him as *God Save the King* was played. With the ceremony over, he went on to Petrograd to review the Kazak cavalry, who were renowned for their horsemanship, and the GHQ in Minsk.

Paget returned to Warren House with two Russian Military Orders, one of Alexander Nevsky and the other of St Stanislaus, given to him by the Tsar, and a new command, the Southern Army. His former adversary Lord French had appealed to the Prime Minister to move Arthur and another soldier, Bruce Hamilton, to commands under him in the UK, because Lord Kitchener had steadily obstructed their appointments, presumably after Paget's criticism of leadership in France. At a large party during the weekend of 6–7 May 1916, Arthur described the defence arrangements in the South of England, where only half of his new six divisions were properly armed. With the depressing talk and bad weather, the 18 lunch guests did their best to liven up the afternoon. The girls and boys danced and sang, and the Grand Duke Michael Mikhailovich, grandson of Tsar Nicholas I, took off his coat and joined them, while his daughter, the Countess Anastasia de Torby, and others played a good rubber of bridge.

Lady Paget had invited more distinguished guests for the weekend of 15–16 July. Coincidentally one of them was Starr Jameson, leader of the controversial Jameson Raid during the Boer War that had led to the resignation of the previous owner of Warren House from the British South Africa Company. Jameson had gone on to become Prime Minister of the Cape Colony and leader of the Unionist Party, had been created a baronet in 1911 and had returned to England in 1912. General Paget returned to Warren House on the

Sunday morning from his temporary home in Brentwood. He was by now in command of a line of defence which ran from Sheerness to Dover, but had only three out of five divisions remaining as the others had been called to France to reinforce the troops after great losses. Unfortunately, he was not in a good frame of mind. Repington recalls: 'We happened to walk through the dining room where there was luncheon laid for 20 people and he said "Good God!" and went off.' Despite Arthur's disappearance upstairs, and the rain, which wasn't just falling in France, the guests submitted to the charms of Warren House and after a cheery lunch played picquet and listened to the tea-time songs of Miss 'Hoity' Wiborg, which made them all laugh.

There was a stark contrast between what Arthur had to deal with and the atmosphere at Warren House. He was concerned that the Home Defence troops were drained and in his opinion could not resist an invasion; at the same time he'd been asked to find 10,000 troops to send to France, but only had 6,500 men, including some of his officers and trainers available. At Warren House the war was far from his guests' minds. His wife had invited the Duchess of Sutherland and other wealthy guests, who after games of tennis, an evening of 'much talk and much bridge, and a great rag', finally retired to bed at 3am, only to do the same the next night. It is hardly surprising that Arthur Paget was in no mood to join in.

Bertie Paget returned home from the Somme on a week's leave in November 1916 and joined his brothers and parents at Warren House with Lady Asquith, Lady Pembroke, the Duchess of Marlborough, Lords Annaly and Blandford and Jack Cowans. So popular had these weekends become that 12 more people, who had proposed themselves for lunch that weekend, were put off. While the house guests ate and drank well, Jack Cowans described the difficulties he was having feeding the troops because food supplies

Sir Arthur Paget was honoured by a performance of Mathilde Kschessinska, the Russian ballerina and former mistress of the Tsar

CHURCHILL AT WARREN HOUSE

The Right Honourable Winston Churchill, MP and his fiancée, Miss Clementine Hozier, c.1908

as Lieutenant Colonel commanding the 6th Battalion of the Royal Scots Fusiliers in France. Lady Paget had been very anxious about her husband's meeting with Winston, but the two men were quite friendly and both agreed in condemning the strategy in France, a view that was echoed by another guest, Arthur Balfour, who had succeeded Churchill as First Lord of the Admiralty. Later Churchill, who was to become quite a talented artist, spent some time painting in the beautiful Japanese garden at Warren House.

In September 1916, Winston Churchill and his wife Clementine were among those invited to Warren House for the weekend. Lady Paget had known Winston since he was a boy, for his mother was her friend Jenny, Lady Randolph Churchill. Minnie had written to him in 1908, when he had become a cabinet minister and President of the Board of Trade, and again from Warren House congratulating him on his engagement to Clementine Hozier. More recently she had been at a dinner at Lady Cunard's with Winston and his mother. Arthur, however, had not spoken to Churchill since the Curragh incident when, as First Lord of the Admiralty, Churchill had written Paget such a damning letter that Minnie had had it locked up in the bank. Churchill, however, had resigned from the Government in November 1915 over his role in the disastrous Gallipoli campaign. He had joined the Army, initially as a Major in the Grenadier Guards, then

Winston and Clementine Churchill returned at the end of October 1916 for a second visit to the peaceful Warren House. His great personal and political friend, the Attorney General Sir Frederick Edwin Smith, and his wife were also guests of the Pagets, and their cheerful banter amused the others staying at the house, such as Lady Cunard and the Spanish Duke of Alba.

Letter written by Lady Mary Paget on 17 August 1908 from Warren House to Winston Churchill, congratulating him on his engagement were low. Bertie told them of the fighting at the Somme, and as they sat up late into the night, Arthur despaired about poor Channel defences. Bertie returned to France on 2 December; he spent his last night with his mother and Repington at the Alhambra Theatre in London, watching the musical revue *The Bing Boys are Here*, famous for the song, 'If you were the only girl in the world'. Her son was not the only one to leave that month: Lady Paget's maid, Eliza Jaques, left after 24 years in service. Lady Paget was very upset, for she relied heavily upon her maid. Before she left, Eliza brought out lockets of Lady Paget's old admirers with photographs in them and Lady Paget declared to her guests that she had forgotten all their names!

Soon after his son's departure, General Paget, on behalf of King George V, together with the President of France, Raymond Poincare, travelled to Verdun to present the City with the Military Cross. Verdun, a poorly defended stronghold and salient which protruded over the German line, had been under attack since February 1916. In August, the German army was forced to move some of its artillery north to the Somme, and Verdun obtained enough relief to launch two offensives; by the end of 1916, the Battle of Verdun finally resulted in a tactical victory for the French at the huge cost of 362,000 French and 336,000 German lives. The British award, together with ones from Russia, Serbia, Belgium, Italy, Montenegro and Japan, was as much a morale booster as an honour of bravery. Paget's speech, on behalf of the King, had been written by the British Ambassador: 'It has been a real pleasure for me to award the cross to the heroic City of Verdun. The whole name will forever awaken unforgettable memories of victory and glorious resistance to our common enemy's fierce and reiterated attacks.'

David Lloyd George, the Liberal MP, took over from Asquith as Prime Minister of the coalition government in December 1916. After the failures of the early campaigns, in particular the Dardanelles and Gallipoli, the Liberals had been forced to enter into a coalition with the Conservative Unionists which lasted until 1922. As Prime Minister, Lloyd George headed up a smaller war cabinet, without the support of half the Liberal Party. On 4 April 1917, the United States entered the war, and General John J. Pershing of the US Army left New York on *Baltic II* to assume command of the Allied army fighting in Europe. All wealthy influential American ladies in England immediately seized the opportunity to entertain the General, and Pershing soon found himself in a social tug of war between the Pagets and the Waldorf Astors. He was invited to Warren House for tea and dinner, but Mrs Nancy Astor, with the help of US Ambassador Walter Hines Page, intercepted him and took him off to see the Canadian Hospital project at her home, Cliveden, in Berkshire. It fell to Pershing's Chief of Staff, Major General James Harbord, to ease the embarrassment and bewilderment at Warren House. It was not until shortly after 8pm, some 30 minutes late for dinner, that Pershing and his entourage appeared at Coombe.

BERTIE PAGET

Poison gas was used by both sides during the war. Special Companies of Royal Engineers were formed to attack the German lines, and the Germans responded by using chlorine in pressurised cylinders. The use of gas required the wind direction to be favourable otherwise it would drift back over the troops that had released it. The poison gas Phosgene was particularly potent as its effects were only felt two days after it had been inhaled, by which time it had already damaged the respiratory organs. It was probably Phosgene that

Left: Poison gas was used by both sides during the First World War

Below: Lieutenant Colonel Albert Edward Paget died at Warren House on 2 August 1917, from the effects of poison gas. *Illustrated London News* Roll of Honour

poisoned Bertie Paget who, very ill from the effects, was returned home to Warren House in June 1917.

As his condition worsened, he was moved to a nursing home. His mother, however, continued to entertain. The Grand Duke Michael and his elder daughter Countess Anastasia de Torby spoke of Russia, the revolutionaries and anarchists, telling of how those returning to Russia after the February Revolution were calling on the Grand Duke for financial assistance for the journey. American society ladies discussed whether they should transfer their good works from British to American charities now that the US had entered the war, but agreed that those married to British men should continue to support the land of their husbands. Repington went to see Douglas Haig, who lived just 300 yards from Warren House at Eastcott on Coombe Hill.

Charles Repington recounts a conversation with another guest, Lady Rosamond Ridley, which is quite poignant and shows that there was at least one guest aware of the discrepancy between her life and those at war. Lady Ridley wondered whether it was callous to go on with their life of parties, lunches and the like

when 3,000 to 4,000 men were killed every day on the battlefields of Europe; she thought such behaviour well explained the reasons behind the French Revolution. The reply was that hostesses kept people sane, steady and cheerful, and but for the fact that dinners were shorter, servants fewer, there was a lack of taxis and petrol, and in some places a shortage of sugar, they did not really notice a difference.

But the war changed the lives of the Paget family forever. On 2 August 1917, newspapers announced, 'the death at Warren House, Coombe Wood, of Lieutenant Colonel Albert Edward Sydney Louis Paget

FILMING AT WARREN HOUSE

Towards the end of the war, Warren House was host to the American film director D. W. Griffith. He had made his name directing short films with the American Mutoscope and Biograph Company, but was best known for the film *The Birth of a Nation* in 1915 which had made him and others, like Louis B. Mayer, very wealthy. On the invitation of the British War Office in 1917, Griffith, working for Artcraft (later part of Paramount), travelled to England to make two propaganda films, *Hearts of the World* and *The Great Love*. Both were silent black-and-white wartime melodramas and the latter starred George Fawcett, Lillian Gish and Robert Harron. *The Great Love* was filmed on the Paget estate at Coombe. Here, according to writer Mark Calney, Griffith fell in unrequited love with an English actress Lady Diana Manners, who introduced him to the Astor set. During his time in England, Griffith was granted audiences with Queen Alexander and Prime Minister Lloyd George, and was wined and dined by British aristocracy. It was therefore inevitable that he would have met fellow American Lady Paget, who offered the Warren House estate as a location for filming. While there is no indication that she appeared in the film, Queen Alexandra and other society ladies like Miss Elizabeth Asquith, Violet Keppel and Baroness Rothschild all made cameo appearances, and *The Great Love* was released in August 1918. Griffith went on to establish United Artists with Charlie Chaplin, Douglas Fairbanks and Mary Pickford.

D. W. Griffith watches footage from his film *Hearts of the World*, in which First World War soldiers fight along a trench, 1918

MVO … His premature death at the age of 38 will come as a great shock to many of his friends.' The resumé of his life that followed told of Bertie's commission to the 11th Hussars after he had volunteered for service at the outbreak of war in South Africa. During that campaign he had shown his considerable military ability and in honour of his service on the staff, he received the Queen's medal and four clasps. On returning to England, he acted as aide-de-camp to the Lord Lieutenant of Ireland and then returned to take up his duties as adjutant to his old regiment. From 1908–12 he was aide-de-camp to his father, then holding the Eastern Command. In 1914 he went abroad with the Expeditionary Force filling various staff appointments, having passed through the Staff College by then. A private family funeral service was held at St John the Baptist Church in Kingston Vale, with the memorial service held at St Peter's in Eaton Square.

Queen Alexandra wrote to Minnie on hearing the news: 'What a terrible misfortune! My heart does indeed bleed for you in your overwhelming sorrow and grief at the loss of your beloved eldest boy Bertie! My King's godson! I do feel for you all so very deeply – I am afraid he must have gone through tortures through that poison gas. It is all too sad for words – My thoughts and prayers never leave you in this saddest of hours.'

In September all the family was at Warren House: the twins had both been injured, Reggie through the knee and Arthur in the foot by a bomb, and Leila appeared worn out by recent events in Denmark. The last good division in the Home Defence had been broken up and General Paget feared for the existence of the Southern Army. Lady Paget was spending her time in London and Paris with her friend Mrs Nancy Leeds. It was only in the summer of 1918 that Warren House was once again open to house guests.

THE FINAL YEARS

The end of the war did finally come on 11 November 1918, and five months later Lady Paget was lunching again with Charles Repington and, by his account, back to her former self. This time their guest was the Grand Duke Dmitri Pavlovitch, considered a possible heir to the Russian throne. Pavlovitch had been indirectly connected with the murder of Rasputin and exiled by the Tsar. He had escaped to Persia and fought for the British during the war. Repington mused, 'Lady Minnie will make him Tsar if anyone can!'

However, she never had the chance. On 17 April Minnie left London for the last time. Accompanied by her American friend Mrs Nancy Leeds, she had both public and private business to attend to in Paris. She must have been aware that there was a flu pandemic in the French capital, but chose to ignore it. Unfortunately Minnie contracted influenza, and on 21 May 1919 with Mrs Leeds at her bedside, she died from a sharp attack of pneumonia. She was 66 years old. Thomas Gold Appleton, a 19th-century American wit, had said, 'Good Americans, when they die, go to Paris.' Sadly, Minnie Paget was already there.

Her funeral took place in Paris four days later. Her remains were then taken from Paris to Warren House and on 28 May to the Church of St John the Baptist in Kingston Vale. A memorial service was held at St Peter's, Eaton Square, where some 46 years earlier she

had been married. She was buried in Putney Vale Cemetery alongside her eldest son. *The Times* wrote a tribute to her:

> Beautiful, clever, ready witted and tactful, Lady Paget possessed gifts that well fitted her to shine as a London hostess. She quickly gained a reputation for the originality of her entertainments. Her card parties were especially popular. Her talent for organising was often used in the cause of charity and that total sum forthcoming from her efforts at the time of her death was stated to be some £28,000, including a bazaar for the Charing Cross Hospital raising £17,000. Just before her death she was devoted to raising £1 million to provide homes for soldiers blinded in the War. At all times she appreciated the importance of friendship between England and the United States and did much to further efforts to develop relations between the two countries.

Minnie left her daughter Leila all her jewels, but her beautiful wardrobe, which had been described so vividly in the newspapers and was the envy of many other women, was sold off. 'In the stark surroundings of a London auction room, in October 1919, all her dresses and gowns were auctioned off to a few friends keen to secure some remembrance of her and eager dealers.' All her frocks, furs, fans, ribbons, parasols and hats were displayed in public for 'discriminating eyes to behold', as the *New York Times* commented. One gown, in black satin with silver beads, made by Worth of Paris just a few months before her death and never worn, went for only £11 10s. The famous Cleopatra Costume from the 1897 Duchess of Devonshire Ball, in which she had made her memorable entrance, fetched just £9 10s. Many other items sold at very low prices. Dress materials were eagerly sought, since such material was scarce at the end of the war: brocades, velvets and French chinon silks by Worth were 33 shillings a yard, while 25 yards of Japanese silk with 10 yards of gauze to match went for just 28 shillings the lot. One newspaper summarised the proceedings: 'The

35 Belgrave Square was the London home of the Pagets for over 40 years, until Mary's death in 1919

frocks which once graced a society leader will soon perhaps be found in the secondhand clothes shops of Bayswater and Whitechapel.'

Repington had written: 'Another old true and loyal friend passed away. I was due at Coombe on 7 June, now Coombe I suppose will be no more. A great loss to her many friends and a hard blow to Sir Arthur following the death of his brilliant soldier son Bertie a little over a year ago.' Warren House and the lease of 35 Belgrave Square belonged to Minnie. In her will she bequeathed them both to Arthur, for his use, and their unmarried children. She did, however, give him the option of selling Belgrave Square and its contents, which is what he did just two months after her death:

> 35 Belgrave Square and 35 Belgrave Mews – An exceedingly choice town house on the south side of this fashionable square, directly facing the large ornamental gardens and a few minutes' walk from the park. The excellent accommodation includes 11 bedrooms, bathroom, wardrobe and linen rooms, a handsome double drawing room and boudoir, three

reception rooms, and an ante room on the ground floor. Electric passenger lift. Two staircases and ample domestic offices. At the rear are two garages and stabling with rooms over. The whole held for about 52 years with a moderate ground rent. With possession. Messrs Trollope by Auction, 31 July 1919.

The house was not sold on at the auction, but Messrs Trollope did manage to find a private buyer in December 1919. Lady Paget's mother's summer house, Villa Marietta, in Rhode Island, and its entire collection of paintings and decorative arts was sold in June 1922.

General Sir Arthur Paget retired from the Army, outliving his wife by nine years. He stayed on at Warren House, but no longer entertained on the same scale as before. During the colder and damper months of the year, he left England for the south of France and Chateau Garibondy, the villa his mother had owned, with his sister Amy for company.

He had always been a keen golfer. As early as 1886 he had been a golf committee member at the Cannes

Left: Arthur Wyndham Paget (1888–1966), photographed in New York, June 1911. Inset: Arthur and Reginald Paget, twin sons of Sir Arthur and Lady Paget, spent two years 'roughing it' on their mother's ranch in California

Country Club in Mougins and in 1911 he and the Rt Hon Arthur Balfour MP had played the inaugural match at Coombe Hill Golf Club. Paget had even played on the links at Newcastle County Down during his time as Commander of the Forces in Ireland, causing much speculation as to the reason for his visit to Ulster, which turned out to be purely a holiday! In his retirement he, and almost 180 people a day, played golf on the Riviera with the likes of Viscount Gladstone, Mrs Winston Churchill and Lord Wolverton. He was a good player and had also been involved in the Army Golf Championships since its inception in 1904, retiring as president when he became too old for the sport, the vote of thanks proposed by his replacement Lord Haig. Arthur

continued to sail yachts as he had done in the past with Edward VII, though none as large as *Britannia*.

In his seventies his health began to fail him. In August 1924 *The Times* noted that, 'General Sir Arthur Paget, who for some weeks has been seriously ill at his residence Warren House, Coombe Wood, is making satisfactory progress. He was visited regularly at Warren House by his daughter Leila and her husband Ralph, his surviving twin sons Reginald, who had married an American in 1921, and Arthur.' Three years later *The Times* reported that, 'General Sir Arthur Paget left for Cannes after spending the summer at Warren House; he is expected to make a long stay.' The warm weather in the South of France must have suited him, for Arthur spent Christmas in Cannes and did not return to Warren House until the following summer. This was on the occasion of his son Arthur's marriage to Rosemary Lowry-Corry, the daughter of a Brigadier General, at the Guards Chapel, Wellington Barracks. He returned to winter again in Cannes and died there on 8 December 1928 aged 77.

The Queen sent a telegram to the Paget family: 'The Queen greatly regrets to hear of the sad loss suffered by you and your family, in which her majesty truly sympathises, and knows how much the King will share their feelings, for in Sir Arthur Paget both the King and Queen lose a very old friend and one who has rendered valued and devoted service to three successive sovereigns.' The columns of *The Times Court and Social*, which for so long had included his name, covered the funeral in its usual manner:

There was a large and distinguished congregation at the funeral service for General Sir Arthur Paget at the memorial Church of Saint Georges at Cannes. Representatives of the Duke of Connaught, the Brigade of Guards, the Coldstream Guards, the Scots Guards, as well as Deputy Mayor of Cannes, the Sous-prefect of the Alps Maritimes, the British Vice Consul, Royal Thames Yacht club, all the Riviera yacht clubs and regatta clubs, Sir Alan and Lady Johnstone, Colonel and Mme Jacques Balsan, his brothers, sisters, sons and daughter. Memorial service for the Colonel of the Buffs (East Kent Regiment) held in the Warriors Chapel in Canterbury Cathedral.

General Sir Arthur Paget was finally laid to rest in Le Grand Jas Cemetery in Cannes, on the Riviera where he and King Edward VII had spent so many happy times.

Le Grand Jas Cemetery, Cannes, the burial place of General Sir Arthur Paget, GCB KCVO PC (Ireland)

5

1932–54

THE TALE OF THE DAME AND THE DIPLOMAT

DAME LOUISE MARGARET LEILA WEMYSS PAGET GBE (1881–1958)
AND SIR RALPH SPENCER PAGET KCMG CVO (1864–1940)

W ARREN HOUSE passed to Dame Leila Paget and her husband Ralph through a deed of family arrangement four years after the death of her father. Since Ralph's retirement ten years earlier, the Pagets had been living in relatively modest accommodation in Pett Farm, Sittingbourne, Kent. Under the terms of Sir Arthur Paget's will, Leila became a wealthy woman and over the next 22 years, she used her money and Warren House to support the humanitarian work for injured servicemen and the Serbian nation for which she had become so well known.

Leila Paget was quite different from her extrovert, highly sociable mother. She was 'a gentle self-effacing woman, with dark grey eyes, long dark eyelashes and a brilliant complexion, who never sought fame or

Opposite: The central fountain in the terrace garden at Warren House

Above: Detail from front of entrance porch

honour'. As a young girl she was believed to have had a delicate constitution and showed no liking for the endless rounds of parties and entertaining which so amused her mother. Instead she would winter in the warmer climates of the South of France or Arizona. She was a debutante, presented at court in 1901 while her father and elder brother were away fighting in the Boer War. On 28 October 1907, she married Ralph Spencer Paget, a distant cousin, whose family was also descended from Henry, 1st Earl of Uxbridge. Her mother had just purchased Warren House and the wedding, a quiet low-key ceremony, took place at the local church in Kingston Vale.

RALPH PAGET'S CAREER

Ralph Spencer Paget, 17 years older than Leila, was a diplomat. By the time of his marriage he had already spent 20 years in the diplomatic service, serving in six countries on four different continents. He had an

Ralph Paget (1864–1940), photographed in the late 1880s

·WALERY·
·PHOTOGRAPHER TO THE QUEEN·
V R
·164·REGENT·STREET·
·LONDON·

excellent command of foreign languages, especially German – his mother's native tongue – but also Arabic and Turkish, and possibly Mandarin and Cantonese. As a diplomat he was following in the footsteps of his father, Sir Augustus Berkeley Paget, who had been the first British Ambassador to the capital of the newly united Italy in 1876; later, when Augustus was Ambassador to Vienna, Austro-Hungary, in 1888, his son Ralph served as an attaché under him. Ralph Paget went on to Egypt where he served under Evelyn Baring, 1st Earl of Cromer, who was initiating his reorganisation of the country and its finances; then in 1891 to Zanzibar under Sir Gerald Portal, where he witnessed the beginnings of British colonialism in East Africa. After a year in Washington, he was sent as charge d'affaires to the British Legation in Tokyo, arriving on 1 July 1893.

He spent six years in Japan, and was promoted to Second Secretary in 1895 for the work he had done at the British Embassy during the period of the Sino-Japanese War 1894–5. Later he worked under

Below: Japanese troops launching an attack on the Chinese fleet at Port Arthur (Lushunkou), 1894, during the Sino-Japanese War, when Ralph Paget was a diplomat with the British legation in Tokyo

Louise Margaret
Leila Wemyss Paget
(1881–1958)

diplomat Sir Ernest Satow. Not long after he arrived, he was praised in a Tokyo newspaper for his attitude towards the Japanese Government: 'Mr Paget has plenty of springs and autumns to come, the future of great promise is before him, and he will certainly make his name as a diplomatist of mark.' *The Times* many years later wrote: 'Japan still retained its charm of unspoilt remoteness and was well known to few Europeans, other than sailors and missionaries. Paget delighted in his time there and travelled extensively through the islands. He was happier in the distant posts than in the normal, urban and urbane diplomatic atmosphere of Europe.' He left Kobe for Cairo and the boat home on 15 May 1899.

In 1901, he was sent as charge d'affaires to the Legation in Guatemala to protect the economic interests of the British Empire. However, he found both the climate and the habits of the Central Americans difficult to tolerate, and must have been very relieved when in 1902 he was sent to Siam, as charge d'affaires to the Bangkok Legation. He was put in charge and eventually became British Envoy Extraordinary and Minister Plenipotentiary in Siam. His main political task was to negotiate a border treaty between Siam and British Malaya, and defend British interests against German rivalry in the region. Paget's success was instrumental in Siam remaining on the side of the Triple Entente during the First World War.

Contrasting views of Bangkok. Right, from *Le Petit Journal*, 1893; above, a city street, photographed *c*.1910

VUE DE BANGKOK
Capitale du royaume de Siam

MARRIED LIFE

In 1907 Ralph Paget, by then 43 years old, married Leila Paget, the 26-year-old daughter of his relative General Sir Arthur Paget. The wedding guests, although few in number, reflected the social status of both families and included the American Ambassador and her mother's friend, Consuelo Yznaga, the dowager Duchess of Manchester. Lunch was served at Warren House after the ceremony. Ralph (who had just been created a Commander of the Royal Victorian Order) and Leila Paget honeymooned in Paris, visiting Aunt Fanny Reed, and then travelled as newlyweds to Siam. It seems that Leila Paget was not in the least bit concerned about the possible hardships of living far from her family. While preparing to leave, she asked a friend, 'What kind of soap must I use for kitchen purposes, for I expect to do my own washing when I reach Bangkok.'

In a farewell letter written two years later to the King of Siam, Ralph described the years he and his wife had spent in Bangkok as 'one of the happiest periods' in their lives. However, it does not seem that this was entirely the case for Leila, who found the climate and noise difficult to bear and soon became unwell. The Siam Legation was situated in an area of

Bangkok which was noisy and polluted. On one side was the river, where passing boats sounded their horns continually both day and night, competing with the hooters of the two rice mills opposite the Legation and the banging of construction workers building a third mill. Whenever the wind blew from the East, the compound of the Legation was filled with ash. Electric trams rattled up and down New Road clanging their bells and, in the early hours of the morning, after the partying in the bar opposite had finished, the bell in the neighbouring Temple rang out calling the faithful to prayer. The pressure of newly married life in a tropical climate also took its toll on Ralph who wrote to a friend in February 1908. 'We are giving a Ball tonight and the whole house is upset and I do not feel in the best of tempers so excuse the short letter. Being a bachelor had its disadvantages in *some* points.' Leila's fragile ill health suffered and she returned to Warren House in the summer of 1908, where she remained until late October. Increasingly during her husband's diplomatic postings abroad, she spent the winter in her grandmother's villa in Cannes, where the weather was far milder.

By 1909 Ralph Paget had been appointed Minister Resident to Munich, the capital of Bavaria, the first British posting in the region for 20 years. Although he had been knighted that year by Edward VII in the Birthday honours for his work in Siam, Ralph's position in Munich did not warrant his presence in important diplomatic discussions which were taking place in Berlin at the time, and he was openly excluded. In his book *The Foreign Office Mind*, T. G. Otte explains that Charles Hardinge, the Permanent Secretary for Foreign Affairs, preferred to appoint diplomats who shared the same views and opinions as himself. Ralph Paget had a rather accommodating attitude towards Germany, which Hardinge believed to be absurd. Paget's views may have been influenced by his mother, Lady Walburga Paget, who was German, as

well as his father's role in the Embassy in Vienna. As Anglo-German relations worsened, Ralph Paget remained unconcerned by the increase in Germany's naval spending, declaring that Germany was merely maintaining its rightful trade links with its colonies. Paget's views meant that he found himself in 'prolonged exile in the diplomatic backwaters', such as Munich and Stuttgart, doing little more than public relations exercises like helping to lay out the first nine holes of the newly established Munich Golf Club. Perhaps his mother-in-law was trying to build bridges when she invited Ralph and Charles Hardinge to Warren House for the weekend house party of 22 May 1909. Nevertheless, Ralph remained in Munich until July 1910, when he was sent to another 'diplomatic backwater', Belgrade, the capital of Serbia.

THE BALKANS

The Balkans had returned to peace after the dramatic events of 1908, the Young Turks revolution, the Bosnian crisis and Bulgarian independence, and to Ralph Paget the posting may not have been very interesting. However, the Serbs soon found themselves in competition with other European countries for foreign investment. As armament recommenced throughout the region, Serbia once more became a politically sensitive area. Britain and Serbia had had a good diplomatic relationship for a number of decades, although the murder of the Serbian King and Queen in 1903 put a strain on the relationship, as Britain was a monarchy. Serbia was of no great economic or strategic use to Britain, except for the fact that her main adversary was Austro-Hungary, a strong ally of Germany. Britain was very interested in the future of the Ottoman Empire and keen to keep as many states on side as possible. Sir Ralph Paget's brief was to maintain Britain's neutral stance, even though the

Below: Bulgarian soldiers in formation travelling through the mountain pass of Belogradchick on the Serbian border during the Balkan Wars, 1912

Serbians perceived Britain as an ally. A couple of months after their arrival in November 1910, he and Leila were visited by General Sir Arthur Paget who was on his way to Bulgaria on the Orient Express. Under the guise of bestowing honours on British allies, Sir Arthur had conducted a number of secret diplomatic missions on behalf of Britain, and always ensured that his son-in-law remained informed of all diplomatic activities in the Balkans.

It was a difficult and not particularly enjoyable posting for Sir Ralph, who took a pro-Austrian stance, believing Belgrade leadership to be utterly obstinate and unreasonable. His initial lack of interest and awareness meant that he did not attribute much importance to the Balkan states and more often than not misinterpreted or underestimated the significance of political events. When a Russian-induced alliance between Bulgaria and Serbia over the future partitioning of Turkish-held Macedonia was joined by Greece and Montenegro, and the four states attacked Turkey, Ralph Paget became more and more pessimistic about the future. In October 1912, he wrote that the views he conveyed to the Foreign Office in a private letter may have given the wrong impression of the situation in the Balkans, by then in a state of crisis.

Leila Paget's delicate health had forced her to spend previous winters away from her husband in the warm air of the South of France, but the plight of the Serbians, and a little persuasion from her friend Mabel Grujić, the American wife of the Serbian Under-Secretary for Foreign Affairs, kept her in the Balkans. She had found her vocation running a military hospital in Belgrade during both Balkan wars. As a tireless worker who made many friends, she gained considerable experience in offering medical care and relief to both Serbian and Bulgarian patients. Although the First and Second Balkan Wars of 1912 and 1913 highlighted the instability of Europe, they seem to have brought the Pagets together for a while. Ralph wrote, 'For about three weeks before the war started, I had to spend hours in the Chancery every day cyphering and deciphering, and if it had not been for my wife who helped me I could never have got through.' Nonetheless, Ralph's attitude towards Serbia and its people remained negative: 'Although I do not want to ask for leave at a moment which may be inconvenient, I have not been over well [he had had influenza] and shall be glad to get away the first moment the situation seems to be sufficiently clear to permit it ... I really cannot think of what is going to happen. I fear this is the end of Turkey in Europe. I am very sad, for the Turk with all his faults and abuses was a gentleman while these people are common to a degree and the very reverse of gentlemen.'

Britain played an important role of mediator in the crisis and Paget, before returning to England in August 1913, was involved in the peace negotiations which, by the beginning of 1914, saw the end of the Ottoman Empire and Turkey virtually out of Europe, limited to the area around Constantinople and Adrianople. The number of independent countries in the region increased, including Romania, Serbia and Montenegro (by now doubled in size), giving rise to nationalist sentiments. Greece became the most important power on the Aegean; even the ill-defined state of Albania became nationalist, while Bulgaria was left bitterly resentful. This settlement and the spread of nationalism were to determine the future behaviour of the Balkan states and their allies. Ralph and Leila took a well-deserved holiday in the summer of 1914, travelling via New York and Los Angeles to a ranch in Southern California, from where they visited Leila's twin brothers Arthur and Reginald in Inyo County. While they were away, a Serbian revolutionary murdered Archduke Ferdinand, heir to the Austrian throne, in Sarajevo, capital of Bosnia (annexed by Austria), and war broke out.

Three months after Britain's declaration of war against Germany, Leila was back in the Balkans, commanding the first Serbian Relief Fund hospital; her husband had returned to the Foreign Office in London. The Serbian Relief Fund was an organisation supported by public funds raised in England to help the Serbians, and was accountable to both its committee and the Government. On her return to Serbia, Leila established a 600-bed unit outside Skopje (Uskub) in the south of the country, now Macedonia. Skopje was the main military and administrative centre for the region, and the relationship between the hospital unit and the Serbian Government authorities was entirely her responsibility.

Above: The Romanian prime minister's reception for Leila Paget (seated in the middle) and 60 of her nurses, 1916

Right: Leila Paget's typhoid hospital on the rocky mound in the centre of Uskub (Skopje), winter 1915

Leila must have astonished her family and their social circle, for none of them expected pale, delicate Leila to take on more than a trip to the spas in the South of France, let alone the war-torn Balkans. Although there is no evidence to link Leila Paget with the Women's Suffrage Societies, she may well have been influenced by their call for non-professional women to do useful work. After all, despite being born into an aristocratic family, they were not particularly wealthy and her two younger brothers, Arthur and Reginald, had worked for the Northern Pacific Railroad in the freight offices of St Paul, Baltimore, before the war.

She arrived back in Serbia at the height of the Austrian invasion. The Serbian army was retreating and conditions were appalling. Hospitals overflowed with wounded men, lying exhausted in dirty, disease-ridden wards. Nurses wore a makeshift germproof uniform, described by Mabel Potter in *Women Wanted* (1918): 'Their trouser legs were tucked into boots, and

Nurses of Leila Paget's hospital in their makeshift germ-proof uniforms. *Illustrated War News*, 1915

an overall tunic fastened tight around the neck and waist; beneath the uniform their arms were wrapped in bandages soaked in Vaseline and petroleum as protection against the flying insects and vermin.' How protective this was is open to question, since typhoid,

dysentery, tetanus and typhus were rife and the death rate was very high. Surgeons performed almost 400 operations a day, but constant exposure to disease meant that at any one time only half the staff were well enough to work. They had little or no warning of the arrival of new patients: once, 120 badly injured service men arrived overnight. The water supply was erratic – they could be cut off without warning for hours and sometimes days. The patients worsened through lack of drinking water, and the staff could not clean, disinfect or cook either. They had to buy oranges and lemons at exorbitant prices and left the men to suck the juice. The typhus epidemic was of particular concern, until Leila managed to persuade the local bureaucrats and General Popović, the Governor of Skopje, to open an isolation block to stop typhus from spreading. She recruited Austrian prisoners, who had recovered from the disease and therefore had some immunity, to man the isolation block.

But Leila did not escape disease herself: in March 1915 she and her chief medical officer were both struck down with typhus, eventually becoming unconscious. Newspaper headlines in Britain and New York feared her dead. Concerned, Ralph left immediately for the Balkans, and was relieved to find his wife alive but seriously ill. He remained with her until she was well enough to travel. Leila returned to Britain and her parents, first staying at Warren House, then travelling to Cannes to regain her strength in the warmth of the Mediterranean sun. She went back to Serbia a few months later and was dealt another blow. Her cousin, Richard Chichester, who had been working with the Serbian Relief Fund as secretary, contracted typhoid and died three weeks later in Belgrade. Leila and her nurses continued to treat the sick and dying as the Austro-German and Bulgarian armies advanced towards Skopje. She even persuaded Governor Popović to allow her to travel to Salonika to appeal to the French and British commanders for help for her unit, but to no avail.

Just before the outbreak of the First World War, Sir Ralph Paget had been appointed Assistant Under-Secretary for Foreign Affairs in London. But because of his previous experience in the Balkans, in April 1915 he was temporarily appointed British Commissioner for the Red Cross relief work in Serbia; it was his father-in-law, General Sir Arthur Paget, who had recommended him for the role. The General's advice was heeded for he had officially travelled through the Balkan states to confer military

SERBIAN RED CROSS

SERBIAN
RED CROSS
ROADSIDE
DISPENSARY

HELP THE DISPENSARY FUND
BY SENDING A CONTRIBUTION TO
THE SERBIAN RED CROSS SOCIETY IN GREAT BRITAIN
9, ENNISMORE GARDENS, LONDON, S.W. 7.

First World War
poster appealing for
funds for the Serbian
Red Cross Society

assistance from the French and British commanders, had been trying to move her patients and nurses to safer cities, but there was no transport. She made the decision to stay and become prisoner of the Bulgarian army, reassuring herself that her family's association with the Queen of Bulgaria would mean that she and her staff would be fairly treated. When Ralph arrived, she convinced him that it was best if she and her staff remained in Skopje.

She wrote: 'About 4 o'clock in the afternoon of 21 October, my husband arrived by motor car from Nish to see what our position was, and if anything could be done to extricate us from it. But it had been hopeless from the start, unless we had chosen to sacrifice the Serbians who needed our protection. He left for the north four hours later in order to save other Red Cross Units whose retreat from the country was not yet cut off.'

The day after Ralph left, the Bulgarians took Skopje. As she had anticipated, Leila and her staff were held as prisoners of war, and spent four months under enemy rule in Sofia. 'For myself I resolved to remain, whatever happened. I knew the chances were that I, and any who stayed with me, would be safe in the hands of the Bulgarians; that if I stayed it might mean protection for all the Serbians, both wounded in the hospitals and civilians in the town.' Like many British aid workers during the First World War, she and her workers were, for the most part, free of any moral dilemma and worked with both warring sides in the hospitals. Leila claimed that even the Axis forces learnt lessons in civilisation from the British whose presence 'had a most desirable effect on the Bulgarians and Austrians whose behaviour there is free from such cruelty as is reported to have occurred elsewhere'. She wrote: 'These were strange times. In the common struggle for mere existence, it did not occur to anyone very much who were friends and who were enemies.' For her humanitarian work under

decorations on Russian and Serbian military commanders and, undoubtedly, to discuss future alliances in the region. Ralph returned to Serbia for purely humanitarian duties, co-ordinating the work of several British medical missions.

When in 1915 the Austro-Hungarian, German and Bulgarian armies attacked Serbia for a third time, Ralph Paget made significant efforts to hold the British humanitarian missions together and organise their withdrawal far from the borders into the central and southern region, away from the advancing Bulgarians. On 15 October, the Bulgarian army cut the railway line, and with the Germans and Austro-Hungarians occupying Belgrade, all other forms of communication were no longer reliable. Concerned for his wife's safety, Paget drove to Skopje, where Leila was in charge of all civil affairs as the Serbian command was about to retreat from the city. Leila, having failed to get

Peter I, King of Serbia, with the Mayor of Uskub

extremely stressful conditions, Leila Paget was awarded the highest honour available to a woman by the Serbian Government, the Grand Cordon of the Order of St Sava, which was presented to her by King Peter of Serbia.

She narrowly avoided being used by the Bulgarians for their own propaganda purposes and managed to convince them to allow her staff to care for the entire refugee population of all nationalities in that part of Serbia. She bravely stood up to the Commandant when rumours that there were spies among the Serbian patients threatened the safety of the unit. The Serbian Relief Fund kept many alive on sacks of rice and flour bought from the Bulgarians, who were also persuaded to pay for new shirts and socks for the injured. Meanwhile, her husband Ralph had reached other units and was leading huge numbers of British workers on a long and arduous climb to safety across the mountains of Montenegro to Albania, and then on to Italy. Many of them wrote later of their hunger and fatigue, the confusion and the frustration, and Ralph Paget's 'extreme competence, and judicious guidance'. In Albania, he organised soup kitchens for the Serbian refugees who had gathered there, and finally led 180 British and Russian soldiers, cattle carts, pack ponies and horse-drawn carriages to the port of Medova on the Adriatic. While some continued east, Paget and the

British and Russian humanitarian units and a large number of refugees commandeered a French steamer and, escorted by an Italian destroyer to fend off the Austrian submarines, they left the Balkans for Brindisi, where 120 people landed on 18 December 1915. For his efforts, Ralph was awarded the First Class Order of the White Eagle by King Peter of Serbia.

The Germans arrived in Serbia in December 1915 and, sensing that there would be a real change in their treatment and that there was a desire among her staff to leave, Leila managed to negotiate repatriation for her entire unit with the Bulgarian Queen Eleonora and the Bulgarian Red Cross. She wrote: 'When the last day of distribution came there were pitiful scenes of tears and lamentation among the refugees, for until that time we had been their only hope and protection in the desolation that had surrounded them, and their future outlook was very cruel and inhospitable.' Although personally offered safe passage through Austro-Hungary, Leila refused to leave until her staff could come with her. She returned to London via Romania (where she and her staff were honoured by the Prime Minister) and through Russia to Petrograd. Arriving at King's Cross Station with 54 members of the Serbian Relief Fund, and two seriously injured soldiers, on 3 April 1916, she was met by her parents and Mr Bertram Christian, chairman of the Serbian

Relief Fund. In appreciation of all that she had done, George V honoured her with the title Lady of Grace of the Order of John of Jerusalem. Notwithstanding, she had to defend her actions with regard to her relationship with Queen Eleonore and the Bulgarians: 'Since my return home, I have learned that the terms of mutual civility upon which we lived with the Bulgarians have given rise in certain quarters to criticism and misunderstanding, it being specially suggested that I acted injudiciously in allowing myself to be a guest of the Queen of Bulgaria while a prisoner of war. I was never the guest of the Queen of Bulgaria, but like all the rest of my mission, stayed in Sofia as a guest of the Bulgarian Red Cross.'

DIPLOMACY IN DENMARK

Sir Ralph Paget's return to England and the Foreign Office coincided with Sir Charles Hardinge's return from India where he had been Viceroy since 1910. The relationship seemed to have improved and Hardinge appointed Paget and Sir William Tyrrell, a senior Foreign Office clerk, to undertake a thorough review of British war aims. In so doing, Paget became one of the most important British foreign policy-makers. The Foreign Office Committee on War Aims completed their report on 7 August 1916, and Ralph Paget took up a post his father had once held: Minister to Denmark. It was in Denmark in the early 1860s that Ralph's mother, Lady Walburga Paget, had suggested that the Danish Princess Alexandra might be a suitable bride for the young Albert Edward, Prince of Wales. Lady Walburga and Alexandra remained good friends for many years after she became Princess of Wales and eventually Queen, and Ralph and Leila's relationship with the royal couple was also strong.

The main purpose of British diplomacy in Denmark was to limit Danish exports to Germany while maintaining good relations with the Danish Government. Denmark had declared, 'favourable neutrality' towards Germany, but it was in their interests to maintain good relations with Britain to ensure that they kept themselves out of the war and still benefited from trade and shipping. Ralph expressed his thoughts in a letter to Lord Hardinge in November 1916: 'I cannot say that I find the position at all easy in some respects. It is disheartening and aggravating to realise that tons upon tons of foodstuffs daily find their way from Denmark into Germany and yet to be unable to do anything much to prevent it.' Writing to the British Naval attaché in Scandinavia, Paget is far more straightforward: 'I may tell you from a purely selfish and personal point of view, there is nothing I should like better than to see all imports to Denmark cut off, for I think it presents the one chance for me to get away from a climate and life which I cordially dislike.' Leila Paget who often acted as a messenger between Copenhagen and London because it was unsafe for the men to travel back and forth without rousing suspicion, attempted to ease her husband's frustration in a meeting with the Under-Secretary of State for Foreign Affairs, Lord Robert Cecil. She asked him to send her husband a clear and definite statement of British policy in Denmark. Although Cecil agreed that Ralph was entitled to such information, he could give no more than general advice.

As was perhaps to be expected, Leila Paget became President of the Copenhagen bureau of the British Red Cross Society, and through a sense of duty to British prisoners of war (POWs) she had also, somewhat reluctantly, taken on the position of President of the Copenhagen Bread Bureau and leader of its committee. Her reservations were not related to the work involved (indeed the wife of the British Ambassador to Switzerland, Lady Grant Duff, had initiated the highly successful Berne Bread Bureau in 1915), but the unsavoury character of the Bureau's director Marcus Warre Slade, a minor aristocrat, lawyer and former King's Counsel in Hong Kong.

The Copenhagen Bread Bureau was governed by the Central Prisoners of War Committee (CPWC) in London, and its chairman was Sir Leander Starr Jameson. The CPWC was responsible for sending food parcels and clothing to British POWs. White bread, baked in Bedford, was one of the largest single foodstuffs sent, but during transit in the hot summer of 1916, the bread became mouldy and inedible, so it was decided to transfer the operation to Copenhagen, contracting local bakers to bake the bread using flour imported from Britain. Here the operation relied on the help of local volunteers, organised by Slade's wife, and local transport, made up of horses and carts, to take the bread to the border where the shipments were handled by the Danish Red Cross. Danish rye flour was sometimes used which the POWs did not like, and occasionally the Germans stopped the supply causing the bread to go hard. Although they dispatched 73,502 loaves of bread during March 1917, the Board of the Bread Bureau was severely criticised by the CPWC in London for neglect, omissions and failure. The Board members in Denmark felt that the blame lay squarely at the feet of Marcus Slade and his wife, who were both quite dominant and difficult to work with. Leila Paget was persuaded to write to the CPWC in defence of the committee and to explain how difficult it was not only to persuade volunteers to join, but have their own voices heard because of the 'objectionable personality' of Mr Slade and his wife. The CPWC turned on Marcus Slade and accused him of not keeping them informed of the difficulties he was encountering. In retaliation to the letter and before resigning, Slade made a disgraceful verbal attack on Lady Paget and a furious Ralph Paget stepped in to defend his wife, not only against Slade, but also the CPWC members who did 'not have the decency to uphold her'.

In May 1917, with concerns over the German advance along the Baltic Coast and in the light of his fury over the Slade affair, Ralph decided to send Leila and other women in the Legation home for their own safety. He took a week's leave to accompany Leila to Bergen in neutral Norway, from where she took a boat to England. However, the situation at home was no happier. The death of her brother Albert Edward on 2 August 1917 at Warren House came as a dreadful blow to the already exhausted Leila, and prompted Ralph to return to Coombe on a leave of absence from Copenhagen.

Despite being in Copenhagen, the Pagets were often consulted on the situation in the Balkans. Ralph exchanged views with Hardinge, and the husband and wife used their influence to try to save some alleged conspirators against Aleksandar, the Serbian Prince Regent, for whom they felt true affection and friendship. Global recognition came in August 1917, when Leila became the first recipient of the Medal of Honour of the Federation of Women's Clubs in her

Opposite: Leila Paget was awarded the Dame
Grand Cross, GBE, by George V for her work
for the Serbian Relief Fund. She is pictured
here on the stairs at Warren House dressed for
the Coronation of Elizabeth II, 1953

mother's home town of New York, and in London she
was awarded the Dame Grand Cross, GBE, by George V
for her work for the Serbian Relief Fund. Leila, now a
Dame in her own right, continued to be involved in
the fate of the Balkans. She raised funds in aid of the
Serbian Red Cross alongside its president and the
Premier, Pašić. In August to September 1918, her
clandestine communications with a Bulgarian diplomat
attached to the Red Cross may have been an attempt to
persuade the Bulgarians to withdraw their allegiance to
the Central Powers. In December, *The Times* published a
letter from a representative of a former Central Power,
a very grateful Government Commissioner of the
Hungarian Red Cross, Countess Károlyi:

> I do not know in which part of the world is living now
> Lady Paget, who has been the last and preserving
> friend and nurse of the unfortunate Hungarian
> prisoners of war abandoned to starvation and dying of
> typhoid fever. Lady Paget treated them as if they had
> been British soldiers. She provided blankets for them
> when they were nearly frozen with cold in their rags;
> she had the sick isolated, disinfected and fed, the dead
> buried. The Hungarian invalids who knew her said
> about her: 'She has been a mother to us, she has been
> God's angel amongst us.' In the name of the
> heartbroken mothers I bow to this great heart.

After the First World War, a street in Belgrade was
named Ledi Pažet ulica, in her honour.

A NEW POST

Ralph Paget, by now 54, was feeling disillusioned
about his career. He longed for a more active post, for
a greater abundance of fresh air and more exercise, 'a
man's proper existence' according to his friend Sir
Theo Russell to whom he wrote: 'I think sometimes
when one gets under the weather one gets most
awfully depressed and dissatisfied with one's self and

is liable to feel one has been a failure in every respect.'
Due to Theo Russell's influence, Ralph Paget was
offered the newly created post of British Ambassador
to Brazil, after the King had raised the status from a
legation to an embassy. Ralph wrote a note of thanks
from Copenhagen: 'I do not think my wife would have
faced another winter here and though I would have
gone through with it myself had it been necessary, I am
more than glad to escape it.' Leila was delighted with
her husband's new posting.

The German Armistice had been signed on 11
November 1918 and ten weeks later the peace
conference took place in Paris. Ralph Paget should
have been among the British delegates, including
Viscount Hardinge and Sir William Tyrrell, who
travelled from Charing Cross to Versailles for the Paris
Peace Conference of 1919. It was here that almost all
the crucial solutions for territorial settlement in post-
war Europe, which he and Sir William Tyrrell had
proposed in 1916 in the Paget–Tyrrell Memorandum,
the first official political agenda, were adopted by the
governments of Europe.

Diplomats gathered at the peace conference in the Hall
of Mirrors in Louis XIV's palace at Versailles, 1919

Colonel Percy Harrison Fawcett asked Ralph Paget – his friend and the Ambassador to Brazil – to lobby the Brazilian government for funds to launch an expedition in search of a lost city he called 'Z'

On 6 June 1919, King George V and Queen Mary gave a banquet at Buckingham Palace for the President of Brazil, Dr Epitácio Pessoa, and his wife and daughter. They arrived in London by train on a four-day visit and Ralph Paget, as HM Minister in Brazil, was there to meet them. They had lunch at the Mansion House, where the Lord Mayor of London welcomed the President on behalf of the City of London and looked forward to developing business relationship between the two countries. The President acknowledged the great debt that his country owed to Britain for helping Brazil in the areas of capital and labour, and hoped that the bonds which united the two countries would continue to strengthen.

Ralph Paget was sworn a member of the Privy Council in August 1919. The next month he left Liverpool on the Pacific Liner *Quilpue* for the West Indies, where he was employed on a special mission, before transferring to the battle cruiser *Renown* to complete the journey to Brazil. He arrived in Rio de Janeiro in October to be welcomed by President Pessoa. However, despite all the preparations, Ralph, who was suffering from bad health, had been reluctant to go. Furthermore, the unexpected death of Leila's mother, Lady Mary Paget, earlier in the year must have impacted on their plans. In the end only one year was spent in the heat of South America. Despite this short period in office, another diplomat, Ernest Hambloch,

wrote fondly of Ralph: 'He was a man of remarkable personality, and one of the most clear-sighted Chiefs I have ever worked under. His advice was always helpful and encouraging and he had a gift for getting harmonious team-work done by his staff.' Ralph asked to resign on 7 August 1920 so that he 'might devote himself to personal affairs'.

Before he left, Ralph lobbied the Brazilian Government to help his friend, British explorer Colonel Percy Harrison Fawcett, to launch an expedition into the jungle in search of a lost city which Fawcett called Z. Paget returned to Britain and retired from diplomatic service. In 1925 Fawcett vanished without trace. A few years later the Pagets were visited in London by one of the many people attempting to discover Fawcett's fate in the jungle. When handed a necktie purporting to belong to Fawcett, the Pagets passed it to a servant who they believed had the skills of a medium. She told an incredible tale of capture, poisoning and death at the hands of native tribesmen.

IN RETIREMENT

Leila and Ralph Paget passed their time quietly in England. While they did not have any children of their own, Ralph agreed to be godfather to his nephew, Viscount Robert Ivor Windsor, who was the son and heir of the Earl of Plymouth and Ralph's sister Alberta Victoria. Where once they played their part on the world stage, their interests now became more parochial: in 1924 Ralph won prizes at the 46th Annual Dairy Show in the Horticultural Halls of Islington for his homemade 'medium-coloured extracted honey' and the couple became involved in animal welfare, making financial donations to the Animal Defence Society for the humane slaughter of animals at abattoirs. As the Treasurer for the People's

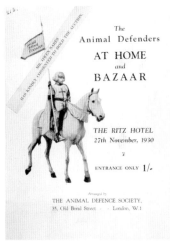

Left: A mobile People's Dispensary for Sick Animals clinic attends to animal flood victims in London, 1928

Below: Poster advertising a fundraising event for the Animal Defence Society at the Ritz Hotel, 1930

Dispensary for Sick Animals, Ralph wrote, 'One must regard the People's Dispensary for Sick Animals of the poor not only from the aspect of relief of suffering, but also from the point of view of its great moral value to its community.' It was a subject in which he became very involved: he also contributed an article entitled 'Civilisation and the Animal' to the January 1927 edition of the magazine *The Animals' Advocate*. Perhaps influenced by his time in the Far East, Sir Ralph Paget also allowed his name to be used in endorsing 'Count Mattei Herbal Remedies', and he made donations to the London Homoeopathic Hospital.

In early December 1928, Leila and her brother Arthur, her uncle Lord Queensborough and aunt Cynthia Tothill gathered at the bedside of General Sir Arthur Paget as he lay dying in Cannes. Father and daughter had a close relationship and on Arthur's death Leila benefited from a 1924 codicil to his will inheriting all his cash in the bank, personal securities and the proceeds of his life insurance policies. Leila was entrusted with making suitable arrangements for her father's servants and others who had worked for him. Everything left to Leila was exempt from the

covenant and trusts contained in her marriage settlement made in 1907, and became hers absolutely. By 1930, Ralph and Leila had left Kent and were living in Warren House full time.

Although Sir Arthur Paget had made provision for his son Arthur, he left little to Arthur's twin Reginald, who in 1920 had married an American actress. This was ultimately of little consequence, as Reginald died, aged 33, on 11 June 1931, at his home, Villa Toki Ederra on the outskirts of Biarritz, following complications after surgery. His body, like that of his mother and elder brother, was returned to Warren House and buried in Putney Vale Cemetery, as was his wife Minna when she died five years later.

Throughout the 1930s, the Pagets lived peacefully at Warren House, and Ralph took regular trips to warmer climates. In 1934 he went to Freetown in Sierra Leone, returning to Plymouth on the liner *Adda*, and a couple of months later he left for Madeira for a three-week visit. While Ralph was away, the Yugoslav King Alexander and French Foreign Minister Louis Barthou were assassinated in Marseilles on 9 October by a Bulgarian conspirator in league with a Croatian group

Below: King Alexander I of Yugoslavia is assassinated in
Marseilles by Croatian terrorists, on 9 October 1934.
Lieutenant Colonel Piollet strikes one of them with a sabre

protesting about the treatment of minorities in
Macedonia. Alexander had succeeded his father, King
Peter, in 1921 as ruler of the Kingdom of Serbs, Croats
and Slovenes, renamed Yugoslavia in 1929. He was
visiting France to finalise negotiations strengthening
the defensive alliance between his country, Italy and
France against Nazi Germany. On hearing the news
and seeing the footage of the assassination, the first
ever to have been filmed, Leila Paget went to Belgrade
to attend the huge state funeral.

In 1936, the Pagets had new neighbours: Leila's
distant cousin, Richard Gilbert Hare, the second son
of the 4th Earl of Listowel, and his new wife Dora
Gordine, an Estonian, hailed as 'possibly the finest
woman sculptor in the world'. The tranquillity of the
area and a long association with Coombe and Warren

House had inspired them to build Dorich House
overlooking Richmond Park.

In August 1938, the 73-year-old Ralph Paget retired
from the People's Dispensary for Sick Animals, as one
newspaper at the time reported, 'owing to taking up
permanent residence abroad'. Whether this was the
case or not, by the outbreak of the Second World War,
his health was poor. On 11 May 1940, just a month
after the Germans had occupied Denmark and the day
after the Germans invaded Belgium and Holland, Sir
Ralph Paget died at St Raphael in France. A year before
his death he had transferred the mortgage on Warren
House to his brother-in-law, the Earl of Plymouth. His
will was simple: Leila was his sole executrix and he
bequeathed everything he owned to her. Ralph was
buried at Putney Vale Cemetery.

Left: Lilian Phillips, convalescent nurse at Warren House 1942–5

Below: A young patient, Bobbie, with whom Lilian used to play table tennis

THE CONVALESCENCE HOME

Britain was at war and soon after Ralph's death, Leila, despite her 60 years, served actively again on Red Cross and welfare committees, and transformed Warren House into a military convalescence home. In November 1942, a young nurse called Lilian Phillips had just finished her six weeks' training at Kingston General Hospital, and as one of the best on her course, the 21 year old was sent to Warren House War Hospital, where she remained until 1945. The following is her story in her own words.

Just one wing of Warren House was kept aside for Lady Paget, who was in her 60s when I first met her, the rest were turned into hospital wards. The patients would come to us from Kingston Hospital after they had been patched up, and we would then take care of them until they could be discharged.

I tried to imagine as I walked from room to room how this beautiful house must have looked before it was turned into a hospital. Instead of rows of beds on polished floors, surrounded by bare walls, there would have been thick carpets and fine furniture. In the

entrance hall was a big open fireplace that one could sit right in without getting burnt. The fire was lit in the winter on visiting afternoons and this made the hall very welcoming. At visiting times there was always a nurse on duty in the entrance hall; sometimes when it was my turn, the patients would keep me company. In the long gallery that led off from the huge entrance hall, I could imagine how the walls were once covered in beautiful paintings. Perhaps some were portraits of ancestors, long gone. The long gallery led into the garden room that led out onto a lawn. Leading off the garden room was the ballroom which was kept locked. Stored inside were all the furniture, carpets and lots of other treasures belonging to Lady Paget. Sometimes when a servant opened the door to go inside to collect something, I would peep in. It was very large indeed. I could imagine many couples dancing, the music playing – it seemed a different world.

The dining room led into the games room. This room was still used as a playroom. I used to play table tennis with a young man called Bobbie, who had a beautiful face, thick brown curly hair and lovely grey-green eyes. He was about 22 when he came to us and almost permanently in a wheelchair. He died very young, such a great pity, as he was always so cheerful and so attractive. The nurses loved him. The next room was the library which led out onto another part of the garden and was used as a ward as well.

Along the long corridor towards the back stairs was the kitchen and a second pantry, our dining room and a small sitting room where the nurses would have a cup of tea after lunch; there was also a small office for the Head Sister. The walls of the long corridor were lined with cupboards with sliding doors, right the way along. These cupboards were filled with tins of food. When I made my way along the long, dark corridor to the pantry, with a tray of used dishes after our meal, I would shine my torch on the ground in order to avoid treading on the dead mice. Two huge cats lived at Warren House. They used to go out at night and hunt for mice, then bring them in and lay them all in a row along the corridor. They didn't eat them as they were much too well fed to want mice. A flight of stairs led up from this end of the corridor to Lady Paget's quarters.

A wide curving staircase led up from the entrance hall. The solid oak banisters were beautifully carved and polished, and the wooden treads must once have been covered with thick carpet. Upstairs was a long veranda with many rooms used as wards for 'up patients', those that could walk around. All the rooms had names like the Boudoir, the Blue Room, the Sun Room, the Morning Room, the King's Room, the Queen's Room and many others.

There were about 13 acres of grounds surrounding the house. These were divided into gardens and lawns, with a sunken garden, a rose garden, an Italian garden, a Japanese garden and a large lake, all beautifully kept. There were many gardeners. The nurses could take the patients for walks around the grounds, some in wheelchairs, some on crutches, or we could play tennis and golf with the fitter ones on the two courses nearby, all in our off duty time, of course!

We had plenty of good food, all cooked beautifully. Food was rationed and most people had very little. Lady Paget was well stocked up; it seemed she had been preparing for this. Breakfasts were very good at Warren House. Tea was ready on the beautiful set table and a lovely cooked breakfast was keeping hot on the hot plates – fried sausages, eggs, bacon, tomatoes, sometimes even potatoes and mushrooms. There was plenty of toast and we each had our own ration of butter. If you were lucky you could have some homemade marmalade. Bobbie's mother used to make it and bring some in for me! We had lots of poultry – chicken, duck, partridge, and pheasant – and many fish dishes, either poached or baked with delicious sauces. The poultry was always roasted and served with roast potatoes and a huge variety of vegetables, including leeks and asparagus, the likes of which I had never eaten before, having been brought up as a poor London kid. Cabbage and stew had been my main diet before then. The puddings were good

Below: Lilian (kneeling front left) with nurses and patients at Warren House. Right: Lilian (in front) with nurses on the lawn at Warren House

Left: Loggia garden and fountain. In the foreground are two cypress trees, given to the Pagets by the Queen of Portugal on a visit to Warren House in 1913

Below: Only one wing was retained for Lady Paget's use. Bedrooms such as this were emptied of their furniture and put to ward use

too: lovely fruit sponges with cream, or fruit pies with delicious custard, so creamy that I'm sure it was made with real cream. With the evening meal we were given cider to drink from pretty amber-coloured tumblers shaped rather like tulips opening out. Wine was served on Lady Paget's table. The cutlery was all solid silver, heavy stuff which Lady Paget's butler, Armstrong, would polish every week. The cups and saucers used for tea were very pretty, delicate, patterned bone china; the teapot, jug and sugar basin were all silver, of course. Everything was served on fresh white tablecloths. The patients thought they had come to the Ritz, especially after having had to rough it in the forces.

The nursing staff and sisters dined on a long table in the same room as Lady Paget, whose separate round table she shared with her guests and secretaries. One secretary was a titled lady who lived quite near, the other was a Frenchman, who lived with his wife in an annex to Warren House. We nursing staff were also waited on at table by Armstrong. He was a tall,

distinguished-looking man with greying hair. He said very little, only speaking when spoken to, exceptionally well mannered, always addressing Lady Paget as 'M'Lady … yes M'Lady, no M'Lady, very good M'Lady'. He was a strong person like his name, with a very strong character.

I remember when his only son was killed. On his first leave, the son came to Warren House to visit his parents. I remember seeing this tall, ginger-haired, young man in an air force uniform walking along the corridor on his way to the servants' quarters. He was with his wife and held a baby in his arms. They looked so happy, but sadly the next week we heard that he had been killed. I believe he was a pilot. So very sad. Poor Mr and Mrs Armstrong were so upset. Mrs Armstrong, the head cook, had to go off duty, but Mr Armstrong would not stop work; perhaps he found that that was the best way to get over his sad loss.

There were many people working in the kitchen, and pantry, cooking for us and the patients, and many

Above: A late 19th-century photograph of what are now two rooms known as Orchid and Wisteria. Right: A southeast-facing reception room known as Magnolia. In Lilian's words: 'I could imagine how the walls were once covered in beautiful paintings, perhaps some were portraits of ancestors long gone …'

servants in the house, many, many maids: ward maids, kitchen maids, parlour maids, housemaids. The ladies' maids would look after Lady Paget, taking care of her clothes, sewing, washing, running her baths, giving her breakfast in bed. General servants were usually foreigners. Some were Polish Jews, some German Jews, those who had managed to escape the death chambers in Germany, but most of whom had lost their husbands or families. Lady Paget had taken them in to live and work for her.

As well as being a good, kind person, Lady Paget did not mind helping out whenever any of the servants were off sick. I went into the pantry one day and was surprised to see Lady Paget on her hands and knees scrubbing the floor. I was so amazed I had to say, 'Lady Paget, you shouldn't be doing this!' 'Why ever not?' she said, 'I can do this as well as anyone.' That's just

one example of what she was like, for she was an intelligent and down-to-earth lady. She did some gardening too. She also ran the library and would lend out her many books to the patients. In this way she would find opportunities to chat to them and get to know them. They loved her, though I am not sure if many of them knew who she was.

When we were on night duty, which lasted for four weeks at a time and came round twice a year, we would take Lady Paget a tray of tea around midnight. She never went to sleep until she had had her tea. We were able to have a little chat with her then. She was always so eager to get to know people. I wished I could have chatted to her for longer and found out more about her life, but there never seemed enough time. Her first name was Leila, though we never called her that.

She was very tall and slim, always wore an overall covering her clothes during the day. In the evening when she came down for the evening meal, she was always very elegantly dressed in long gowns, wearing lots of jewellery. She always wore long earrings, even in the day when she was working.

Some of the patients were unable to return to their units after they had been discharged since they were so badly wounded and could not get work. So Lady Paget would take them in and give them work. They were so grateful. Some would help in the library, some as gardeners, and one man was an extra butler when Armstrong was off duty. One man was a clock winder. He would be responsible for keeping all the clocks going in the house and there were lots of them. One was a night watchman who would lock up all the doors and gates at night. They were all ex-patients.

I was a resident nurse. There were about five other resident nurses and four resident sisters and Sister Campling, the Head Sister. We all occupied the top floor, where we had bedrooms, bathrooms and a sitting room. All the other nurses and sisters lived nearby at home with their parents. Daughters of ladies lived at Hampton Court. But in spite of us all being such a mixed bunch, we all got on well together. I learnt from the servants who had been with Lady Paget

for many years that she and her husband used to entertain many important people before Warren House was turned into a war hospital. I could imagine the huge gates to the drive being opened to admit the guests with all the pomp and circumstance that went with it. Sometimes I would stand at the gates in my uniform trying to imagine the scene.

Sister Campling did not permit us to talk to the servants. At one time I became friendly with a young Polish Jew, a daughter of one of the kitchen staff. Her father had been taken to a concentration camp and of course there was no hope of seeing him again. I could have learnt a lot from her about the cruelty in Germany, but sadly our friendship was short-lived. Sister Campling got to hear and put a stop to it, telling me I should not be friendly with the servants who were beneath me. I disagreed and told her so, but there was nothing I could do. I didn't see the girl again, perhaps she had been told to leave, I don't know.

Patients of a high rank would have private rooms to themselves where possible. Some were lords and generals, friends of Lady Paget, and although they did not want this special treatment, snooty Sister Campling insisted. She, unlike Lady Paget, was a real snob. We did have some patients who were not in the forces. Donald Pears was one. He told Sister Campling he was a singer, a famous singer, so she gave him a private room. I had never heard of him but I think he was a kind of popular singer. One day I entered his room without knocking. He was cross with me and said I should always knock before entering his room. I told him I was a nurse and that he was a patient in my care, no different to all the other patients. However

I did notice that he tried very hard to be friends with me after that. He liked to be popular with all the nursing staff. He did fancy himself! On one occasion he told me I had a lovely face and he would like to make up my face for me. I laughed and said 'Can you imagine me sitting in your room having my face made up by you and in walks Sister Campling?' and he replied, 'Oh, that would be fine she's a friend of mine. I would make up her face too!' I thought that was very funny. I just had to tell the nurses when I joined them at dinner that evening. I was telling my story at the table and of course there was lots of laughter. Sister Campling's ears pricked up at hearing her name mentioned and wanted to know what was so funny. Well, at that moment I wished the floor could have opened up and swallowed me! I looked around at the nurses not knowing what to do and they all said, 'Go on Philly, go on, tell her.' So I did. All the sisters were quite amused. Sister Campling blushed and looked quite sheepish, but I think she quite liked it. I am sure Donald Pears had managed to get on the right side of her with a bit of flattery.

Every Christmas the nurses did a show for the patients. It was November 1942 when I first arrived and met all the nursing staff in the nurses' sitting room. As I entered the room, all the nurses looked up and said, 'The Spanish Lady!' and everybody cheered. You see, they were looking for someone to take the part of a Spanish lady and as I had black hair, I was just the person. Another nurse and I danced to the music from *Carmen* and to this day, whenever I hear this music I think of that first day at Warren House. I was only involved in that first Christmas show. The next Christmas I was on night duty, so I missed all the fun, and for the third Christmas in 1945, Lady Paget had arranged for some of her friends who were famous artists to perform. She did know a lot of famous people. I remember Phyllis Neilson-Terry acting a piece from a play she was doing and I think she sang. She was quite old then. Then there were two famous pianists who played on two grand pianos. I seem to remember that one performer was Ralph Richardson, but it's difficult

to remember names after all this time. Lady Paget would organise performances during the year and all the patients who could walk were able to go to the shows, and the bed patients who were well enough to sit up could be wheeled along to the huge music room. Some of the nurses, who were not looking after the patients, would wait on the performers, bringing them food and drink after the shows.

Once when I was on duty we had a very bad air-raid. We got a phone call from Kingston Hospital saying that part of the hospital had been bombed and could we prepare to take about 20 patients. We woke up all the day staff, moved all the walking patients upstairs, and the long gallery was made ready to receive the overflow of what we thought would be all the young wounded men. You can imagine our surprise when the great door of the entrance hall opened and in came lots and lots of stretchers and wheelchairs, all carrying lots of old men. I don't think there was one of them under 90. They all looked pretty bewildered poor things! We knew immediately what had happened. The surgical ward had been damaged, so all the young men from that ward had been moved to the old men's ward and all the old men sent over to Warren House. We knew that the nurses at the General Hospital were very envious of us nurses at Warren House ('The Land of Plenty') and I'm sure they thought that we ('The Glamour Girls') had very little to do and they would give us some extra work for a change.

In July 1945 the war ended. Gradually everything at Warren House came to an end. We no longer admitted new patients. Some patients got better and were discharged; others went off to other hospitals. Gradually the nursing staff dwindled, and a lot of the servants left too, as Lady Paget no longer needed them all. A year later, after my husband Will got his demob and came home from Egypt, Lady Paget invited Will and me to visit her for afternoon tea at Warren House. It was lovely to see the House back to how it had been before the war. All the carpets and furniture were back in place – it was so beautiful! Lady Paget was a very wise person. She took life as it came, but she too

missed all the patients and all the bustle of the hospital wards of the old days. I continued writing to Lady Paget and we sent Christmas cards to each other until she died.

LEILA AND SERBIA

Leila's association with the Serbian people was reawakened when in April 1941 the Axis Powers invaded the Kingdom of Yugoslavia and split it into four separate provinces under foreign rule. The independent state of Croatia became a Nazi puppet state ruled by a fascist militia, the Ustase, who were responsible for the persecution, murder and expulsion of many Serbs and Jews. General Draža Mihailović led the Serbian Chetnik anti-German and anti-communist resistance movement. A staunch royalist, he was supported by the British and US and the Yugoslavian Royal Government of Peter II, in exile in London. Leila Paget corresponded with Dr Milan Gavrilović, the Minister for Justice of the Government-in-exile and was well acquainted with Professor Slobodan Jovanović, a former literary critic and Prime Minister of the Yugoslav Government in exile from 1942–3. She provided help and support with her knowledge, contacts and money, and even helped the Serbian anti-

war poet and romanticist Miloš Crnjanski to obtain British citizenship.

In 1944, Allied help shifted to a rival resistance movement, the communist Partisans under Marshal Tito, because of apparent collaboration of the Chetnik units with the Germans. Western governments' attempts to unite the exiled Royal Yugoslav Government in London with Tito's Partisans failed and eventually became obsolete when elections of 1945 were won by the communists. But Leila's commitment did not waiver. A newspaper correspondent for *The Times* explained: 'When the British and United States government withdrew recognition from the Royal Yugoslav Government in London, she privately helped and encouraged many Serbian politicians, diplomats and intellectuals who were suddenly left destitute by this action. After the War, though her weakened health did not allow her to play an active role in affairs, her home was always open to all who came seeking help, advice or understanding.'

One such family were the family of Dr Pazaratz who escaped from Serbia at the end of the war, and made their way with two very young sons, Velimir (Velia) and Dusan (Dookie), via Italy and France to London. It is Velia, later called Bill, Pazaratz, who tells the story.

Upon arrival in London, our parents approached a local Serbian Church for temporary financial support. The church introduced us to Lady Paget, who was well known for assisting Serbian immigrants. My parents spoke no English, had no money and had two very young children to look after. Following that initial meeting, Lady Paget offered to take on the full responsibility for me and my brother's upbringing, to look after our health and education. My parents were thrilled and agreed. Lady Paget called me Velia and my brother Dookie, and we called her Aunt Roxolor. My mother Mirjana adored Lady Paget and was forever grateful to her for taking such great care of her children during these difficult years. Lady Paget also sent regular packages of food and supplies to our parents who lived in a one room flat on Robert Street in London; this was to allow our parents to concentrate on finding employment. Our mother managed to locate a few cleaning jobs, while our father studied English medical terminology, for he was determined to achieve accreditation as a medical doctor, his profession in Serbia. Lady Paget paid for our education at a private boarding school. She attempted to enrol us in some of the more prestigious schools, but she was rebuffed due to the discriminatory policies of those schools (we were immigrant children). Troubled by this prejudice but undeterred, she managed to locate a new boarding school for Catholic boys that had recently started and needed the funding. So, from 1945 to 1951, my brother and I attended Penrynn School (now Winterfold House) in Worcestershire, but during the school holidays we lived at Warren House where our parents would visit us on a regular basis.

Our old bedroom, on the top floor, had a sloping ceiling, a balcony and adjoining bathroom. The bedroom opposite to ours on two occasions was occupied by one of two young Serbian men that we understood were in medical school and receiving some form of assistance from Lady Paget. Being mischievous, my brother and I managed to make each of these students (who weren't very friendly) furious with us because we messed up their belongings. We had a much stronger bond with Aunt Roxolor than they did and we took full advantage.

While living with Lady Paget at Warren House, we spent hours in her company, and I adore my memories of the extreme loving care lavished on both my brother and myself by Aunt Roxolor. Many of the films we attended with her and many of the conversations we had while walking around the vast property, feeding stale bread to the birds, were designed by her to raise us as socially aware and responsible adults. Lady Paget possessed a very strong social conscience, and took every opportunity to discuss socially important and

ethical issues with my brother and me. The lessons were presented to us in small but regular doses, using language and examples tailored to our level of understanding. To this day 60 years later, I still have a strong sense of the values she held, and the behaviour she would have wanted of me and my brother.

At Warren House, Aunt Louise [Louisa Beatrice Folkett, the housekeeper at Warren House] was put in charge of our daily routine. She made sure we got up in the morning, attended breakfast, got ready for any trips we might be scheduled to take, and generally kept tabs on us to make sure we did not destroy the house while playing. She reported to Aunt Roxolor on our diet and general health. Aunt Louisa would hand over her childcare responsibilities each weekend to Aunt Marie. An evening ritual I remember to this day was a bath, followed by pyjamas, followed by storytime in bed while eating a large bowl of fresh fruit. We brushed our teeth and then received reassurance by Aunt Louisa or Aunt Roxolor that we were safe, since my brother and I indicated regularly that we were afraid of the dark.

Lady Paget provided the staff with very strict and specific instructions regarding any interaction with us. For example, the morning after an attempted burglary to the house (of which there were several), the staff were instructed not to discuss the event in our presence in order not to frighten us. While Lady Paget was a very compassionate person and treated her staff with great kindness, their relationship was never the less governed by the very strict rules of the era. Each side was mindful not to cross certain lines, and great respect was accorded in both directions.

We did not eat regular meals with Aunt Roxolor because she explained that she did not always eat meals, and when she did she had a very restricted diet. In order to promote proper nutrition for her two charges, she had us eat meals at regular times with up to a dozen staff in their dining hall, presided over by the head butler. One staff member would monitor our intake and report back to Lady Paget who had definite opinions on nutrition and what constituted a proper diet. This was just one of many ways she was greatly

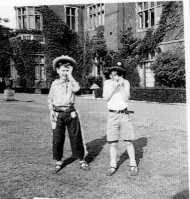

Left: Leila, 'Aunt Roxolor', spending a day on Brighton beach with Velia and Dookie, and their mother Mirjana Pazaratz

Below: The brothers playing on the lawn at Warren House

ahead of her time. We had afternoon tea every day with Lady Paget in the Sun Room, just outside the billiard room. She served a special rum cake that my brother and I craved, which contained real rum and was loaded with sugar, so we were only allowed a tiny sliver each time as a special treat. Each day she would play any current records (purchased at her favourite record shop in Oxford Street) on a small gramophone in the room. We were allowed to change the needles, but due to our youth and possible damage to the records someone else would place the tone arm on the record. She also had a television in that room, and I can remember she would view the *Little Women* series on that set.

Lady Paget would regularly collect a large number of stale bread loaves, crumble them up into a large wheel barrow, and go around the entire back of the property placing the bread in the bird feeders. My brother and I would accompany her, although we really didn't help her at all. She would allow us to run around and play games as long as we remained within her sight. She even gave us permission to dig for 'buried treasure' in a spot near the back of the property that was hidden by vegetation where an unexploded WW2 bomb had once been found.

Aunt Roxolor only became visibly upset with us once during our entire stay with her. This occurred on

'Aunt Louise' relaxing by the fireside, and Mirjana and her sons in Trafalgar Square during a trip to London

the occasion of our breaking a very large and probably very valuable vase. We struck it whilst riding our bikes, tipping it over and breaking it. Again, very much ahead of her time in terms of parenting skills, we would receive short rational admonitions from her when our behaviour got out of hand. This was always followed by verbal reassurances of her love.

Whenever required we would be driven into London by Mr White [Wilfred H. C. White] the chauffeur, Aunt Roxolor always accompanied us in the limousine. These trips had many purposes: shopping for clothes at Harrods, haircuts, visits to doctors, or to catch trains back to school from Paddington. We saw movies, annual Pantomimes, visited the Zoo, and sometimes spent the day with our parents. Mr White regarded the limo as his domain and we were forbidden to so much as touch the shiny exterior or door handles ourselves. Lady Paget and Mr White kept up a running quarrel each trip centred on the speed at which he was driving. While being perfectly respectful, he would hold his own in the discussion without allowing her to dictate the speed for much of the trip.

Every summer she would reunite us with our parents for a one week holiday in Brighton, sometimes coming with us and spending a day on the beach.

I have spectacular memories of Christmas in the Ballroom when Lady Paget organised a large festive event which was attended by dozens of people including many children. We found out later that Lady Paget insisted that her friends bring presents for the children, including for my brother and me. One year, Aunt Roxolor invited the son of the headmaster Mr Arbuthnott to join us as he was in my brother's class. At an appropriate time the lights in the ballroom were dimmed and we could hear Santa's sleigh bells getting louder and louder. Then the side window was opened and Santa stepped in with a huge sack of gifts. It was during one of these Christmases that my brother and I received our first two-wheeled bicycles, mine was red and my brother's was green. Since it was winter time we spent the remainder of our Christmas vacation learning to ride in the long basement hallway with 'Yorky' (one of the household staff) and anyone else he could find to catch us at either end of the hall.

In 1951 my father left for Canada to pursue his goal of regaining his medical accreditation, something that was not possible in Great Britain. While he was making arrangements for us to join him, Lady Paget confided in my mother her fears that my brother and I could not be looked after as well in Canada as she had looked after us. She proposed that we stay with her at Warren House until my parents had established themselves. She even offered to help my parents financially if they agreed. Looking back I understand she had bonded with us as if we were her own. I understand the emotional turmoil she went through when she 'lost' us. My mother understood this at the time and was forever grateful to Lady Paget for shielding her children from the daily difficulties encountered by other immigrant and refugee children in London.

THE PAGET PAPERS

Leila had spent many years collecting and assembling letters, documents and other papers relating to both her and her husband's side of the Paget family. She had enlisted the help of the Deputy Keeper in the Department of Manuscripts of the British Museum, Mr H. R. Aldridge, and a friend Mr Ernest Hambloch, and hoped to present the collection to the Trustees of the British Museum for preservation in the Manuscripts Department before her death. It was her wish that public access to the Paget Papers should be left to the discretion of the British Museum Trustees, in view of the fact that some of the letters and documents were from members of the royal family.

Ernest Hambloch had been on Ralph's staff in Brazil before becoming the British Consul in Brazil and Commercial Secretary of the British Embassy and a long-term guest at Warren House from 1942–3.

Hambloch first coined the phrase 'economic militarism' when in 1939 he described the Nazi ideology of using military power to invade other countries in order to gain economic advantages. He also wrote books about the new regime imposed on Brazil in 1937 and militant Italy. It is easy to see why Leila entrusted him with preserving the history of the Paget family, and paid him generously.

The work was not completed before her death, and many of the manuscripts were still in tin boxes at Soames House. She left instructions that all her own private papers should be destroyed after her death, and not included in the manuscripts. In accordance with Leila's wishes, Hambloch spent four years producing typed transcripts of documents dating back to 1801, and he added his own typed and handwritten notes to the pages. His work was bound and presented by Lady Phyllis Benton, Ralph's second cousin, and her family to the British Museum, along with the originals, which now make up 30 volumes of what are known as the Paget Papers.

We sailed for Canada in August 1951. Lady Paget was so emotionally distraught she could not bring herself to accompany us to the boat for a send-off. Although she vigorously opposed our move to Canada, where my father became a medical doctor after years of re-certification in a new language, we kept up a written correspondence. Unfortunately these letters do not survive, but the memories and love will always be with me and my brother, for she was very much like a beloved and doting grandparent, even though we called her Aunt.

Leila Paget was a donor to the Church of St Sava in Lancaster Road, London, and the Serbian Club, as well as being a supporter of dozens of Serbian emigrants who remained in Britain after the Allies reorganised the communist regime in Yugoslavia. In 1947, she and a number of other notables, including Violet Bonham Carter and Rebecca West, wrote a letter to *The Times* concerning the displaced Yugoslavians and Russians who had put themselves under British and US protection, but whose future was uncertain. She also erected a bronze monument to General Draža Mihailović, head of the Chetnik resistance movement, who had been tried for war crimes and executed by the communists at the end of the war.

In 1954 Leila, then 73, decided to sell Warren House to Imperial Chemical Industries (ICI) to help raise funds for Serbian emigrants. She moved across the Coombe Estate to a smaller property, Soames House, where she spent the last four years of her life, kept company by Marie Kovacević, a loyal and devoted member of staff. Dame Leila Paget died on 24 September 1958, and was buried alongside her husband at Putney Vale Cemetery. Queen Marie of Yugoslavia and Princess Tomislav were among those present at the memorial service at St Sava, the Serbian Orthodox Church. Author Kosta St Pavlović wrote a year after her death: 'Lady Paget in her life had three loves; love for the birds, love for the flowers, and love for Serbs. She spent all her money helping Serbs, she sold the house where she grew up, alienated from the park she cared so much for, the flowers that she nursed, birds that she fed daily at dawn. She died with one thought, "May all forget me, I don't care. But it will be hard on me if my Serbs forget me!"'

6

1954–2000

THE TALE OF THE CHEMICAL GIANT

IMPERIAL CHEMICAL INDUSTRIES (1926–2008)

F OR JUST OVER 80 years, Warren House had been a family home, witness to the trials and tribulations of family life, but also to the wider social and political scene. All this was to change: in the autumn of 1954, the house became the property of Imperial Chemical Industries Ltd (ICI), the largest manufacturing company in the British Empire.

In purchasing Warren House as a new residential management training centre, ICI saved the building from almost certain demolition, which by the 1950s was an increasing trend in the fate of big country houses. During the Second World War many large houses had been requisitioned by the War Office, gardens had been ploughed up and planted with crops, or used as army camps. In the years that

followed the war, social, political and economic pressures, such as increasing taxation and a shortage of staff, meant that families were unable to occupy their large homes as they once had. The big country house was no longer the centre point for local communities, providing employment and housing, as well as supporting local churches, schools or hospitals. Furthermore, wealthy owners were keen to sell as death duties imposed by HM Treasury were charged at a maximum of 80 per cent of the total value of the estate. Many were sold for institutional use, others were adapted or demolished.

Like many other country house owners at this time of austerity, Dame Leila Paget decided to sell up. She was nearly 73 years old with no heirs, except her younger brother Captain Arthur Wyndham Paget. It was also said that she sold Warren House to raise funds for members of the Yugoslav Government in exile. Whether for them or for her own financial reasons, she must have been relieved when ICI agreed to purchase

Opposite: The Ballroom, modelled on the Hall of Mirrors at Versailles, and restored in 1986

Above: One of the Della Robbia reliefs originally in the loggia, built into the facade of the London Room

185

Warren House from the drive, *c*.1958

the house and 13.82 acres for £30,000. This was not much more than her mother had paid for the property in 1907. Leila may have raised more if it had not been for the 1947 Town and Country Planning Act passed by the post-war Labour Government which in establishing the concept of planning permission for land development, and compulsory purchase order, forced depreciation in land values. It may explain why Leila did not sell all of her land to ICI. She retained a large wooded plot to the southeast which stretched almost as far as Warren Cutting, and ensured that she maintained all rights to it, perhaps with the intention of developing the land herself.

With the help of her faithful staff, all the fine English and French period furniture that had filled the rooms of Warren House was packed up, the Chinese and European porcelain carefully wrapped, and vast numbers of books were taken away. Paintings and drawings by 19th-century French artist Jean-Baptiste Mallet, 18th-century landscapes by Venetians Canaletto and Bernardo Belloto, portraits by Sir Thomas Lawrence and George Romney, caricatures by

Thomas Rowlandson, and other works by well-known artists, including Peter Tillemans who had retired locally to Richmond in the 1720s, were all removed, leaving bare spaces on the sun-bleached wallpaper. Carpets and rugs were rolled up, the television and phonograph records were all loaded into the Hillman estate van. After 47 years, the last member of the Paget family to live at Warren House was driven out of the gates by Mr White, the chauffeur, in her 1952 Humber Pullman limousine. They were not going far; her new home at Soames House on Coombe Hill Road was just a mile away. She lived there quietly, with a few staff, until her death four years later.

THE NEW OWNER

ICI had been extremely successful since its creation in 1926. The organisation was the result of a merger of four companies – Brunner Mond, Nobel Explosives, United Alkali Company and British Dye Stuffs – to create one huge company whose first year turnover was

ICI corporate advertisement, promoting staff benefits. *Punch*, November 1956

£27 million. Over the next two decades the company's commitment to research and development paid off, with the invention of the acrylic plastic Perspex, as well as polyethylene and a fibre known as Terylene, the most widely used synthetic fabric ever. They also produced explosives, fertilisers, insecticides, dyestuffs, non-ferrous metals and, with DuPont, co-developed Dulux paints. It was the largest single manufacturer of wrought non-ferrous metal products in the British Empire. In the 1940s and 1950s ICI also established a pharmaceutical division, which developed two important products: an anti-malarial drug, Paludrine, and an anaesthetic agent, halothane. The 1950s also saw the arrival of another fabric known as crimplene, which became popular throughout America.

At the time that ICI purchased Warren House, the company employed 74,000 workers and 25,000 staff and foremen across 11 manufacturing divisions, as well as a pharmaceutical division and Central Agricultural Control (the company's organisation for marketing agricultural products). It employed thousands of people in and around each divisional headquarters which spanned the UK: from the alkali division in Winnington, Northwich, Cheshire, to Billingham in Stockton-on-Tees, County Durham; dyestuffs in Blackley, Manchester; general chemicals in Liverpool; the leather cloth division in Hyde, Cheshire; the lime division at the Royal Exchange in Buxton; metals in Witton, Birmingham; the Nobel division in Ardeer, Stevenson, Ayrshire; paints in Slough, Berkshire; pharmaceuticals in Wilmslow, Cheshire; plastics in Welwyn Garden City, Hertfordshire; salt in Liverpool and Dublin, and the Wilton works in Cleveland. In addition, there were Scottish Agricultural Industries Ltd in Edinburgh, Plant Protection Ltd in London, ICI Estates Ltd, ICI Savings Bank Ltd, Imperial Chemical Insurance Ltd, Housing Associations at Thames House Estates, and eight other associated companies. Members of every trade union appeared on the payroll from anhydrite miners to turbine attendants, electricians to pottery makers. Professional staff ranged from accountants to veterinary surgeons, chemical engineers to estate managers. The business operations were divided into four UK regions: Midlands, Northern, Scotland and Northern Ireland, and Southern, each under the leadership of regional managers. The Board consisted of 20 members, 15 executive and five non-executive members. In 1950 these included such heavyweights as Sir Peter Bennett who was also on the board of Lloyds Bank, Lord Glenconner and Viscount Weir. ICI was a very large, powerful company with a capital value in round figures of £64.5 million.

The purchase of Warren House was not an unusual one for this organisation since they already owned and occupied four others, having taken advantage of the relatively low price of country houses. Winnington Hall, Northwich, Cheshire, a Grade I-listed country house owned from the 1870s by the Brunner and Mond families who built a chemical factory in the area, was converted to a club for the use of Brunner Mond staff and subsequently for senior staff members of ICI's alkali division. Marbury Hall, also near Northwich, originally a family home, later housed POWs and was the base for the Polish Free Army during the war. It was purchased by ICI in 1948 to house their employees, with single men living in the main building and the old POW huts converted into family bungalows. One former employee, recalling ICI's ethos of 'caring for staff beyond the workbench', has fond memories of Christmas parties for workers and their families at Marbury Hall in the mid-1950s, where every child received a gift from the company. Wilton Castle, near Redcar, a Grade II-listed, 19th-century mansion built on the site of a medieval castle, was bought in 1945 by ICI, who used the house as offices and developed the

park into a golf course for staff. South of Wilmslow in East Cheshire, Fulshaw Hall, a Jacobean-style former manor house listed Grade II in 1951, was bought by ICI and used as offices for the Corporate Management services of its new pharmaceutical division.

On 17 June 1955, at the 28th Annual Meeting of ICI Ltd at Wigmore Hall, Dr Alexander Fleck, the chairman, announced the purchase of Warren House to the shareholders:

> I should like to make special mention of the residential training centre which we have recently opened at Warren House on Kingston Hill, Surrey. We intend to bring together in this training centre many of the educational and other study courses for staff which the company has developed since the war, and to extend them still further. This new centre with its residential facilities, will give greater opportunities for closer contacts between senior executives and other employees in the company's service. The board are particularly concerned with the training of those on whom the responsibilities of higher management may one day be expected to fall, for without imaginative management in the boardrooms as well as efficient management in the factories, no business can prosper continuously.

ICI AFTER THE WAR

Although turnover was high, ICI had struggled to be profitable after the Second World War. An anti-trust suit in the US meant that the co-operation on prices and markets that had once existed between ICI and

A postcard from an ICI employee on a course at Warren House to his daughter in Middlesbrough in June 1957

Left: A photograph of one of the many groups of ICI staff who received training at Warren House. This is Finance & Management Course No. 6, lined up in October 1962. A young John Harvey-Jones, future ICI chairman and CEO, is seated in the centre of the front row

Below: Senior secretaries at an ICI conference at Warren House in 1964

DuPont, together with their mutual exchange of technical information, was brought to an end. Despite opening a huge chemical complex at Wilton in 1952 to counter the effects of an increasingly competitive British chemical market, most of ICI's productive capacity was outmoded, and many believed that its old-fashioned management style was a hindrance to growth.

Changing the way things were done through management education and training was therefore seen as one of the elements essential to future success. With the absence of a significant national business school within British universities before 1965, large companies such as Unilever, Shell and ICI had to teach these skills in-house. Initially management training was seen as highly elitist, given only to graduate high-flyers, those on a pre-planned career progression, and as part of succession planning. But by the 1960s ICI was involved in what became known as open systems planning, where training became a common experience for managers, professionals and shop stewards. ICI training schools were established across the country and provided in-house education not just to managers but across the workforce from the apprentices, to secretaries and analytical lab assistants.

For the next 30 years, Warren House was host to hundreds of ICI senior management staff, trainers and external consultants. The rooms that had once been family living areas were turned into classrooms, the satin dresses and hushed tones of Victorian and Edwardian high-class society replaced by grey-suited gentlemen, and sometimes primly dressed secretaries,

The ICI in-house bar at Warren House was located in the room just to the right of the entrance hall

Sir John Harvey-Jones (1924–2008), Chairman of the Board and CEO, addressed divisional managers in his usual charismatic way, one night after dinner at Warren House in 1982

discussing strategies and personnel management. The small kitchens provided three meals a day for these residential guests, served in the large dining room where the conversations took a very different tone from those of the past. The practical bedrooms offered few home comforts for these gentlemen, but the benefits to the company were measurable. ICI's fortunes began to see gradual improvement in the early 1960s. An ICI pharmacologist, James Black, pioneered the development of Propranolol, the first successful beta blocker and one of the most important contributions to 20th-century medicine. However, still a little risk adverse, ICI would not back his ideas for a new drug to counter stomach ulcers, and he resigned from the company in 1964. High capital investment in Britain, Germany and America in the mid-1960s reduced production costs. Sales in Europe rose by 33 per cent every year from 1967 until the early 1970s, by which time productivity was also on the increase. ICI had negotiated a highly competitive price for its supply of newly discovered North Sea gas, which it used to produce plastics and paint, as well as ammonia for its ammonium nitrate fertiliser at a price far lower than its competitors, provoking government intervention. As the products became more competitively priced, so wages increased and there was an improvement in labour relations.

However, the company's profitability ebbed and flowed throughout the 1970s. When Prime Minister Edward Heath led Britain into the Common Market in 1972, ICI initially concentrated its investment in the US. However, seven years later ICI chairman Maurice Hodgson credited Britain's membership of the Common Market for the marked increase in the company's annual sales in Western Europe from £235 million in 1972, to £1,053 million in 1979. He said that ICI had increased exports to the EEC four times faster than overall demand for chemicals had grown, and that where ICI plants had been installed

throughout Europe, ICI exports from the UK had increased 20 per cent over the previous 12 months. ICI was no longer dependent on its home market and once again had become one of the world's top three chemical companies. Its traditional business of chlor-alkali and paints were strongly supported by the newer profitable petrochemicals business and thriving pharmaceuticals division. However, in 1980 the Chancellor of the Exchequer, Geoffrey Howe, raised interest rates to curb inflation, and as a result the value of sterling rose dramatically. In nine months ICI's profits of £600 million disappeared and it reported a loss of £200 million. By the end of 1981, a third of its customers had gone out of business.

JOHN HARVEY-JONES

The tide turned in 1982 when the charismatic John Harvey-Jones was appointed Chairman of the Board and Chief Executive Officer (CEO). Harvey-Jones, a non-chemist, had joined ICI in 1956 as a junior training manager at Wilton, had been chairman of ICI's petrochemicals and plastics division, and on the main Board of Directors since 1973. Soon after his appointment as CEO, he addressed a cross-section of ICI top divisional managers one night after dinner at Warren House:

We have first class management, but it has become excessively bureaucratic and political. We've adopted a value system that is ponderous, negative, and unanxious to share risk and not willing to give headroom. What is the pattern for the next ten years? Instability and change will characterise it. It will be a repositioning decade, with lots of new patterns and shifts of power. Growth as we've known it will be greatly reduced. No company can exist without growth; therefore we have to make it by pinching the markets of competitors, outdating his products and developing new ones. We need a new attitude to risk – we minimise risk, we don't maximise opportunities. The biggest risk of all is to take no risk. We have to be more flexible, because we won't read the future right. We need to have the ability to move fast, more market sensitivity, more openness and trust, greater tolerance of differences and more courage in dealing with others. Individuals have the answers, not ICI as a group. The size of the board will be reduced. Senior management is about getting people to own the problem and do something about it, not passing it up. Leadership is about getting extraordinary performance out of ordinary people.

Many years later the *Guardian* newspaper wrote:

Harvey-Jones was a swashbuckler, who was miraculously made chairman of ICI. And this at a time when the rest of the country's heavy industry, British Leyland, Triumph, Norton Motorcycles, mines, shipyards and steel industry were disappearing down the commercial plug hole in the real world of unemployment and collapsing industrial economies,

and ICI had just clocked up its first ever quarterly loss. Everyone expected the company, a bellwether of British manufacturing, to appoint a grey suit, but instead it got John Harvey-Jones, with his shock of dark hair, moustache, baggy brown suit and wild ties. Under his watch ICI quickly recovered.

Jones led the change in company focus away from outdated products and a reliance on bulk chemicals and fertilisers to drugs and speciality chemicals and paints. He concentrated on higher profit margins, cut costs, reduced the main board from 14 to eight, laid off workers and closed plants. Over the next six years ICI's workforce was cut by a third, it stopped making polyester and exchanged polythene for PVC. Even the company's impressive headquarters at Millbank in Westminster was put up for sale, though not sold. Harvey-Jones scrapped all controls except profit, cash and strategic direction, and began to give the customers what they wanted rather than what ICI had traditionally produced. By 1983, profits had doubled on the previous year to $939 million and one year later ICI was the first British company to break the one-billion profit barrier.

By the time Sir John Harvey-Jones resigned his position as chairman in 1987, he had been awarded a knighthood and voted Britain's Industrialist of the Year. Sales in the company reached £10,114 billion, and had a market value of £7,038 billion; with subsidiaries throughout the world, it employed 118,600 people. Harvey-Jones's leadership had begun to change the corporate culture within ICI. There was now a real commitment to getting the best out of teams of people, diverting the concentration from political in-fighting to customers, suppliers and competitors, and thereby achieving a competitive advantage in the world outside the company.

Harvey-Jones believed that there was no such thing as bad troops, only bad leaders: 'It is extremely difficult to teach grown up people anything. It is however relatively easy to create conditions under which people will teach themselves.' It is hardly surprising therefore that the company decided to make substantial improvements to Warren House, which by the mid 1980s was not only a venue for training ever-increasing numbers of senior management, but also served as a management retreat, a quiet place where executives could come to discuss strategy away from the distractions of divisional offices.

THE WARREN HOUSE REDEVELOPMENT

By late 1985, ICI were on the hunt for an architect to take on the enlargement and refurbishment of Warren House. ICI wanted the quality and standards of a five-star hotel, with a complete range of audio-visual facilities, and yet also wished to retain the feeling of an English country house. They had originally approached East Molesey-based architect Ivor Cunningham for ideas on how the gardens might be developed, and it was to him that they turned once more in 1986. Cunningham had been in partnership with Eric Lyons and, working in conjunction with Span Developments, they had created over 2,000 homes in London and the Southeast over 30 years. They were best known for 'reuniting post-war estates with their picturesque outdoor setting' and 'synthesising buildings with the natural environment', most notably the World's End development, King's Road, Chelsea, and Parkleys in Ham, Richmond. Eric Lyons had died in 1980, so it was 60-year-old Ivor Cunningham and his team who took on the work at Warren House.

The planning strategy was to arrange the enlarged and more complex facilities in organised function groups, to provide independent access to all rooms, and to retain as much of the existing fabric of the

Architects Eric Lyons (1912–80) in the centre and Ivor Cunningham (1928–2007) on the right. Cunningham was commissioned by ICI to refurbish Warren House in 1986

building as possible. The original building had 29 bedrooms of which only two had en-suite bathrooms. The written brief was set out during 1986, enlarged during a process of collaboration between the architects and ICI's Personnel and Training Manager Michael Broaden, Senior Personnel Training Officer Arthur Tait and Headquarters Personnel Manager Tony Bloxham, and finalised in September that same year. Their proposals finally received planning consent in January 1987. With ICI's own engineering department filling the role of project engineer, Cunningham and ICI selected Lovell Construction (London) as management contractors, and each phase of works was allocated to 94 separate sub-contractors through a competitive tendering procedure. The contract period was 15 months, from January 1987 to March 1988, and its value, £2.85 million, excluded furniture.

To finance the redevelopment, ICI took the decision to sell off two separate parcels of land adjoining Warren House. The smaller site to the northwest of the main house encompassed the land behind the gardener's cottage and greenhouses, the site of the red tennis courts where once royalty and politicians played and the northern entrance stretch of the original carriage driveway. The second, much larger site to the south included the majority of the garden, many fine trees and shrubs, as well as the large pond and famous water gardens. From a list of seven developers, and following a careful selection process, Octagon Developments, a local housing developer, was chosen. In spring 1987, Octagon Developments paid £3,440,000 for both parcels of land. They built a group of linked but detached houses on the smaller plot. For the bigger site there

Above: ICI employees explore the Japanese water gardens

Right: One of the lead cranes, a gift of Edward VII, as seen today

had been a condition of sale that no building would obstruct the view south to the pond from Warren House; in accordance with this and to maintain the quality and spaciousness of the land, Octagon planned three apartment blocks.

When the developers started work, the Japanese gardens were in poor condition. This may have been because it was just too much work for Frank Potter, the head gardener who lived in the gate lodge with his family, and Ken Burch and his assistant John Perez, or perhaps there had been not enough investment from ICI. The old Victorian pumping system that had pushed the water around the network of ponds had rusted away, making the waterfalls a thing of the past. The area was heavily overgrown, stone steps had crumbled and the wooden handrails had rotted.

Although they managed to refurbish the pavilion which overlooks one of the lower ponds, the tea room, where once sat the two kylins from Peking, was beyond recovery and had to be demolished. Octagon installed a new pumping system and brought the ten cascading waterfalls to life again; they employed Pantiles Nurseries who replanted the whole area with the acers, rhododendrons and other shrubs that Veitch had introduced. Fortunately, many of the trees planted by famous visitors to Warren House survived the 1987 storms, and the view across the lawns from the house remained much the same. Finally the bridges were restored and repainted, and three new bridges added. The lead cranes, part of a set given to Edward VII who had in turn given them away as presents to his friends, were cleaned and took up their positions once more among the water lilies.

In an interview with the *Surrey Comet* newspaper in June 1988, Cunningham described the work on Warren House as one of the most challenging and complicated yet satisfying projects he had worked on:

It was very complicated because I had to keep all the walls of the existing structure. My aim was to make the building super-efficient for its new purpose whilst at the same time retaining all its country house appearance and atmosphere. Many overseas executives who come here have arrived straight from Heathrow or Gatwick and this will be the first English building they have entered and it is important that it should have the right ambience. Without being immodest I think I can say that what I have done is an improvement on what I found. The main task was to design and build a new conference room, the London Room. We used handmade Swanage bricks to match up with the

Below: The Persian Smoking Room photographed in the late 1890s, and left, how it looks today from a similar angle

original ones. We restored the Ballroom cornicing to its original white and replaced the chandeliers. In fact the original Ballroom is now two rooms made by re-positioning a couple of columns and putting in new doors and partitions and replica mouldings. The former Kitchen now joins with the Persian 'smoking' room to create a new dining room, but all the old features, the mouldings and panelling have been retained and extended through into the new space. They transferred the dado and some of the cornicing into the former kitchen area to give continuity. The original dining room with splendid pine panelling has been transformed into the Lounge, while the new kitchen has been located in the former laundry and housekeepers' office area. The only part of the house to be demolished was the Orchard Room, a heavy structure put on 70 years ago, in around 1918, and a kitchen storage area, which has been replaced by a swimming pool, sauna and exercise room looking across the kitchen garden.

Cunningham, like Devey just over a hundred years earlier, enlarged the house. A new small meeting room was created outside the main staircase window and its external walls shaped to reduce its impact when seen through the nearby lounge window. The original halls and lobbies were retained, and with the use of glazing

he transformed the Italian loggia into small offices; keen to preserve the original external appearance, the glass is set back behind the line of the columns and the ornate arches. Four Della Robbia rondels depicting figures with garlands of fruit were removed from the back wall of the loggia, repaired and cleaned, then repositioned on the external facades of the new air-conditioned conference room and inside the leisure area. Originally, access to the ballroom from the entrance hall passed through three other rooms. To overcome this, Cunningham created, partly from within the existing building, a new glazed corridor attached to the windowless northern side of the southern link. From this corridor all five meeting rooms, both conference rooms and new offices in the loggia could be accessed, therefore ensuring that each was self-contained. He increased the number of bedrooms from 29 to 45, by adding five new rooms to the main house, nine new rooms in the original stables annex, and extending it to add two further rooms. Every study bedroom was fitted with individual computer and TV terminals, and with clever use of partitioning the designers ensured that each one had an en-suite bathroom. One internal and one external staircase was removed and replaced by two

new internal staircases and one external, and a first-floor link added to connect two parts of the building previously separated at that level. The contractors renewed heating, lighting and communications networks. Work to the existing external finishes was limited to repairs, and cleaning was kept to a minimum to retain the patina of time.

The choice of carpets, curtains, upholstery materials and paintwork was co-ordinated using the ICI Colour Dimension range. Carpets had to be made with ICI fibres, paints, varnishes and stains were ICI Dulux, while the kitchens were all designed in collaboration with ICI's central catering service head, John Salisbury.

Because the original entrance and part of the drive was included in the land sold for housing development, a new driveway was laid out on the axis of the house's entrance porch. Newly designed, electrically controlled, steel entrance gates were hung from brick piers topped with the original stone pier caps of the magnificent Paget entrance. A small enclosed formal cloister garden, centred on a new fountain, was created in the outside area flanked by the new corridor, conference room and entrance hall and overlooked by the famous Devey wall-mounted sun-dial. The remaining four acres of gardens and lawns remained much the same, trees were planted along the northern boundary to screen the new housing development and to match the existing mature trees which screened the new apartments on the southern boundary. A steel railing was erected in the more open part of the garden

where there is a view down to the Japanese water garden, allowing a full sight of the cedar planted by Edward VII. Three-quarters of the original winter garden, a glass-roofed structure heated by its own boiler and containing a large Pulhamite stone grotto adjoining the billiard room, had already been demolished and remodelled in 1980. Some repairs were made to the remaining grotto in 1987, as well as fountains and a number of garden ornaments. The gazebo which had stood a little further from the house on the site of the new apartments was relocated once more within the grounds of Warren House.

The contract was delivered on time and to budget, the house increased by just over 36 per cent from 2,375.2 square metres to 3,234.07 square metres. The new chairman Sir Denys Henderson was delighted with the results: 'The new facilities are absolutely splendid and will clearly stand us in very good stead for the enhanced training efforts. What struck me particularly was the way in which the architect has managed to blend the traditional with the modern to produce an overall effect which is both thoroughly functional but also pleasing to the eye. It represents a major accomplishment.' In 1989 Warren House once again opened its doors, and for the next ten years it served as a venue for conferences and training, used by ICI directors, senior executives and staff. Qualified chefs and sous-chefs prepared executive dinners from the new kitchens, the bread and butter pudding creating particularly happy culinary memories for some.

In 1991, Lord Hanson, a Conservative industrialist and owner of Hanson plc renowned for leverage buyouts, purchased 2.8 per cent of ICI and started a takeover bid. In direct response, ICI chairman Sir Denys Henderson hired Goldman Sachs to look into Hanson's business dealings. They discovered that Hanson's partner was running racehorses at shareholders' expense and Hanson duly backed down from the takeover bid. Two years later ICI separated the

Right: The gazebo was relocated within the grounds

Below: Cunningham added nine new bed-study rooms in the original stable block, and two more in an extension to the building

bioscience business – agrochemicals, pharmaceuticals, seeds and biological products – into a new and independent publicly listed company, the Zeneca Group. The result was a substantial increase in company profitability. A new CEO, Charles Miller Smith, once a director at Unilever, was appointed in 1994. Miller Smith led ICI away from bulk chemicals with the 1987 $8 billion purchase of Unilever's speciality chemicals businesses. This was the beginning of many changes within ICI. To finance these acquisitions it sold the Australian subsidiary and its polyester chemicals business. The new strategy was to invest in higher-growth and higher-margin business, such as electronic chemicals. In the final month of 1998, ICI formed Uniqema, a speciality chemicals unit, formed by merging five members of the ICI group. Between 1997 and 2001 ICI made more than £6.1 billion in divestments and spent £5.7 billion in acquisitions.

Just as the company's headquarters at Millbank had become redundant after the 1993 demerger of the business, so these later changes had a knock-on effect on Warren House. With ICI's staff reduced from

100,000 to 12,000, company use of Warren House dropped from 100 per cent to 20 per cent between 1997 and 1999. The company started selling their residential, conference and meeting facilities to other blue-chip companies, and the house was now staffed by a third party. The Senior Board still used the House as a retreat venue, but the usefulness of the training facility had diminished.

ICI put Warren House, Wilton Castle and Winnington Hall up for sale in 1999. Fortunately, none suffered the same fate as Marbury Hall which was demolished in 1969, just three years after ICI had moved out. While Wilton Castle was converted into residential apartments and its surrounding golf course acquired by its members, and Winnington Hall is now offices, Warren House was sold to a small business consortium. They continued to run the house in much the same way as it had been by ICI, as a residential training centre used by global corporations such as SmithKline Beecham, British Telecom, Barclays Bank, British Gas, the Capital Group, Glaxo Wellcome, Centrica and ICI's own creation, Zeneca S A.

EPILOGUE

I N DECEMBER 1999, Warren House and its garden features were listed under the Planning Act of 1990 as being of special architectural and historic interest. The building and four acres of land had just been bought by a group of local businessmen, and English Heritage undoubtedly wanted to preserve the building and prevent any redevelopment of the site.

The house was sold again in 2005 to the present owners who are keen to maintain its historic value. The structure of the building today is much as it was in Victorian times. The original 1860s red-brick with burnt-brick diaper work and decorative brickwork of Hugh Hammersley's rebuilt mansion appear dark, in contrast to George Devey's similar patterns of the 1884–5 extension. The stone dressings and tiled roof are still in place, as are many of the original metal-frame windows and fittings, set in the stone mullioned windows and transoms. The original entrance is now set back in a small courtyard where, mounted on a

Opposite: The front entrance today

chimney stack, is the Hammersley and Eden Crest: three rams and three bushels. A blue and gold sun-dial, dated 1884, continues to display the time to anyone who cares to look. Above the moulded arch of the later stone entrance porch, the original Wolverton Crest badly weathered and aged has been replaced by a perfect replica.

The original Devey stone blind arcade leads into the 1880s square-panelled entrance hall and large fireplace, then to the inner hall where the original open-well oak staircase, with its 'exuberant foliate balustrade, square newels, ornate ball finials and gadrooned drop finials', is the same one Gladstone climbed two steps at a time. The doors and panelling are replicas, but the brass furniture is original. The timber and brass radiator cupboard, with Corinthian columns and a gadrooned frieze, displays the Paget emblem, which reappears in the baroque friezes and ceiling mouldings of the former ballroom, said to be based on the Hall of Mirrors in Versailles. In Wolverton's dining room (now the lounge), Devey's original fireplace once warmed important dinner guests. In the corner of Sir Arthur Paget's smoking room (now the dining room)

Upstairs, bedrooms from the 1880s, with their classical details, still exist. Two principal bedrooms display mouldings similar to the ballroom; presumably these belonged to Sir Arthur and Lady Paget. One bathroom still retains its marble interior, installed for the visit of King Edward VII. Attached to the south of the house, the nine-bay loggia is now enclosed internally with glass, and contains the Della Robbia rondels, installed by the Pagets.

Most importantly, Warren House is still a working house, run and maintained as it has been since 1870, by a team of dedicated staff. Its location and proximity to London, combined with the peace and tranquillity of the country setting within the Coombe Estate, make it an ideal venue for conferences and training. Offering both residential and day events, the house has 46 luxury en-suite bedrooms and all the 21st-century conveniences of technology. The house and grounds also provide the perfect setting for private meetings, events, weddings and funerals. The various styles and sizes of the ground-floor rooms provide the management with the flexibility to meet customers' needs. The lounge is open to casual visitors and friends for refreshment after a long walk in Richmond Park, or even a champagne afternoon tea. Not surprisingly the

is an angled chimney with Oriental tiles, and an Islamic-inspired dado and door panels set with small mother-of-pearl stones, perhaps on the instruction of Lady Mary Paget. In the ceiling of this and the adjoining room are coloured glass panes, the dappled light from which once fell on the billiard table where Edward VII played.

team have received many awards and accreditations for service, and client testimonials speak for themselves.

For well over a century, Warren House has remained one of the finest houses on the Coombe Estate. This book has been a true account of past scenes played out under its roof, between its walls, on its lawns and beneath its trees. There has been drama, tragedy and romance. The higher echelons of society – royals, aristocrats, generals, diplomats, politicians, leaders of industry – appeared in the spotlight like actors in leading roles. With Warren House as their stage, they dined, discussed important matters of state, entertained and gave generously to charity. The old characters are

now long gone, the scenery has changed somewhat, and today Warren House is open to all. Those that come to stay, to wed, to celebrate, to mourn, to tread its boards, all add their story to its history. Warren House remains as welcoming and as accommodating as ever, creating memories for all who visit. Indeed there is no 'end to this strange eventful history'.

AFTERWORD

Genealogy has entered popular culture, helped along the way by the digital age, celebrities and television. Archives, once located in the dimly lit basements or dusty corridors of long-forgotten buildings, are now located in brightly lit and well-ventilated modern buildings, full to bursting with researchers of all ages, classes and cultures accessing thousands of documents online. It is no longer merely the pursuit of aristocrats arguing legitimacy, claiming inheritance, or establishing power and status. In this ever-changing world, more and more of us want to know where we came from.

This book is a result of my interest in both genealogy and history. I have been researching family history, my own and others, for nearly 20 years. The satisfaction comes from not just discovering ancestors' names, dates and relationships, but tangible evidence of their lives, through which they can be understood in the context of the world and time in which they existed. My parents bought Warren House in 2005, and with that my own family history became inextricably linked to the house and its former owners.

Warren House, the building and gardens are English Heritage Grade II listed, but other than this, there is very little evidence of the lives of the inhabitants and even some debate as to who they had been. However, one photograph (reproduced on page 127) taken on 22 May 1909, which hung on the wall by the Ballroom, grabbed my attention. King Edward VII sits on a wicker chair, ankles crossed, spats visible, cigar alight, surrounded by 15 others, just outside the Italian loggia in the garden at Warren House. In the foreground a small puddle, presumably overflow from the fountain,

threatens to dampen the hemline of Lady Johnstone's dress. Intriguingly, standing in the back row on the far left, her face almost covered by the huge brim of an elaborate hat, is the tall, elegant figure of Mrs Alice Keppel, society hostess and long-term mistress of the King. For me this was too much to resist. Who were all these people and what had brought them to Warren House? I set to work researching every one of them and the result was illuminating – they were not just royalty but MPs, viceroys, diplomats, aristocrats, American women and the future Baroness Eugene de Rothschild. I was hooked! Who else could have lived here? Who were they? What did they do? And how did they come to own Warren House? I spent the next two years, between school runs, homework and bath times, researching every aspect of Warren House, its owners and their lives. I discovered that every former owner, without exception, played an important role in the society of their day, and I was determined that their tale should be told. I've had some help along the way and I am extremely grateful to Graham Senior-Milne, descendant of the Hammersleys for his generosity and support and enthusiasm for genealogy; also to Mrs Lilian Phillips and Bill Pazaratz for sharing their photographs and their wonderful memories of Warren House, which have really brought the story of Dame Leila Paget alive. Thanks must also go to the team at Third Millennium for their professional guidance, but most of all to my family for their support and patience with what has been a long and rewarding experience.

V. K. L. Good, December 2013

INDEX

Principal coverage of a topic is entered in **bold**. Illustrations are entered in *italics*.

The Hammersley family members are entered by reference to their relationship to Hugh Hammersley.

The Glyn family members are entered by reference to their relationship to George Grenfell Glyn.

Cawston family members are entered by reference to their relationship to George Cawston.